M000167475

ON THE WAY

ON THE WAY

My Life and Times

FRANK DENIUS

WITH THOMAS M. HATFIELD

BRISCOE CENTER
FOR AMERICAN HISTORY
THE UNIVERSITY OF TEXAS AT AUSTIN

Distributed by Tower Books,
an imprint of the University of Texas Press

© Copyright 2016 by the Dolph Briscoe Center for American History, The University of Texas at Austin.

All rights reserved.

Printed in the United States of America.

First edition, 2016

Requests for permission to reproduce material from this work should be sent to Office of the Director, Dolph Briscoe Center for American History, The University of Texas at Austin, 2300 Red River Stop D1100, Austin, TX 78712-1426.

∞The paper used in this book meets the minimum requirements of ANSI/NISO Z39.48-1992 (R1997)(Permanence of Paper).

Frontispiece: Frank Denius and Tom Hatfield. *Photo by Marsha Miller, the University of Texas at Austin.*

Unless otherwise noted, photographs are courtesy the Denius family.

Library of Congress Control Number: 2016944751

DEDICATION

To my comrades in arms
The men of Battery C, 230th Field Artillery Battalion
Thirtieth Infantry Division
"Old Hickory"
U.S. Army
England, France, Belgium, Holland, Germany
1944–1945

Contents

Foreword

THEY HAD TO GROW UP FAST . . .

. . . unimaginably fast, as viewed from today's perspective. But the no-alternative, lightning-quick need to assume adult responsibilities—often the gravest responsibilities—must have been central to the extraordinary achievements among those whom Tom Brokaw has memorably called "the Greatest Generation."

Whenever I hear Brokaw's label, my mind turns inevitably to Frank Denius, my neighbor, friend, and colleague of two decades' standing, but, more important, the finest exemplar whom I have encountered of what the Greatest Generation experienced and achieved. This book is his story, rendered by Denius himself in partnership with Tom Hatfield.

At age nineteen, Frank Denius crossed Omaha Beach and entered combat. Within nine weeks, dire conditions forced critical responsibilities upon him, as his unit came under heavy fire and was cut off from relief. Far before he was twenty-one, he had fought his way across Europe and had linked up with the Russians across the Elbe. He had been awarded four Silver Stars for gallantry under fire, a Presidential Unit Citation, and two Purple Hearts. He had learned about fate and fear; he had received deep lessons about leading and working with people; and he had acquired a powerful drive to make the best use of his education after the war.

He had already chosen his university, too, and that is a big part of the later story.

Important early sections of this book are about Denius's formative experiences in the Second World War. They are powerful, and they cause any reader to search his or her soul in wonder over how he or she might have held up under a year of such pressure. But without the actual test, only God can know. Frank Denius went through the test.

But most of this book is not about war experiences. Rather, it is about the much larger part of Denius's life after the war.

He was discharged in October 1945 and was enrolled in the University of Texas within a week, on the very edge of the enormous wave of GIs who would overtake and help to remake American higher education. In this book, we have good glimpses into the phenomena that made up that time and that scene. Denius pushed through his undergraduate years and then through the University of Texas School of Law.

The reader joins him as he enters one of Austin's leading law firms, one having a catholic practice and blue-chip political connections. The Austin of that era—in the late 1940s—was just a regional town hardly bigger than a hundred thousand in population. But it was the capital city of an important state; it had drive from Lyndon Johnson and from the University of Texas; it would develop its own brand of magic; and it was destined for explosive growth. In the seven decades since the end of the Second World War, Austin has become a metropolis of more than two million and has established a presence among the centers of global creativity.

Frank Denius—always versatile and with good judgment ever at the ready—witnessed it all and was a participant in a remarkable array of key events. Most of this book is about Denius's experiences through those seven decades in which Austin and Texas and America were transformed into their contemporary forms. The reader has a chance to sit in on the history—to see how Texas operated in Lyndon Johnson's prime, to experience practical steps taken by practical people to desegregate Texas under new law, to observe power plays in the Texas energy industry, to watch interested, able alumni helping a fine regional university to become a global leader. For anyone who lived through the changes that Denius experienced, the history described here connects personally. For others, more remote from the events themselves, who would just like to understand more about what gives Texas its rather distinctive character, this book is an exceptional resource.

The book is written in the first person. It is an autobiography assembled from a great many conversations between Frank Denius and Thomas Hatfield, which Hatfield carefully recorded and edited into well-chosen, fluid chapters of a life and career. The reader benefits from Thomas Hatfield's extensive experience with biography and from his great historical knowledge of the personalities, events, and places of the Second World War.

Everyone who knows Frank Denius is well aware of his extraordinary devotion to the University of Texas. Over the seven decades since he first enrolled, he has performed a great range of gracious and wise services on her behalf. He loves her indeed, but he has never been blinded by his devotion. During my eight years as president of the university, I came to treasure Frank's clear-eyed perception of the university's real needs and his consistent wisdom about how to get her to the right place. He is the truest, rarest kind of friend. This book shows something of how those qualities arose—of how growing up fast and responding with truth and judgment in the critical moment produced a man who could help mightily to build a sound society for seventy years beyond.

LARRY R. FAULKNER
President Emeritus
The University of Texas at Austin
November 30, 2015

Introduction

FRANK DENIUS AND I WERE WELL ACQUAINTED before we began collaborating to produce this memoir. Over several decades we had talked from time to time about the Second World War, Texas politics, and the University of Texas, which together comprise about two-thirds of the narrative. When we began concentrating on the book, I tried to systematically collect information from him with one-on-one interviews that were duly transcribed. Eventually I had some thirty hours of these interviews. At the outset I prepared for each interview by making a list of logically sequenced questions intended to elicit important information about a period or episode of his life. As the interviews became less superficial, we delved into more personal and subjective topics, which were often more interesting than those provoked by questions. As drafts of chapter manuscripts emerged from my computer, Mr. Denius and I met frequently over lunch and in his office to discuss them. Such discussions inevitably produced more information for the next draft, especially as he became less restrained and more willing to tell me things that made the whole of an anecdote or period more transparent. An example of this is the *in camera* operating philosophy of his law firm, espoused by wily senior partner Edward Clark, a philosophy Mr. Denius described to me only shortly before I gave the book manuscript to copy editors. Countless impromptu telephone conversations ensued with more stories or corrections to previous stories or manuscripts. Even now, I can hear him saying, "Don't ever change your cell phone number!" In addition, he invited me to travel with him to speaking engagements with students about leadership, freedom, and democracy. At other times we visited projects benefitting from Cain Foundation benevolence, and we both journeyed to Europe several times for World War II–related activities while the book was in progress.

As an altruist with profound intrinsic motivation, Mr. Denius has participated in many worthy ventures, some small and others large, but invariably useful in terms of the public good. The stories here preserve his memories of how these beneficial social, economic, and educational developments came about. By correlating Mr. Denius's life story with his accomplishments and motivations, I hope to inspire others with generous inclinations to devise their own ways to provide effective leadership for worthy causes.

Here the reader can also find firsthand accounts of how things got done in Texas Democratic Party politics from the late 1940s through the 1960s, insights about how Austin got the "jump" on other cities during the era of Mayor Tom Miller (1933–1961), and accounts of machinations to win natural gas contracts for Texas cities. Also found are numerous stories about the University of Texas, most notably the dismantling of the last legal barriers to racial integration, the expansion of the campus east and south, and the complexities of making decisions about the Brackenridge Tract. Frank Erwin is here—Denius defending him while disagreeing with him—and a lifetime of Longhorn football legends, especially of Mr. Denius's friendship with Darrell Royal and Mack Brown, who says, "Frank has been to more practices than I have." Mr. Denius's personal idealism and aspirations for exceptionalism in ethical practices at UT Austin will appeal to all highminded devotees of the burnt orange and white.

This account of Frank Denius's life was written at the insistence of his countless friends and admirers. In this task, I was privileged to be his handmaiden, his willing and happy accomplice. Although this is his story, it unintentionally—and perhaps inevitably—reflects many of my passions and perspectives, at least to the extent that they overlapped with his. This is particularly true in reference to the University of Texas, his and my alma mater, to which both of us have devoted most of our lives.

I could not have helped Mr. Denius as I did without significant assistance by the superbly professional staff of UT Austin's Briscoe Center for American History, particularly David Zepeda, Echo Uribe, Holly Taylor, Margaret Schlankey, Brenda Gunn, Catherine Best, and Don Carleton, executive director of the center and author of several books that were prototypes for this one. Lynn Fowler, executive director of the Effie and Wofford Cain Foundation, retrieved substantive records that lent detail and authenticity to the text. In similar ways I had the able assistance of Janis Rebold and Rebecca Carfer in Mr. Denius's law office. In Frank Denius's hometown of Athens, Texas, I was grateful for Sarah Jane Brown, Felicia Cain, and John Cain for finding and sending me an important photograph. Mr. Denius's late wife, Charmaine, encouraged me in my work, which was augmented by their daughter, Charmaine McGill, and her husband, Gordon McGill, as well as their son, Wofford Denius, and his wife, Beth. My wife, Carol Sutherland Hatfield, an award-winning magazine editor, helped me structure the manuscript and accompanied me across battlefields of the Second World War that Mr. Denius knew—all with no less enthusiasm than my own.

The book's title was derived from the traditional shout of American artillerymen—"On the way!"—when they have fired the cannon and the projectile is out of the barrel.

THOMAS M. HATFIELD
Dean Emeritus of Continuing Education
Director, Military History Institute
Briscoe Center for American History
The University of Texas at Austin

France, August 1944

Headquarters 30th Infantry Division
Office of the Commanding General
Award of the Silver Star Medal
Citation

Staff Sergeant (then Corporal) Franklin W. Denius, 38 480 234, 230th Field Artillery Battalion, United States Army, is awarded . . . the Silver Star for gallantry in action from 7 August 1944 to 12 August 1944. When the enemy launched a determined counteroffensive in the vicinity of Mortain, France, designed to reach the sea and divide American armies in France, Sergeant Denius distinguished himself as a member of a forward observer party directing artillery fire in support of an infantry regiment. Despite intense enemy pressure, which included an attack by paratroopers, considerable armor, and large infantry forces, Sergeant Denius and his companions remained valiantly at their vulnerable post for seventy-two hours without rest, directing artillery fire which was a contributing factor in thwarting the German effort. In spite of direct tank, artillery, and small arms fire, which were directed on their positions, Sergeant Denius and his small group displayed gallantry and an indomitable fighting spirit in keeping with the highest traditions of the Armed Forces.

Leland S. Hobbs
Major-General, Commanding

· · ·

I want to begin by telling you why this citation was written. In the late summer of 1944, I was one of about 665 American soldiers surrounded by German troops, most of them Nazi Stormtroopers, for six days and nights on a ridge called Hill 314 near the French town of Mortain in southwest Normandy, about fifty miles inland from Omaha Beach. The siege ended about noon on August 12, when other GIs came to take over our foxholes and assume responsibility for the defense. During the previous night the Germans had withdrawn from their positions around the base of the hill. By holding out for those six days, we denied the enemy two essential objectives. One was the main road of the region, which ran through Mortain. The second was Hill 314 itself, which was what the military calls the critical terrain because it was the highest point of land for miles around, giving an advantage to whoever held it. Those of us on Hill 314 did not do this alone; we were part of the U.S. Thirtieth Infantry Division, which was itself part of a much larger American force.

The enemy's enormous counterattack was designed to split the two American armies that had broken through German defenses some thirty-five miles north near the city of Saint-Lô. If the Germans had succeeded, they could have attacked each of our armies separately and probably inflicted great harm. Many top-level commanders and historians say that by withstanding the enemy attack on Hill 314, we saved the Allies' breakout from Normandy. No one disputes that it was an important event in the ultimate defeat of Nazi Germany.

The countryside was quiet on the morning of August 6, 1944, when we went up on Hill 314. We relieved elements of the U.S. First Infantry Division, the famous "Big Red One," who had driven the enemy from the hilltop a few days earlier. Since they had not seen a German for two days, they told us it was a quiet sector. They could not have been more wrong. When we came down from the hill on August 12, 273 of us—40 percent—had been killed, wounded, or were missing. When a man was missing, it usually meant we did not know what had happened to him. He could be a prisoner of war, a deserter, dismembered, even vaporized by high explosives, or simply disoriented and lost. It happened.

I was a nineteen-year-old corporal assigned to assist Lt. Charles A.

Bartz, the leader of our artillery forward observer team; the others were radio operator Sherman Goldstein and his assistant, and a jeep driver, Louis Sberna. The enemy attack began just before dark the first night with sporadic artillery fire that gradually intensified and was followed by an attack by their infantry up the hill. They got so close that I lay on our radio to keep them from hearing its squawking static or incoming messages. During the entire night, I was in the same shallow hole with Lieutenant Bartz and Sherman Goldstein. Goldstein and I had been in combat for two months, but it was Bartz's first experience.

Through the night, Bartz was nervous and jittery. When I tried to talk to him, his replies did not make sense. Lt. Robert Weiss, another forward observer, saw him the next morning and said he had the "pale stamp of death on his face." Shortly after daybreak, Bartz blurted out, "I can't take it. I cannot take it anymore. You'll have to take over." He then crawled into a hole and I did not see him again until we were relieved on August 12. I did not have to think twice about what to do. By training and experience, I knew that my job was to assume his duties. His predecessor had been killed three weeks earlier as I stood only an arm's length away, and I had taken over from him.

On Hill 314 the difference between living and dying was mostly luck, but what was the difference between Lieutenant Bartz and me? I was as scared as he was. I pondered this question for decades before concluding that I was able to manage fear and he couldn't. When he hunkered down in a foxhole and said, "You'll have to take over," he forced me to choose between controlling my anxieties and fears or breaking down and neglecting my duties. His failure forced leadership on me. Effective leaders—whether in boardrooms, classrooms, courtrooms, or on battlefields—must manage their fears and worries, lest they fail in their duties and infect others with similar distractions, impairing their ability to function. As Gen. George S. Patton advised, "Do not take counsel of your fears." Confidence begets confidence. Self-control is the key.

Over the decades since Hill 314, I have contemplated why I was able to maintain my composure then and in all the trials of life that have followed. I always reach the same conclusion. The answer goes back to my family in Athens, Texas; to the examples they set for me, to the values they taught, and the preparation for life that they insisted on. They could be trusted, and they made good, balanced judgments. They were conscientious, and they persevered in their undertakings. I grew up feeling secure and confident about them and myself. The happy childhood they gave me has been a lifelong source of strength. That's the best explanation I have for my conduct on Hill 314, which was a turning point, the watershed event, for the life I have lived, although I did not realize it until much later.

CHAPTER 1

Athens, Texas, and the Cain Family

W HEN I WAS LEARNING TO READ, I could not understand why every edition of our local newspaper, the *Athens Daily Review*, had a spelling error near the top of the front page. The mystifying sentence was right under the masthead: "Athens and Henderson County noted for peas, potatoes, pot ash, petroleum and *ph*urniture." Gradually, I realized it was a deliberate mistake to publicize the fact that those five products were the economic basis of the area. The livelihood of every person depended on producing one of them, unless they had a business selling them or other goods, like my grandfather, Smith Cain. Grandpa Cain sold just about everything in his Spot Cash Store on the town square. I never knew why he called it the Spot Cash Store because I don't think anyone ever paid him cash for anything.

If anyone asked me about Athens, I usually began by telling them about the town square. If you wanted to meet someone or find them, it was the place, especially on Saturday afternoon when people came to the county seat from miles around to shop and visit with friends. Their cars and horse-drawn wagons lined the square and the streets leading into it. Storefronts stood around the perimeter of the square and the county courthouse was in the center. The surveyor who laid out the square gave it four equal sides and each corner was a perfect right angle as well as a four-way intersection. Although the courthouse was a government building, its four tall white Doric columns gave it the dignified aura of a monument. We were proud that our town was the Athens of East Texas, and the home of the Athens High School Hornets. After the Hornets won the national basketball championship in 1929, 1930, and 1931, the town—in fact, the whole county was in an absolute frenzy for years.

I usually had a job sacking groceries in the Safeway on the square. In front of each business there was a small hole in the concrete sidewalk for a flagpole. During the week of Armistice Day, November 11, flags flew all around the square. Other flags extended from the corners of the courthouse and on a bandstand at the northwest corner of the square where the high school band played. At eleven o'clock—the exact hour of the signing of the cease-fire in France on November 11, 1918, that ended World War I—everyone in Athens paused for one minute of silence that concluded with the fire department sounding its sirens. Except for the banners and flags, Fourth of July celebrations were completely different—noisy with fireworks, bands playing, barbecue and watermelon. These scenes made powerful impressions that I've remembered my entire life.

In 1928, when I was three years old, my mother and I moved to Athens to live with her parents, Mattie Wofford Cain and Smith Cain. She was Frances Carrie Denius, the youngest of their three children. She and my father, Samuel Franklin Denius, were divorced. Mother's next older brother, John, had married her college roommate, Peg Byers. They lived only a few minutes' walk away and had one child, James Byers "Jimmy" Cain, who was two years older than me. Uncle John owned and operated the Ford car dealership in Ennis, Texas.

Mother's oldest sibling, Wofford Cain, graduated from Texas A&M in 1913 with a degree in civil engineering and was a businessman in Dallas, about an hour-and-half drive northwest of Athens. Uncle Wofford (1891–1977) had not yet married and frequently visited us in Athens. (He married Aunt Effie in 1942.) In partnership with his Athens childhood friend, Clint Murchison Sr., he was actively involved in drilling, producing, and selling oil and natural gas, particularly gas to numerous municipalities in Texas and several other states. Their business relationship seemed almost hereditary. Their grandfathers—B. W. J. Wofford and J. A. Murchison—returned from the Civil War in 1865 to partner in a general mercantile store in the nearby community of Fincastle. However, when the Cotton Belt Railroad bypassed Fincastle in favor of Athens in 1880, they followed, and Athens became the trading center of the county. Even so, they or their forebears, left their mark in rural parts of the county as there are still two places named for them: Murchison, Texas, is a thriving community with a post office, and traces still remain of the village called Wofford.

My mother introduced Clint Murchison to his first wife, Anne Morris of Tyler, whom he married in 1920. After she died in 1926, he and Uncle Wofford shared a house in Dallas. When Uncle Wofford came to see us in Athens, Murchison often came too, and I grew up calling him "Uncle Clint." In the culture of East Texas, it was common for children to refer to a familiar, older man as uncle. Attached as I was to him and Uncle Wofford, I could not have imagined how important both of them would be in my life. Clint Murchison and Wofford Cain were contrasting personalities who complemented each other. Wofford had earned a college degree and wanted everyone to have the same opportunity, but Clint had no interest in college. He was a brilliant risk-taker, extravagant, and entrepreneurial, while Wofford was cautious, reserved, steady, and determined. They implicitly understood each other and never had a disagreement that I heard about.

Uncle Wofford's role model was his uncle and my great-uncle, Reagan Wofford. Reagan had gone to college and conducted himself like the cultured gentleman he was. Never married, he was a business entrepreneur, who successfully explored for oil, and advocated generosity with others. His joy in life was making money and giving it away, especially to his family, his church, and to schools. When Reagan Wofford died an early death in 1923, Wofford Cain had absorbed important life lessons from him, and I would learn from Uncle Wofford. To our intimate family in Athens I should add Grandmother Cain's sister and her husband, Sally Wofford Coleman and Charles Coleman. Mr. Coleman had been mayor of Athens and prospered with two brick factories and a building materials company. To me, he was "Uncle Chick," and she was "Aunt Sha." I called Uncle Wofford "Bubber," and my mother was always "Money" to me. Everyone called me "Teedy." Our nicknames are clues to our affection and informality. The Colemans lived in our neighborhood and had an important, positive influence on the family. When the

Great Depression struck in late 1929 and there was no market for bricks, Mr. Coleman declined to lay off any workers and kept making bricks. He explained, "I've made money by hiring poor people and now they are getting it back." When the economy improved, he had backlogged enough bricks to dominate the regional market. Aunt Sally had graduated from Baylor University and gone on to law school. When Jimmy Cain's mother was stricken with tuberculosis and his parents moved to El Paso for the dry climate, he remained in Athens and lived with the Colemans, who had no children. This arrangement became permanent after Jimmy's mother died in 1930.

Members of our family were frequently in each other's homes, usually for Sunday dinner after church, and for holidays and birthdays. If there were disputes among us, I knew nothing of them. Since there were not many of us, we could easily get together. In the absence of electronic devices, except radio, which was limited by today's standards, we talked, and the main topic was us, our family—our history, where we came from, what we were doing, and where we were going with our lives. The name of the deceased Reagan Wofford, beloved brother of Grandmother Cain and Aunt Sally, was frequently mentioned. There was a lot of "family advising," led mainly by Uncle Wofford, particularly after Grandfather Cain died in 1937. The only children in this family circle were my cousin, Jimmy Cain, and me. As a result, an entire family of mature, high-minded, successful adults doted on two little boys, confirming who we were and shaping who we would become. We were close, and we supported each other.

My grandmother's side of the family was staunchly Presbyterian, but Grandfather Cain was a Methodist. Until his death, the two of them attended the Methodist Church and the rest of us went to the First Presbyterian Church, only three blocks from their home and two blocks off the town square. I was baptized there, married there, have intentionally remained a Presbyterian, and served my congregation at Westminster Presbyterian in Austin as deacon, elder, and trustee. In 1930 Grandfather Cain sold his Spot Cash Store and retired, not because of the stock market crash, but for the freedom to do the two things that he most enjoyed: support Athens High School athletic programs and go fishing when he wanted to. I spent a lot of time with him, fishing. Often I took along my BB gun, and later a .22 or shotgun to shoot squirrels and doves.

Grandfather Cain began taking me to high school football and basketball games when I was three or four years old. He was an all-out booster, going to both the games and the practices. The football field was just that—a broad expanse of unimproved open field with wooden bleachers on each side and no lights. People parked their cars beyond the goal posts at each end of the field. At dusk, the cars would turn on their lights to brighten the field so the teams could continue playing, sometimes with a white football so the players could see it better. When I was small, Grandfather would wrap me in a blanket and take me to football games in his Model T Ford. His influence explains why athletics became important to me, and in turn fostered my competitive spirit. If I take on a project, I want it to be successful. I want to be in the top bracket of anything I do. Grandfather Cain shaped my value system and inspired me to be a positive and contributing citizen of the whole community. Uncle Wofford's values were much like my grandfather's. After Grandfather died when I was twelve years old, Uncle Wofford became the primary male figure in my life.

My teachers were also important to me. When I entered the first grade in the Athens grammar school in 1930, my teacher was Miss Odie Mae Norwood. My second grade teacher became the mother of Lowell Lebermann, later my friend and fraternity brother as well as a Distinguished Alumnus at the University of Texas. One of my favorite stories concerns an incident in the fourth grade. My teacher, Miss Jennie Boone, kept a Victrola in her classroom. She played classical music pieces for us— Beethoven, Schubert, and Chopin. Then she'd discuss in detail how each was written and who wrote it. At the end of the week, she would play them back, and we were supposed to write on paper the name of the particular piece of music and hand in the paper.

At the end of the first six weeks, I had a perfect score: Zero! Nothing but mistakes. I loved music, but I couldn't distinguish one note from another. At the beginning of the next six-week session, she announced that we would have a new series and told the class, "I think Frank will be able to listen to this music and get the name right." Then, she played

"The Eyes of Texas," and I got a perfect score. Later she got a recording of "Texas Fight," which I think was then called "Texas Taps," and I did even better. I didn't pass that course on the basis of musical intelligence, but because I volunteered to crank the Victrola. Within an hour I'd crank the Victrola two or three times and always cranked it at the end of the class so that it would be ready for her next class. About this time I got the idea that I wanted to go the University of Texas and become a lawyer. I did not know any lawyers, and there were none in my family. I don't know if Miss Boone had gone to the University of Texas, but she probably gave me the idea or reinforced it. From then on, if someone asked what I wanted to be, I'd say, "I want to go to the University of Texas and be a lawyer."

In grammar school, I made new friends who lived on farms outside Athens. With the construction of paved roads and improvements in school buses, their schools merged with those in Athens, and farm kids came to town more often. One of President Roosevelt's New Deal programs, the Works Progress Administration, helped construct a new junior high school, an addition to the grammar school, and two tennis courts near the high school. In 1937, the WPA and the Athens Independent School District collaborated to build a football field with lights and metal seats. During the six school years that I was in Athens, I played football, basketball, and baseball, depending on the season. Below the high school level, we played tag football rather than tackle. I also learned to play tennis, a game that I have liked ever since.

Among the most vivid memories of my Athens childhood is the weeklong Henderson County Fair in the fall of each year. In addition to the Ferris wheel and the other rides, the most exciting thing was going to the fairground's railroad siding to watch the circus unload the animals and all the equipment required for performances. The circus usually arrived in two trains, one with flat cars that carried the huge tents, and the other with boxcars carrying the animals and all the paraphernalia. The cars were colorful. Wagon-cages were on long flat cars, covered with canvas to protect the bright red and gold paint. Some cars were rolling stables for a half-dozen elephants, each weighing four or five tons and swinging their trunks; and maybe fifty horses of various exotic breeds we had never seen; plus lions, tigers, and zebras. The other boys and

I sat mesmerized on the railroad tracks not far from the railway cars. Watching the elephants help the workers unload the flat cars was amazing; they actually pushed cars along the tracks or pulled them up ramps.

Next came the erection of the huge tent, maybe 300 feet across and 150 feet high. After the boss decided on the location, several hundred stakes, four or five feet in length, were driven most of their length into the ground. It was not a task for weaklings. Several men stood in a circle around a stake, swinging their seventeen-pound sledgehammers sequentially, each swung through a full circle to strike the stake a hundred or more times. All this must be the reason I've had a lifelong interest in circuses and trains. When my grandsons were young, we had great fun watching the circus unload and set up in Austin. About the only hobby I've ever had is collecting model trains dating from the 1930s.

After my grandfather passed away, my grandmother wanted to temporarily get away from Athens to escape the never-ending reminders of their wonderful home life. In September 1937, she, my mother, and I moved to Dallas where we lived in Uncle Wofford's fashionable apartment at the Maple Terrace until we moved to the Melrose on Oaklawn. I attended Highland Park Junior High School for seventh grade. I didn't like living in an apartment house, and I'm sure that the management of the Melrose was delighted to see us leave when school was out in May 1938. They were not used to having young kids playing football in the courtyard and dropping water balloons from the roof.

We moved back to Athens, though we had never really left Athens. Since our apartment was furnished, we had taken only our clothing to Dallas. I resumed working at Safeway. It was a full-time job that on Saturdays began about seven in the morning when I swept off the sidewalk and ended when I swept out the store in the evening. In between I sacked groceries and carried them out to the customers' cars. My break was going home for lunch. I saved my earnings, and Uncle Wofford knew it. One day as he was passing through the checkout line, he said, "Teedy, if you will loan me the money you've saved, I will pay you 8 percent interest." Young as I was, I knew that was quite a deal—8 percent was exorbitant, an outright gift. And there was more.

He added, "When you have enough money, I will use it to buy stock for you in Southern Union Gas," the natural-gas production and distribution company that he and Clint Murchison had founded in 1929. The business was becoming a big success supplying natural gas to towns and cities in Texas, Oklahoma, Arkansas, Arizona, New Mexico, and Ohio. I agreed to Uncle Wofford's proposal, and that was the beginning of beneficial investments in Southern Union Gas that continued for seventy-three years—until 2011, when I cochaired a committee of the corporate board that negotiated the sale of the company for more than fourteen billion dollars.

CHAPTER 2

Schreiner Institute and the Citadel

By the summer of 1938 the adults in my family were keenly aware that another war was probable. Germany had reoccupied the Rhineland, annexed Austria, and was threatening Czechoslovakia. I was thirteen years old and going into the eighth grade. No doubt they discussed what was the best thing for me. In addition to the possibility of war, Uncle Wofford didn't think it was good for me to be raised by my grandmother and mother. Aunt Sha suggested that I should go to Schreiner Institute, an all-male, military school with about 450 students in Kerrville, Texas, that was affiliated with the Presbyterian Church. The idea caught on, especially when Aunt Sha and Uncle Chick Coleman offered to pay for it. My cousin, Jimmy Cain, had just completed his first year there. I looked up to him, and I was enamored with his uniform. I was eager to go. In September 1938, my mother and grandmother drove Jimmy Cain and me to Kerrville, and I enrolled in Schreiner Institute.

Schreiner Institute was a four-year high school and a two-year junior college with ROTC in all six years. At the time, public schools in Texas had eleven grades or years, and Schreiner had the eighth through the eleventh, plus the freshman and sophomore years of college. At Schreiner, the rules were definite, and the discipline was demanding. From the moment the bugle—a real, live bugle—sounded reveille at 6:00 a.m., you knew you were in a military school. By 7:15 a.m., we cadets were standing in formation. Classes began at 8:00 a.m. We wore uniforms all the time, even when we left the campus on weekends. Each student was issued a military web belt and a 1903 Springfield rifle with bayonet, and we had marksmanship practice. We had an hour of close-order drill practice three times a week, followed by a parade each Friday that was graded by the professor of military science and tactics, who also inspected our rooms. Few exercises can compare to close-order drill—marching shoulder-to-shoulder and responding to commands of a drill instructor—for instilling discipline and camaraderie. Sunday afternoons featured a formal parade for the public that was well attended. I played intramural sports and, at various times, managed the football and basketball teams. In my third year, I was promoted to color sergeant, the cadet who carried the flag in all formations and drills. The greatest thrill was carrying the colors in the Battle of Flowers parade in San Antonio on San Jacinto Day, April 21, the date of the final battle of the Texas Revolution in 1836, when Texas won its independence from Mexico. I liked the whole Schreiner experience and it would prove more beneficial than I could have imagined.

At Schreiner, we were too busy to be homesick. We had class or military training during the day, study hall at night, and, if you participated in sports, intramurals or intercollegiate, your day was full. Military training agreed with me. The discipline that it instilled enhanced my performance in academics and sports. I never objected to getting up at six o'clock or five o'clock, or making up my bed. Military training and the discipline that went with it became part of my life. Ever since I went to Schreiner, I've tried to do my best at whatever I've taken on.

Chapel attendance was required on Monday, Wednesday, and Friday at 10:30 a.m. Attendance at a worship service on Sunday in a church of our choice in Kerrville was also required. On the morning of December 7, 1941, I went to church with three friends, including my roommate, Jimmy Barton. After lunch we went to a movie. We came out of the theater intending to hitchhike back to campus, only a couple of miles away. As the four of us were standing there in our dress uniforms, a taxi pulled up in front of us and the driver said, "You guys get in." We said, "Hey, wait a minute. We don't have a nickel." Since it cost a nickel to ride a taxi out to campus, we either hitchhiked or walked. We weren't interested in spending our money on taxi fare. I'll never forget what the driver said. "No, come on and get in. I'm gonna take you. The Japs have bombed Pearl Harbor. You're all immediately due on the campus." The military commander at Schreiner had let the whole town know that cadets should return to campus.

When we got to campus, the student officer-of-the-day and a professor of military science and tactics were standing at the school megaphone, and the bugler was calling cadets to formation. All 430 of us lined up and were told to go to our rooms, get the rifle, bayonet, and military belt that we had been issued, and return to formation. That evening trucks arrived from Fort Sam Houston in San Antonio to collect all military equipment at Schreiner—our rifles, bayonets, two machine guns, and one thirty-seven-millimeter cannon. The equipment was needed for the army, which shows you how unprepared our country was for war. I have often thought about how ill prepared our country was at a time when Germany had already overrun most of Europe, and Japan was challenging us in the Pacific. I am still astonished to think that the U.S. Army needed our small stock of 430 rifles to defend the country, possibly against a Japanese attack in California. We never want to get in that situation again.

Pearl Harbor changed America forever, and it had an immediate effect on Schreiner Institute. That night we were permitted to turn on our radios. "Taps" was delayed until eleven o'clock instead of the usual ten o'clock so we could listen to the news on the only station that reached Kerrville—WOAI in San Antonio. At breakfast the next morning we were told that after our eight o'clock class we should assemble in the auditorium to hear President Roosevelt's speech to Congress, which was followed by Congress's vote to declare that a state of war had existed with Japan since its attack the previous day. After lunch, classes resumed as usual, and that evening we were again allowed to listen to the radio.

On Tuesday, classes were suspended at noon, and the entire student body marched with the institute's band to the Kerr County Courthouse Square in downtown Kerrville. Between seven and ten thousand people were there. An announcer on the public address system gave more details about the disaster at Pearl Harbor and described the Congressional actions that had followed. There were patriotic speeches encouraging men who were eligible for the draft to enlist rather than wait to be called. Afterward we marched back to campus and resumed our usual activities for the afternoon.

The next month, January 1942, I completed my high school graduation requirements and immediately enrolled in Schreiner's college courses. Since graduation exercises were held once a year, I didn't get my high school diploma until May 1942, when I had already earned about fifteen hours of college credit. Then, only five months past my seventeenth birthday, I joined the army, and was accepted into a program that allowed me to attend college for two semesters at the army's expense before going on active duty. The army sent me to the Citadel, the military school of South Carolina, a marvelous military and academic institution, from July 1942 to April 1943.

As a four-year military academy with about two thousand students, the Citadel was comparable to West Point and Annapolis. Our uniforms were tailored and inspections were rigorous, whether in personal appearance, in formations, or in our rooms, where everything had to be in an exact place. I was assigned to the Coast Artillery ROTC unit and to a barracks with only Coast Artillery students. Before classes began, we had two weeks of intensive military drill and discipline, which included an obstacle course on the campus that required running, crawling, jumping, and swinging. We crawled under barricades, climbed fences and walls, and swung—clinging to a rope—across a creek with a full pack. Initially, we were issued a British Lee-Enfield rifle, and later a M-1 Garand Rifle, which the army had recently adopted, a bayonet, and a web belt with a canteen.

We never walked to class. We double-timed, running in formation about three hundred yards to the classroom building. I was made a section leader, which meant that when we got to the classroom, I entered first, saluted the professor, who was also a military officer, and introduced the cadets enrolled in the class. From that one-hour class, we went to other classes. At 11:00 a.m., we went to the parade ground where we had an hour and fifteen minutes of close-order drill with rifles and bayonets and full equipment. Physical exercises were part of the warm-up for close-order drill. Then we returned to our barracks, stacked our rifles and equipment, and marched to the mess hall accompanied by a drum and bugle corps. Fourth-year classmen were freshmen, and that's what I was.

At mealtime we sat on the first three inches of our chair eating a square meal, which meant raising your fork up to mouth level, then bringing it to your mouth in a straight line. We did the same thing with whatever we drank. When we finished, we waited until the bugle blew and everybody marched back to the barracks.

Afternoon classes ended about three-thirty, and we went outdoors to learn tactics and to field-strip machine guns and rifles, eventually while blindfolded. We had exhibitions of army materials and techniques and went through the obstacle course. Several Russian officers came to observe our training. This schedule continued until the first of April, which began the last three weeks of school when regulations were relaxed and we could take our meals like the upper classmen.

On Friday afternoons at four o'clock, we had a formal dress rehearsal parade near the Cooper River, which flows past the Citadel. The river was a breeding ground for mosquitoes and gnats. We were required to wear a full-dress uniform with white gloves and carry a rifle. If you swatted a gnat from your nose or your ear, you had the pleasure of staying in on Saturday and doing military duty. That's when I learned about citronella oil. If I soaked my shirt collar and neck and hair and head under my shako—the Citadel's stiff cylindrical military dress hat with a plume—the gnats and mosquitoes did not bother me. I smelled awful, but everybody else smelled the same. On Friday nights and Saturday afternoons, cadets with passing grades could go into Charleston until ten o'clock. On Sunday afternoons, the Citadel hosted tea dances on campus that attracted girls from all around. But most of the time I just went with other cadets to a movie theater in downtown Charleston on King Street.

The year 1942 was the hundredth anniversary of the Citadel, and we commemorated it by cadets marching in formation through downtown Charleston, ending with a ceremony at the original buildings where the school was founded. The army sent a number of generals for the ceremony, and flew over a formation of planes, which made it a very stirring event for me, then all of seventeen years old.

When I completed the Citadel program in mid-April 1943, I got a letter from the army that I'd be called to active duty in early June. My mother had learned of a special three-week compressed-time intersession program about to start at the University of Texas. I figured the more college credits I had before going on active duty, the better off I'd be. I hurried to Austin, and got there just in time to enroll in two sophomore English courses for six hours credit. Under the wartime class schedule, classes were held six days a week, and I was in class four hours each day.

CHAPTER 3

Private Denius: California to England

AFTER COMPLETING TWO COMPRESSED-TIME COURSES at the University of Texas in May 1943, I went home to Athens to await orders calling me to active duty. When the letter from the War Department came, I was directed to appear at the Henderson County Courthouse by 6:00 a.m. on June 1, 1943. Since the courthouse was only three blocks from my home, getting there was probably easier for me than any of the other seventy-five men I encountered there. At age eighteen, I was one of the youngest—some looked to be about forty. We'd been told to bring only the civilian clothing that we wore and that when we reached our destination—Camp Wolters near Mineral Wells, Texas, about 150 miles west—the army would issue us everything we would need.

The scene around the courthouse square that morning seems quaint today. Most of the people in Athens (population four thousand) were there to see us off. That tells you how unified and determined our country was during the war. My mother, my grandmother, and my great-aunt and great-uncle Coleman were in the crowd along with the high school band, all cheering us. It was an astonishing outpouring of support from the hometown folk, and I left Athens that morning exhilarated, my adrenalin soaring. What a send-off! And exactly fifty-three weeks later, I would go into combat in France, although no one knew it then.

As we left Athens for those fifty-three weeks of training, our transportation—three old Greyhound buses—was another story. Mine broke down after only forty miles, stranding us near Kaufman. The other two went on. Hours later a replacement arrived from Dallas and took us to Camp Wolters, where we arrived after midnight. Despite the hour, we were examined by doctors, issued uniforms, assigned to a barracks, and given blankets and sheets to make up our beds. The medical exam included a humiliating experience that the army imposed monthly to detect symptoms of venereal disease. The exam began with the shouted command, "Drop your pants!" Then each man passed in front of a medical officer, who indicated "pass" or "fail" by the wave of his hand. Afterward we got a short night's sleep before the bugle sounded reveille at five-thirty. We were allowed time to take a shower. I did not yet shave, which saved me precious minutes. After breakfast and cleaning up the barracks, we began taking written tests intended to measure native intelligence and exercises to detect physical limitations. That afternoon, we went to the rifle range for orientation to the range procedures and to fire weapons. So it went for three days.

On the fourth day, about 750 of us boarded a train with our duffel bags. We didn't know where we were going, but we were headed west, and soon learned that we were California bound. What a trip! A troop train was low priority in comparison to those hauling military equipment like tanks, trucks, and artillery pieces. Our train was often diverted from the main track onto sidings, allowing the others to pass. We were fed two meals a day, and it took four days to reach Los Angeles, where we changed trains and went north to Camp Roberts near Paso Robles, about halfway between San Francisco and Los Angeles. An immense military post of more than forty thousand acres, Camp Roberts had a drill field longer than thirteen football fields laid end-to-end, originally for horse cavalry.

After more written tests, I was assigned to basic training for the field artillery. To understand my explanations that follow, it helps to know that field artillery guns are usually aimed at targets several miles away, typically beyond the view of the cannoneers—the men who operate the guns. Since the targets cannot be seen by the cannoneers, they must rely on forward observers, who can see the target, and whose job is to transmit a precise location to a fire direction center (FDC) where other specialists translate the nature of the target and its location into aiming directions and loading instructions for the cannoneers. These three groups made up a field artillery team. It was exciting to watch the team perform their tasks, especially the gunners performing "crew drill"—the big, strong guys who actually handled the ammunition, prepared the shells for firing, picked them up, loaded them, and yanked the lanyards to fire the guns, while shouting "On the way!" I was not one of them, but I was proud to be part of the team.

The individuals within the three groups of a field artillery team had different training. The forward observation team was composed of a forward observer, usually a second lieutenant; an assistant FO, which I would be; and a radio operator. As an assistant FO, my job was to pinpoint the map location of the target described by the forward observer and to call oral instructions for the radioman to transmit to a FDC. To learn the skills required to do this properly, I was placed in a course called "instrument and survey." Other specialists were trained to work in the FDC, making the calculations required by the cannoneers to load the guns to fire on their targets. The calculations took into account differences in the altitude of the gun position and the target, atmospheric conditions, even the rotation of the Earth while the projectile was in the air. This process was complex, and the training was technical and demanding.

Not long after arriving at Camp Roberts, I was made an acting corporal. With five years of military training at Schreiner Institute and the Citadel, I understood military life and soldiering better than most other trainees. I also had an advantage in height. The average American man was about five feet eight inches tall, and I stood six feet two inches. I was not a corporal, but wore an armband with the two stripes of a corporal, identifying me as a squad leader. When reveille sounded at 5:30 a.m. we "fell out in a formation," meaning that we ran out of the barracks and stood in a specified arrangement with the other men in the squad. With two other squads, we made up one platoon of thirty-six men, and our platoon was part of a training battalion. We drilled as a platoon, marched to the mess hall together, and went through our training, day and night, as a platoon. When we lined up in formation, my duty was to see that every man in my squad was there and to salute the officer in

charge, saying, "All men are present and accounted for, Sir" unless someone was missing, in which case, I reported it. A squad was made up of
ten to twelve men. Fortunately, the men in my squad were outstanding
and I had no problems.

For the first month at Camp Roberts, we were housed in permanent
installations, about forty of us sleeping in our underwear on cots in an
unpartitioned area. The place was wide open with everything exposed—
showers, commodes, washbasins. We were together 24/7. If you did not
like someone, too bad. It is difficult to ignore someone in close quarters.
Emphasis was on physical conditioning and classroom instruction in
the principles of artillery and fire direction. Later we bivouacked in the
mountains to learn by doing: giving firing directions and actually firing
the guns. But in this first phase, the daily routine was breakfast, return
to barracks, make up beds, scrub the latrines, and police the area around
the barracks, picking up paper, cigarette butts, and any foreign objects
that were on the ground. I was responsible for what my squad did, or
did not do. Physical conditioning was an important part of every day
and became progressively more strenuous—marches with full packs,
night marches, double-timing (running), up and down hills. My platoon made it through, but I saw men who could not keep up and were
transferred to units with less physical demands.

Training films were a principal means of instruction. Some were
technical, others concerned army regulations and how to stay out of
trouble, but the most memorable were the *Why We Fight* series produced by Frank Capra, explaining the reason the United States was
in the war and what we were fighting for. Capra used actual Nazi and
Japanese film footage to illustrate the evils of those regimes, and it was
convincing. For the most part, the men I was with were conscientious
and patriotic. They wanted to be good soldiers. My generation was not
skeptical or cynical. We had confidence in our government and leaders.

Many men were shocked that basic training was so different from
working at a civilian job. They were not accustomed to doing things
they did not want to do, nor to the possibility of going to the stockade
(army jail) if they disobeyed an order. They were upset to be constantly
told what to do, when and how to do it. The training was stressful, both
mentally and physically, but its purpose was to replace civilian attitudes

with the army's way of thinking—self-discipline, sacrifice and loyalty to comrades, and obedience to commands. I don't want to seem boastful, but it was not difficult for me. I had been in military school since I was in the eighth grade, and it has served me well ever since. I arrived at Camp Roberts already of the opinion that most civilians were too unorganized and undisciplined. Since I was not stressed out by the training, I could concentrate on learning the technical skills of a forward observer, which I found challenging and very satisfying.

Our marksmanship training was with carbines, the lightweight rifle that most artillerymen carried in combat, and we began learning the techniques of surveying-in artillery pieces. "Surveying-in," meant locating the guns correctly on a map in relation to their targets. Only by knowing the precise range and direction between guns and their target could they fire accurately. Lacking today's GPS systems, every time we moved a gun, even at night, we had to survey it in, locating it exactly with newly learned skills in map reading, mathematical calculations, and trigonometry, and manipulating a surveyor's optical instruments and transits as well as using steel tapes and chains. It helped that I'd had four years of math in high school and two semesters of college algebra. Surveying at night was a real challenge. As an indication of how important this training was to me, I have a letter that I wrote to my mother from England a year later (1944) asking her to forward me back copies of the army's subscription journals on infantry and artillery.

Inoculations were on Friday afternoons. For about six weeks we typically got two shots in each arm, while walking straight through an aid station in the hallway of a long building. I don't remember the hypodermic needle so much as the soreness afterward. We thought the best remedy was exercise, and we got it Friday afternoons, preparing for the inspection the next morning by washing vehicles and thoroughly scrubbing our barracks, including the latrines and showers, on our hands and knees.

On Saturday morning we fell out in dress uniforms: olive drab trousers, khaki shirt, and a black tie and green blouse or service jacket. When the inspecting officer stepped in front of you, you immediately went to present arms, bringing your rifle to chest high and opening the bolt, looking into it as you did. He might ask you about your training or to recite one of the eleven general orders for guards on duty, which we were supposed to have memorized. I remembered those orders when arsonists set fire to the Texas governor's mansion on the night of June 8, 2008. Even now, I'd know to post a guard to watch a situation. The first general order back then was "To take charge of this post and all government property in view" and the last was "to be especially watchful at night."

After our first inspection, I was selected the colonel's orderly for one week, the first in my platoon to be chosen. The duty was not difficult. I reported to the colonel each morning and was assigned to work directly with a lieutenant or captain. Usually I delivered orders to subordinates or messages to post headquarters. I did what I was told to do, Monday through Friday, when I went back to my platoon and prepared for inspection the next day.

On Saturday, after the inspection, we marched to a theater near our barracks in dress uniforms, boots spit-shined and polished, and watched more films, often with documentary combat footage. We saw training films about marksmanship with real soldiers, and cartoons featuring a bungling, comical figure called Private Snafu, the fall guy who got lost, could not find a booby trap strapped to his jeep, or load his rifle without smashing a finger. A Looney Tunes cartoon with Bugs Bunny promoted the sale of war bonds. In a film on aircraft recognition, Capt. Ronald Reagan portrayed a greenhorn pilot who could not identify a Japanese Zero. In some films, we saw Russian troops and their army in action; this slight exposure to our erstwhile ally would be useful when we met them on the Elbe River in Germany almost two years later. Saturday afternoons were usually a time for skull sessions with members of my squad about the mathematics involved in being a forward observer. There were more movies on Saturday nights. Then lights out and "Taps" at ten o'clock. "Reveille" was not until seven on Sunday mornings. Church was not compulsory, but my buddies in the squad usually went to a chapel in the area. We had a different chaplain every week. After church we returned to our area, held a formation, and marched to the mess hall.

Training intensified with time. We had a lot of dry runs, rehearsing what we would actually do in combat—identifying the enemy, both ground troops and tanks, sometimes dug in or located in a village, and calling a fire mission to a fire direction center. We had close-order drill every day with forced marches, and night marches up to twenty miles. In the simulated combat exercises, the surveying crew, the radio section, the cannoneers, and the forward observers learned their jobs. After classroom instruction, we'd have practical experience in the field under simulated combat conditions, going through the processes so many times that eventually we could make the necessary calculations in our heads. A drill sergeant quizzed us orally, asking questions and grading us both on our answers and on how quickly we responded.

The reality began to sink in on me that we, the forward observers, were expected to be with the infantry, and out front, often in enemy territory, looking for targets while avoiding detection by stealthy movements and camouflage. Despite the dangers, forward observers had to position themselves to watch a wide expanse of territory. We were taught to use binoculars, although using them in combat was risky because light would reflect from the lenses and give away your location. When I practiced directing artillery fire, a senior sergeant and a couple of officers were with me. I would determine the map coordinates of my position and of the target, and call them to a nearby radio operator who transmitted them to the fire direction center, which refined them and sent them to the firing battery, which then fired several rounds at the target I had selected.

I was fortunate not to lose anyone in my squad for physical or academic reasons. On the rifle range, every man in my squad qualified as a marksman, and I became a sharpshooter. Just about everything we did was satisfying to me, although I'm sure that my enthusiasm faded on long marches. On marches, the platoon sang, always the field artillery's "Caisson Song": "Over hill, over dale, as we hit the dusty trail, and those caissons go rolling along. In and out, hear them shout, counter march and right about, and those caissons go rolling along. Then it's hi! hi! hee! In the field artillery . . ."

From my first experience with close-order drill at Schreiner Institute, I enjoyed it. It is amazingly effective in teaching discipline and self-control, enhancing morale and unit cohesion while instilling the habit of instant obedience to commands. I drilled my squad apart from others, and we taught each other the general orders, even practicing our conduct as guards on duty. Drilling, as well as digging, is fundamental to the making of a soldier. The oldest man in the squad was a thirty-five-year-old draftee named Howard "Howie" Young, a tavern keeper from the south side of Chicago, married and the father of three children. Howie stood 5'10" and weighed about two hundred pounds, a bulk that was reduced considerably by those twenty-mile marches. He was a masterful poker player and crapshooter who knew the odds on every throw of the dice. I'll have more to say about him later.

In November, after I'd been at Camp Roberts for almost five months, I got a forty-eight-hour pass; it was my first opportunity to leave the post. With forty-eight hours leave, you could be gone from Friday evening until suppertime on Sunday night. Three other fellows and I decided to go to Los Angeles by renting a two-door Dodge coupe from a sergeant who made extra money that way. I have forgotten what we paid him, but the big challenge was not in paying for the car, but getting gasoline for it.

The government began rationing gasoline in 1942 after voluntary rationing proved ineffective. Most family cars were issued an "A" sticker for their windshield, and stamps that allowed the purchase of four gallons a week. People whose occupations required considerable driving were issued additional stamps for more gasoline. For a while, A-stickered cars were not driven for pleasure at all. Most people were prudent and walked rather than drove to the grocery store.

When my mother learned I was going to Los Angeles, she sent me two gasoline stamps she had saved, which entitled me to buy six gallons of gasoline. Some people sold their stamps, creating a black market.

My three buddies and I left after the last formation on Friday without staying for supper. Through the night we took turns driving the ten hours to Los Angeles. The speed limit was thirty-five miles per hour and there was no Interstate 5, just Highway 101 with numerous military convoys that really slowed down the traffic. Near Los Angeles, where Highway 101 was the same road as the Pacific Coast Highway, signs instructed drivers to douse their lights so as not to provide navigational clues to Japanese submarines that might be lurking offshore. With dimmed lights, we drove even slower.

In Los Angeles, we went straight to the Stage Door Canteen in Hollywood, which rivaled in size the one in Washington, D.C., as well as the original canteen in New York City. The canteen operated eighteen hours a day, seven days a week, and the sign over the door read, "Through these portals pass the most beautiful uniforms in the world." It could have added "some of the most beautiful women in the world," because movie stars like Marlene Dietrich, Bette Davis, and Betty Grable, the number one pin-up girl of the war, came occasionally to dance with GIs. Entertainers came, too—Bob Hope and Bing Crosby among them.

Although the four of us were privates—the lowest rank in the army—we were treated like everyone else. There was a spirit of equality in all Stage Door Canteens, wherever they were. A nice lady greeted us, saying, "I have just the place for you boys," which I guess we were. The canteen had converted the fellowship hall of a nearby church into a place for GIs to stay for two dollars a night. It was all we needed: bunks, bedding, and bathrooms. Then we went out on the town to see some sights.

I had cousins in the area, and we went to see them at 108 South Palm Drive, off Wilshire Boulevard. We chatted a while over cakes and soft drinks. One of our guys knew a girl attending UCLA, who invited us out to her sorority house. It was midnight or later when we got back to the Stage Door Canteen. On Sunday morning we did a little sightseeing and headed back to Camp Roberts. Our brief trip to Los Angeles was the only time I was away from Camp Roberts during those seven months. It cost me thirty-six dollars, about the same as my take-home pay each month. The monthly pay for a private in mid-1943 was fifty dollars a month, from which a couple of dollars was deducted for an insurance premium. We were paid in cash once a month. Since ten dollars a month was about all the spending money I needed, I used the rest to buy war bonds and sent them home.

On Christmas Day 1943, I made my only telephone call from Camp Roberts. Making a telephone call took too much time. On the entire Camp Roberts, with several thousand men, there were only about a dozen public telephones. They were attached to the wall under an overhang of the roof at the PX—the Post Exchange, the soldiers' store. So many men were usually lined up to use them that you might wait an hour or more just to get your hands on one. There was no such thing as direct distance dial or area codes. An operator necessarily handled every call. When I got to the head of the line and had an operator on the line, I would say, "I want to place a collect call to two-three-two in Athens, Texas." A succession of operators would route my call through their switchboards, eventually connecting to the telephone office in Athens, where the last in this chain of manual operators dialed 232. If I was lucky, my mother or grandmother would answer, and the operator would ask, "Will you accept a collect call from Frank Denius?" It was wonderful to hear their voices, but you can appreciate why telegrams and letters were the main way we communicated.

On New Year's Day, we had the afternoon free, and I listened to the Rose Bowl game won by the Southern Cal Trojans over the Washington Huskies 29 to 0. Then we went to the mountains for eight days of simulated combat, the last stage of our training. January 15, 1944, was graduation day. We were issued a certificate that we had completed artillery basic training and were eligible to be forward observers in the instrument and survey section of a firing battery. We had been cross-trained, prepared for several jobs: to be forward observers, to scout new positions for the guns, and to lay-in the guns—that is, align them to fire accurately on their targets. On graduation day, I could not have imagined that within a few months I would perform all these tasks in a combat environment on the European continent. In the final days at Camp Roberts, I got new orders, granting me ten days delay in route before reporting to Fort Meade, Maryland, near Washington, D.C.

I telegraphed my family that I had a furlough and would be home in about two days, the estimated time to reach Dallas by train. Well, it took almost four days! People today would find it difficult to understand public transportation during World War II. Trains were the main way to get from one region of the United States to another. Commercial air service was very limited, mostly reserved for priority military travel, and considered only a supplement to railroads. In addition to men and women in military service crisscrossing the country, their wives and children were also on the trains, traveling to be near them as long as they remained in this country. Since millions of people were on the move, trains were crowded and seldom on their timetables. The scheduled six-hour train ride from Camp Roberts to Los Angeles took twelve hours, and we missed our connection to El Paso. I say "we" because I had buddied up with Royal Walker from Murchison, Texas, a small town near Athens that I mentioned earlier. Royal had just completed the cannoneer school. Any delay counted against the ten days before I had to report to Fort Meade.

The scene in the Los Angeles railroad station that afternoon was unforgettable. Royal and I had not eaten since early morning, and now we had missed the train to Texas. I went up to a military policeman, showed him my orders and my train ticket, which was a government-issued ticket rather than railroad-issued. He said another train to El Paso was scheduled to leave at seven o'clock that night and, if we wanted to get on it, we should stay right there. "Just sit down and wait," he said, "because there may be a thousand people trying to get on."

We took his advice, sat on our duffel bags, and waited for hours. When the gate to the boarding platform finally opened, we ran, carrying our bags, and got in the fourth or fifth car in time to get a seat; otherwise, we might have stood in the aisle all the way to El Paso. These were not sleeping cars; they were just coaches or chair cars. Almost twenty-four hours were required to cover the eight hundred miles between Los Angeles and El Paso, where we arrived the next night. Again, we were hungry and aggravated that we had already used more than a day of our ten-day furlough. Our government-issued tickets had us going on the Southern Pacific Railroad to Houston, almost two hundred miles southeast of Athens. If we could go straight to Dallas, we'd save time. I went to the Texas Pacific station and learned they had a train leaving for Dallas in two hours. So Royal Walker and I tore up our government tickets and bought tickets to Dallas with our own money. We got to Dallas about ten o'clock the next morning, and I called my mother's brother, John Cain, whose office was only a few blocks away in the Mercantile Bank building. I had not alerted him that I was coming, but he immediately said, "Teedy, I'll get my car and be right there." Royal and I waited in front of the station. Uncle John was there in a few minutes and drove us those seventy-five miles to Athens and home. That's the kind of family I was born into.

My mother and grandmother—and my great-aunt and uncle, Aunt Sha and Uncle Chick—were so glad to see me. For almost a week, they lavished attention on me. Every meal was better than the one before. No doubt they were thinking that this might be my last visit home, but we did not talk about it. Friends of the family came to see me, perhaps for the same reason. Athens was not like it had been, because most of the young men were away in the service, and the girls of my age were either at college or following the fellows they had married—now in the service—around the country, or had gone to work in Dallas or Houston, which hummed with good jobs in defense industries. In the whole town, there were only two girls that I knew and I took one of them, Jacqueline Holland, to Tyler one evening for dinner and a movie. Anytime I left my home, I wore my army dress uniform, as required by army regulations, and my mother had my uniforms tailored. I went to Stirman's Drug Store on the square to see the older men I had known growing up. I visited with the Safeway store manager, who always had a job for me. Uncle Chick promised to give me a thousand dollars if I did not smoke or drink until I was twenty-one years old. I spent my furlough with my family, talking about everything except the obvious—that I was leaving soon for an unknown place from which I might not return. It was a quiet time.

When my departure day finally came, my mother and grandmother drove me about thirty-five miles to Corsicana, where I caught the Burlington-Rock Island Railroad's *Sam Houston Zephyr*, a streamlined passenger train to Houston, where I transferred to the Southern Pacific's *Sunset Limited* for New Orleans, and Jacksonville, Florida, then to Atlanta and up to Washington, D.C., on the Southern Railroad, where I caught a local train to Fort Meade, Maryland. Upon arrival, I was assigned to a training company of one hundred and fifty men who had completed artillery basic training at different army camps around the country. I did not know any of them.

I was at Fort Meade less than three weeks. A few days after I arrived, orders came down that I was going overseas. I did not know where or the unit I would be assigned to. The daily regimen was physical conditioning, usually involving an obstacle course, where live ammunition was fired over our heads while we crawled under barbed wire, hugging the ground; or swung on ropes across a sizeable river, holding on to avoid falling in its frigid winter waters. There was more artillery training as well as long marches with a full pack. Each day seemed a repeat of the day before.

During the two weekends of that brief period at Fort Meade I went to Washington to visit Bob "Shakey" Strain, my old buddy from Athens, who was stationed there after basic training in the navy. Bob would meet me at Union Station and we'd go sightseeing to Arlington Cemetery; the Smithsonian; the Tomb of the Unknown Soldier; the Pepsi Cola Center—a huge facility near Union Station where you could drink all the Pepsi you wanted for free and buy a hot dog or hamburger for a nickel; and the Stage Door Canteen, only two blocks from the White House, where girls came to dance with GIs. We visited the office of the congressman, John Dowdy, from our district in Texas, but not to see him—we went to see Mary Hoy Owens, the beautiful young woman from Athens who worked for him.

On my last weekend in Washington, my mother came by train from Dallas. She managed to get a berth on a Pullman, a railroad sleeping car, and I got her a hotel room near Union Station for two nights. Bob Strain and I met her at the station. One evening she took Mary Hoy Owens, Bob, and me to the Statler-Hilton Hotel for dinner and dancing. We did not talk about this being our last time together before I left the States, but I am sure she was thinking about it.

During the third week at Fort Meade, about a thousand of us boarded a train that traveled north—with the blinds pulled down for reasons of secrecy—to Camp Myles Standish, a staging area some forty miles south of Boston. It was early February 1944 and snow covered the ground. We remained there three days, had more inoculations, and were oriented to our coming sea voyage. One afternoon I got into Boston and stayed until ten that night. I wanted to see the Old North Church from which the famous "One if by land, and two if by sea" lantern signal was sent to alert the patriots of Lexington and Concord. As a schoolboy, Henry Wadsworth Longfellow's poem about Paul Revere's midnight ride had made quite an impression on me.

In conspicuous locations around Camp Myles Standish and in Boston, there were signs that read, "Loose lips sink ships." We were constantly warned not to disclose anything about our unit, our branch of service, not anything! Letter writing was forbidden, and we were quarantined, except for one brief visit to Boston. Despite all this, I wanted to let my mother know where I was. I went into the Jordan Marsh department store and bought her an inexpensive scarf, paid for it in cash, and asked the saleslady to mail it to my mother with a note stating that it was a gift from me. The postmark told my mother that I had passed through Boston.

In the cold, wintry darkness of the early morning in mid-February, about a thousand of us boarded a train for the forty-mile journey to Boston harbor. Other trains joined us on converging tracks as we approached the piers along the waterfront. We detrained in a huge barn-like shed. A band was playing and Red Cross girls were serving hot coffee and donuts, but my hands were so full with a rifle, duffel bag, and back-pack that I could not take any. All we could see of the ship was its huge, battleship-gray, slab-like side bordered with a chain of life rafts. I walked with my squad up the gangplank to enter the USS *Wakefield*, formerly the fast luxury liner, the SS *Manhattan*. Years later I read that the USS *Wakefield* had a maximum capacity of six thousand troops and it averaged eighteen days on round trips between Boston and Liverpool. The vessel was crammed with every conceivable space filled.

The army's method of assigning us to our compartments was very efficient. A sergeant used chalk to mark on each man's helmet his compartment number. Mine was D-10, next to the lowest level, just about waterline in a space that we called "torpedo junction." We slept in hammocks, slung in stacks of four from the ceiling with about eighteen inches between them. Mine was the second from the floor. We were told to put our duffel bags under the bottom hammock and to stay in our hammocks until the ship left port. I hung my helmet over the side and laid my rifle parallel to my body. I do not know how many men were crammed in that compartment, but with their body heat and no fresh air coming in, it was hot! My clothes were soaking wet, and we had nothing to eat, but eating wasn't important anyway. Somehow I went to sleep, only to wake up freezing. The ship had begun to move, and cold air was coming down from those big round vents on the deck. We were in the North Atlantic in the dead of winter.

Life on board the *Wakefield* was simple. We were given a color-coded card indicating when and where to go for meals. We were fed every twelve hours, round-the-clock. We lived in our uniforms, were always ready for chow, and ate from our steel mess kits with a knife, a fork, and a spoon that were sized to fit inside the kit. The cooks sloshed our food into the bowl of the kit. Going through the chow line the first day I encountered Howie Young, my friend from Camp Roberts, the Chicago tavern keeper. We greeted each other warmly. Calling me by my army nickname, he said, "Tex, how much money do you have?" Keep in mind that Howie had three children and a wife, and he always needed money to support them. He had about twenty-five dollars. I said, "I've got a hundred and five dollars." He replied, "If you'll loan me fifty dollars, I'll give you your fifty dollars back from what I win in crap games and split my winnings with you."

Well, any kid that got in a crap game with Howie Young didn't realize that he was playing with a pro. Howie knew the odds on cards, poker, and shooting dice. He never bet on the dice. When he rolled the dice, it was only to keep the game moving, and he always bet against the dice. Shortly before we docked in Liverpool, he paid me back the fifty dollars and gave me my half of what he'd won. My part of his kitty was about $2,100, the equivalent of $28,200 purchasing power in 2014. What was I to do with almost two hundred bills of varying denominations, from one to twenty dollars? I decided to hide them in the equipment I carried, and stuck all those bills in the bottom of my gas mask. Since army regulations prohibited me from sending home more than my normal monthly pay of sixty dollars, the money became a pool that the guys in my battery "C" of the 230th Field Artillery Battalion could draw on for emergencies, perhaps a family crisis back home. When I returned home in August 1945, I still had a couple of hundred dollars.

The *Wakefield*, capable of thirty to thirty-two knots, was so fast that German submarines were not a big scare. Until we reached open water, the ship was shadowed by three or four navy PBY Catalina flying boats, watching for U-boats. Then the *Wakefield* left the convoy and operated as a "lone wolf." In the conversion from the passenger liner *Manhattan* to the troop ship *Wakefield*, a five-inch gun was added to the bow and the stern. The marines on board—about thirty of them—were in charge of the guns. About four o'clock on the first morning at sea, the ship rumbled with shock waves of those guns firing. Down below, we woke up alarmed, concerned that we'd run into a U-boat wolfpack, but it was only the marines test-firing the guns.

We approached Liverpool on a cold, gusty day. Several PBYs and

Royal Navy corvettes met us at sea and escorted us into the harbor, where we docked along the River Mersey. Trucks were lined up on the pier alongside the ship to haul us away to unknown destinations. I was still an acting corporal and had charge of a squad of a dozen men. We were taken to a transit camp that was nothing more than twelve-man tents erected on cold, damp concrete slabs in an open area in the countryside. In groups of three, we coped with the frigid conditions by laying two blankets on the concrete and sleeping under the third, fully clothed and snuggled close together for the body heat. Each member of our squad was on duty for an hour during the night. I took the last hour in order to be awake when the wake-up call came.

Seeing haystacks in an adjacent field, a man in my squad had the bright idea of putting hay under his blanket. I have never smoked a cigarette in my life, but this fellow, like 95 percent of the Americans, was a smoker. He went over to bring hay back, and others followed him, all of them smoking. Suddenly, an Englishman came running out of nowhere, screaming, "Sergeant. Sergeant." I was not a sergeant, but I went to see what he wanted. "Please keep those soldiers away from the hay stacks," he said, because they were actually storage tanks of hundred-octane aviation gasoline—thousands of gallons—covered with hay as camouflage.

The next morning we boarded trucks again for a long ride to a British army camp near Southampton. I was selected for five weeks of Ranger training, including a parachute jump from a C-47. After those five weeks, I was assigned to the Thirtieth Infantry Division, 230th Field Artillery Battalion, and joined the battalion near Billingshurst, about fifty miles northeast of Southampton. I would remain with the 230th battalion for the rest of the war, which would be attached to the Thirtieth Infantry Division. In Billingshurst, we were housed in drafty uninsulated Nissen huts, just metal sheets bent into the curving shape of half of a cylinder. Coal was strictly rationed, and the small English stoves did not produce much heat. At night, German bombers occasionally passed overhead and we could hear the dull thud of bombs in London, some forty miles away. Each day brought more rumors about the invasion—when and where it would occur and who would be in it.

Having mentioned the 230th Field Artillery Battalion, I want to explain what it was because I will refer to it many times in future chapters. The battalion was about five hundred men commanded by Lt. Col. Lewis D. Vieman, a 1938 graduate of Texas A&M from Dickinson, Texas. He was outstanding, a well-trained officer and a splendid gentleman. The battalion had three firing batteries—designated "A," "B," and "C"—each with four 105-mm (4.14-inch diameter) guns, for a total of twelve guns, or as artillerymen said, "tubes." Strictly speaking, our guns were "howitzers," which have a relatively short barrel and fire projectiles on high trajectories that descend at steep angles on targets. They had a maximum range of about seven miles and were particularly useful for firing on targets out-of-sight, on the other sides of hills and ridges. By comparison, a real "gun" fired line-of-sight, directly at the target, as would a ship at sea. I was in the forward observer team for battery "C" commanded by Capt. Merrill S. Alexander, whom I liked very much. He had graduated from the Officer Candidate School at Fort Sill, Oklahoma, the premier training ground for artillery officers. The Thirtieth Division had three infantry regiments—the 117th, the 119th, and the 120th, each with three thousand soldiers. They were the fighting troops who were in closest contact with the enemy. My battery "C" would usually support the 120th. We were like business partners with the 120th Infantry Regiment, and the business was killing Germans. All told, the Thirtieth Infantry Division had about seventeen thousand men.

On April 4, we vacated our camp to make room for invasion troops and moved inland by motor vehicle. The move confirmed that the Thirtieth Division would not be involved in the initial assault in France. Our new encampment was on the grounds of an estate called St. John's near the town of High Wycombe, about thirty miles west of central London. Team training for artillerymen continued for two weeks at a British army post on the Salisbury Plain, some ninety miles west. Then, we went to the east coast of England for infantry exercises under rolling artillery barrages.

Both Gen. Dwight D. Eisenhower and Gen. Bernard L. Montgomery (the British general) came to inspect the division. Montgomery made a speech. "The young Germans are tough, very tough," he said. "There is not much you can do with them except kill them. We kill them." The generals were terrific morale boosters, but it was our division artillery commander, Brig. Gen. Raymond S. McLain, who really fired me up. He told us that forward observers were the most challenged and exposed men on the battlefield. They had to think fast under extreme stress and work silently on and behind enemy lines. He emphasized that the enemy would regard us as high-priority targets because we had the ability to bring destructive artillery fire on them. The general called artillery the "King of the Battlefield," which was an apt descriptor because it was the greatest killer.

When the invasion began on June 6, we were eager to go, but were told that the Thirtieth Division would not go into action for several days. Nonetheless, we stripped our equipment and personal belongings to the essentials and put everything in readiness to go. It was a good thing because, suddenly, on the afternoon of June 8, whistles blew all over the place and officers began shouting, "Load up! Load up! Get in your trucks! You've got forty-five minutes." Most of us thought it was another practice, but it was not a dry run. The 230th Field Artillery Battalion was bound for Southampton and Normandy to replace, we learned later, a field artillery battalion of the Twenty-ninth Division that had landed on D-Day and had been virtually destroyed. We would take their place and the rest of the Thirtieth Division would remain a few days longer in England.

We got to Southampton—about seventy miles south—before dark after passing through villages where people waved, gave us a "thumbs up" for victory, and called out "God bless you." In the port area, the military police escorted our convoy to the head of the line, and we began waterproofing our trucks and howitzers. That night we slept in the trucks or beside them in the rain. The next morning we loaded onto two LSTs, the acronym for "landing ship, tank." One flew the Stars and Stripes and the other the Union Jack. I was on the British ship. Both pulled away from the dock and dropped anchor in the harbor.

CHAPTER 4

Normandy and Hill 314

L ATE ON THE AFTERNOON OF JUNE 9 we weighed anchor for Normandy with a barrage balloon tethered to our LST swinging high above. The flat-bottomed vessel seemed to slip sideways on the sea, but the crossing was uneventful. By dawn the next day we were within sight of Omaha Beach. I knew nothing of the landings, over to the right on Utah Beach, and the thump-thump-thump sound of heavy artillery firing was incessant. There may have been a thousand ships in view, from small landing craft to heavy cruisers. Even battleship *Texas* was out there, but if I saw it, I did not recognize it. The shoreline was littered with the wreckage of landing craft, trucks, half-tracks—vehicles of all kinds, tipped over, underwater, or half-submerged. A high bluff rose a couple hundred yards beyond the beach where I could see a tent hospital.

Our vehicles drove from the LST directly onto the shore, but we—the foot soldiers—climbed over the side of the ship and, clinging to rope ladders, we jumped into an LCI (landing craft, infantry) that took us to the beach. My most vivid memory of coming ashore in Normandy is jumping from the ship into the landing craft that was pitching both up and down and from side to side. I hardly got my feet wet as we landed at the mouth of the first ravine east of the present American cemetery, called the "Colleville Draw." An antitank ditch about five hundred yards long had blocked the mouth of the ravine until our bulldozers had filled parts of it, creating bridges for vehicles and walking soldiers. With others in my battery, we walked up the slope on the right side of the draw, passing a pair of German artillery bunkers that had been plastered. By mid-afternoon—still June 10—we had driven our trucks about a mile inland to bivouac near the village of Colleville-sur-Mer. The stench of death was unavoidable, with dead Germans along the roads and bloated cows in the fields, feet sticking straight up. Under a roadside wooden cross lay the bodies of four American soldiers covered with flowers by French civilians. We moved cautiously, observing the lines of white tape that marked minefields and peeking over hedgerows to get the lay of the land. Men began walking bent over in the "hedgerow stoop" to stay out of the sight and gunfire of the Germans.

Shortly after we landed, a U.S. Navy liaison officer joined my forward observer team. He could talk "navy," and we began telling him the map coordinates of German installations, which he transmitted to warships lying offshore, which then fired on them. That night, we surveyed in our guns, using flashlights and lanterns, as we had learned at Camp Roberts. By daylight, June 11, we were firing in support of the Twenty-ninth Infantry Division and we'd captured our first prisoner, a sniper caught unaware as he tried to find a hiding place near the headquarters of the 115th Infantry Regiment of the Twenty-ninth Division. He was lucky not to have shot anyone we knew. We began having casualties, minor wounds from shell fragments, and then a sergeant in another forward observer team was killed while trying to get in position for a firing mission. His death was the first of someone I knew, and it got my attention, because his duties were the same as mine. I learned later that he was Staff Sgt. Edward Smith of "C" Battery, killed by a German machine gun while with a forward observer party that ran into a German roadblock.

There are similarities between football and war. In war you are playing for keeps and cannot afford to lose. When University of Texas football coach Mack Brown called on me to speak to the team, as he did before the Oklahoma game in 2011, he mentioned my wartime experiences with men killed and wounded. I told the team that, unlike combat in war, if you lose in football you can walk to the dressing room.

The attack of the Twenty-ninth Division was relentless, almost straight inland, and making steady, though costly, progress toward the city of Saint-Lô, about twenty miles from Omaha Beach, and the center of the regional road network. The Twenty-ninth was more than halfway there, and more divisions were coming ashore to broaden the front and put more pressure on the Germans. The Second Infantry Division came along the left side of the Twenty-ninth.

My parent Thirtieth Infantry Division began landing on Omaha during the night of June 13 and was inserted on the right flank of the Twenty-ninth in the gap between the two main American forces attacking inland, one from Utah Beach on the Cherbourg Peninsula and the other from Omaha Beach. The 230th Field Artillery Battalion was released from the Twenty-ninth and returned to the Thirtieth. This change involved us marching at night about fifteen miles northwest to a site between the towns of Isigny and Carentan where the Germans were still within a couple of miles of the English Channel. This was the weakest and most vulnerable stretch of the American front. A single road ran along the coastline, and our defenses were shallow. Holding it was vitally important, so that if the Germans launched a massive counterattack on one beachhead, the other could reinforce it. We were in the low-lying area between the meandering Vire and Taute Rivers, with numerous drainage ditches and hedgerows so dense with shrubs and trees that they were practically dikes. Almost any movement in the soggy marshland was difficult. Each hedgerow was a natural fortress that provided excellent concealment for the Germans. Typically, they dug in and camouflaged their tanks at the corners and defended the open fields between them with machine guns, making our advancing infantrymen vulnerable to crossfire.

Unknown to us in the lower ranks—and I was only private first class—Gen. Omar N. Bradley, the overall American ground commander, had decided to hold all captured ground, but not to advance in our area. "Maintain vigorous patrolling and an active defense" was the order. Bradley needed time to bring more forces ashore and to take the port of Cherbourg before attempting a major attack here. Thus, for three weeks we patrolled aggressively, trying to persuade the Germans that a big offensive might come at them anytime. The main objective from Omaha Beach remained Saint-Lô, with Cherbourg the objective from Utah Beach. We were in the middle, holding the vital though shallow link between the two beachheads. Patrolling proved difficult for several reasons. If attempted during daylight, broad spaces had to be crossed in view of the enemy, and the nights were at their shortest of the year—about four hours—leaving little time to reconnoiter enemy positions under the cover of darkness.

Although General Bradley said we were to hold in place and not advance, for us in the frontline, every day was intense and hazardous. On a typical day, we fired about 375 to 400 artillery rounds and encountered plenty of mines and booby traps, some hidden under dead Germans and Americans. About the first of July we began planning for the Thirtieth Division's long-awaited attack toward Saint-Lô, about fifteen miles south. Using the road from Carentan to Saint-Lô (N 174) as our axis of advance, my 230th Artillery Battalion would support the division's 120th Infantry Regiment, which was to cross the Taute et Vire Canal, take a crossroads village called Saint Jean-de-Daye, and continue on. The Twenty-ninth and the newly arrived Thirty-fifth Infantry Division were on our left, advancing toward Saint-Lô from the east and the north. The Thirtieth Division's goal was to reach the high ground west of Saint-Lô along a long straight road that led to Périers, a smaller town twelve miles west.

First Silver Star

Our attack jumped off at 1:00 p.m. on July 7, and we gained ground steadily. By the end of the day, we had fired 2,437 artillery rounds and Saint Jean-de-Daye was in our hands. In liberating the village, the 120th Infantry Division, which we were helping, advanced beyond it, then doubled back to take it from the rear. We'd also had several casualties in our forward observer teams, but the Thirtieth Division's infantry had gotten ahead of other U.S. units on both of our flanks and we projected like a finger into the German lines. This forced us to defend on our left and right flanks as well as to our front. As a result, for the next three days we had heavy fighting with little forward progress. At the end of July 11, the fifth day of our offensive, the Thirtieth Division had taken more than thirteen hundred casualties, and the rest of us were dead on our feet. Things would get worse. In the next four days, we took almost two thousand more casualties. For the army, "casualties" refers to those killed, wounded, taken prisoner, or simply missing—unaccounted for.

On July 17, while pressing the attack inland toward the road that ran from Saint-Lô to Périers, the incident occurred for which I was awarded my first Silver Star. My three-man forward observation team was out front, led by Lieutenant Miller, who had joined us the day before. He was so new that his name had not been entered on our roster, and I have forgotten his first name. He may have come in the night before, which is when we usually got replacements. As his assistant, I stayed right with him and did whatever he said. Our radio operator, Sherman Goldstein, was about ten steps behind us. The spotting rounds from our firing battery's guns were impacting near the target, but not close enough to have the desired effect. Miller was trying to get a better view of the target so he could call back instructions to adjust the fire. Unfortunately, he stood up to look over a hedgerow at the wrong time, using his binoculars, and was hit by machine gun fire. He died instantly.

There was nothing for me to do except take over and carry out our mission. As I started to peep over the hedgerow, Goldstein shouted, "Stay down, Tex." I crawled to a less exposed place where I could see two German tanks with about twenty infantry on foot advancing toward us. Miller had called the map reference correctly and the battery was firing, but the rounds were not hitting close enough. I shouted to Goldstein something like "one-hundred over, seventy-five right." This improved the accuracy. When our rounds began hitting close or on the target, I called "Fire for effect" and all guns in the battalion fired—twelve 105-mm howitzers. Most of the Germans fell immediately, either for safety or from wounds, and the tanks backed up fast. Goldstein may have saved my life when he shouted, "Stay down, Tex." To be decorated for gallantry in the face of the enemy, someone must see what happened and report it, and that could have only been Goldstein.

A few days later my battery commander, Capt. Merrill Alexander, with his jeep driver behind the wheel, drove me to the division headquarters, lodged in a farmhouse, where our commander, Maj. Gen. Leland S. Hobbs, awarded me the decoration in a special ceremony. Hearing my citation read before the assembled staff of the division with men from my battery present was an unforgettable and highly emotional moment. I was nineteen years old and, although I have received numerous awards since then, the award of this Silver Star was like none other. This proud, yet humbling, experience has enabled me to accept others without altering my routine or inflating my sense of who I am.

Private First Class Franklin W. Denius, 38480234, 230th Field Artillery Battalion, United States Army, is awarded the Silver Star Medal for gallantry in action on 17 July 1944, in France. Private Denius was a member of an artillery forward observing party advancing with an infantry unit. To complete their mission, it was necessary to move some distance in advance of the leading infantry elements. During the adjustment of fire, the officer in charge of the observing party was killed by enemy machine gun fire. Private Denius, although having no previous experience in observing fire, completed the mission by accurately adjusting the fire of his artillery unit. The initiative and perseverance shown by Private Denius to carry out his mission, at the risk of his life, are highly exemplary and reflect the highest credit on himself and the Armed Forces. Entered military service from Texas.

When we reached the Saint-Lô to Périers road four days later on July 20, the Thirtieth Division had lost more than three thousand men in the eight miles since we crossed the Vire et Taute Canal on July 7. While we were slugging forward, with heavy losses and small gains, General Bradley was also frustrated with the overall failure of American forces to gain more ground across the entire front. As a tactic to break through the enemy defenses, he proposed saturation bombing of a limited area directly in front of us on the other side of the Saint-Lô to Périers road, more or less our boundary with the Germans. The area he selected was a rectangle about three miles along the road and one mile deep on the German side, the south side. The codename for the plan was *Operation Cobra*. This technique—"carpet-bombing"—had been pioneered a few months before in Italy around the town of Casino. The intention was to pulverize German defenses and kill or stun the men in or near them. We would then rush across the road and penetrate through their positions before they could recover. Just before the bombs began falling at noon on July 24, we—my Thirtieth Division—and the Fourth and the Ninth Infantry Divisions, which had come in on our right—were to pull back a safe distance from the road. Once the bombing was concluded, these three divisions would spearhead the attack, followed by three armored divisions.

On the morning of July 24, more than two thousand bombers took off from their bases in England for *Operation Cobra.* Just before noon, we heard them coming from the north. Unfortunately, about the time the bombers left England, heavy clouds blew in over the target area, obscuring it to crews, who had to be able to see the ground to bomb accurately. An attempt was made to call them back, but some did not get the message, and about 350 B-17s and B-24s continued on. Some of them dropped their bombs on our side of the road, killing or wounding more than 150 men of my division. It was tragic, but "c'est la guerre," as the French say, and the bombing mission was rescheduled for the next day.

On July 25, the bombers came again in full force. With the roar of thousands of engines, they came in, formation after formation, each with several hundred planes, flying steadily through black puffs of German antiaircraft fire. The magnificence of the sight is impossible to describe. Then came the thunderous noise, with the ground trembling as bombs exploded nearby. There was the horrible sight of bombers bursting in flames in mid-air, blowing up and falling to the ground. Unbelievably, the aiming error of the previous day was repeated and there were about 800 casualties—more than a hundred killed, about five hundred wounded, and two hundred hospitalized with PTSD, or "combat exhaustion." Among others killed was Lt. Gen. Lesley J. McNair, the highest-ranking American officer to die in the European Theater.

On both days, I was only a few hundred yards away, near the village of Hébécrevon in the northeast quadrant of the intersection of the north-south road from Saint Jean-de-Daye to Saint-Lô and the east-west road between Périers and Saint-Lô. Despite the casualties, we accepted the mistake as an inevitable consequence of war and, when the bombing ended, we crossed the road to close with the enemy. The attack went well, and we pushed on. I directed artillery fire immediately in front of our advancing infantry to eliminate the remaining enemy tanks and infantry. The next day we pulled to the sides of the roads and let the tanks pass through us to pursue the fleeing enemy. General Bradley's breakthrough plan was a big success, and the tanks made rapid progress. Advancing with the infantry, we mopped up behind them. The Germans could still put up a strong resistance, but they had few prepared positions between Normandy and their own country. Within a week we were twenty-five miles further into France, three times the ground we had covered from the landing beaches in the previous six weeks.

A week later, on August 2, we were pulled back a few miles, away from frontline fighting to the village of Tessy-sur-Vire. The Thirtieth Division had been in combat continuously for fifty-one days and my 230th Field Artillery Battalion for fifty-five days. We didn't know how long this break would last, but we knew to clean our weapons and equipment. We needed to rest and absorb hundreds of replacements, most of whom required further training. For the first time since leaving England on June 9, I brushed my teeth, had a shower, and put on clean clothes. Each afternoon American Red Cross ladies served us coffee and donuts. Movie stars Dinah Shore and Edward G. Robinson came with a USO (United Service Organizations) show to entertain us. With his gangster, tough-guy image, Robinson was almost sinister looking. Dinah Shore was the big hit, singing her most popular recordings, like "Blues in the Night" and "You'd Be So Nice to Come Home To." She left the stage and walked among the troops. I was sitting on the ground, and she leaned over and gave me a kiss on the cheek. Later, my buddies teased me about it and asked which I liked best, the shower and clean clothes or the kiss. I said it was a tie.

Robinson wanted to meet a German POW, but we'd sent them all to the rear. Not wanting to disappoint him, a German-speaking American sergeant from Milwaukee was brought before him, wearing an enemy uniform. Guarded by two GIs with tommy guns, the impostor gave an arrogant "Heil Hitler" salute and was haughty in his manner toward Robinson, a professional actor who was fluent in German. Robinson never realized he was being conned by an amateur.

Mortain and Hill 314

Our break from combat lasted only three days. About 9:00 p.m. on August 5 we were told to prepare to move, and four hours later we crossed the I.P. (initial, or starting point) under a bright moon. Our destination was the town of Mortain, about thirty-five miles south, where we would relieve units of the First Infantry Division, the famous "Big Red One." My observation party consisted of Lt. Charles A. Bartz, the forward observer; our radioman, Sherman Goldstein of Toledo, Ohio; our jeep driver, Louis Sberna of Benwood, West Virginia; and me, Bartz's assistant. About ten o'clock that morning we drove into Mortain, a picturesque town of about sixteen hundred people spread on the slopes of a ridge that rose sharply on our left, to the east. The Cauce River flowed through a deep valley to the west. There was no obvious war damage. The crest of the ridge was 314 meters above sea level and therefore labeled Hill 314 on our maps. It was the highest point of land we had seen in Normandy, the kind of prominence that soldiers call the "dominant terrain." Mortain's main street ran through the center of the town and was the major east-west road in the region.

We were there to support the Second Battalion of the Thirtieth Infantry Division's 120th Infantry Regiment. On the hilltop, the GIs that we would replace showed us their foxholes and firing pits. We were glad to see these because the ground was hard with solid rock just beneath the surface in many places. Their diggings were shallow and not intended to contain a strong enemy attack, but we were not worried. The "Big Red One" men had not seen any Germans or been shelled for two days. We accepted responsibility for the defense of Hill 314 shortly before two o'clock on the afternoon of August 6, and the First Division men cleared out, still telling us that it was a quiet sector. They had not been gone thirty minutes before a German plane flew overhead, apparently on a reconnaissance mission. However, we saw no great cause for concern.

We, the artillerymen, were partners with the infantry. Their job was to hold Hill 314, and our job was to help them by bringing to bear on the enemy the firepower of our big guns located six to eight miles behind us. The Second Battalion had about 650 infantrymen on the hill. We, the artillerymen, numbered about a dozen and consisted of two forward observation parties. The counterpart to Lieutenant Bartz in the other forward observation team was Lieutenant Robert Weiss, who would publish in 1998 an excellent book—*Fire Mission!*—about the battle.

Lieutenant Bartz and I walked around the hilltop with our maps, familiarizing ourselves with the terrain. The hill was well suited for defense, with large boulders, and dense undergrowth. It was more vulnerable on the east and northeast sides, which sloped up gently and were in the direction of enemy forces, but the north, south and west sides were steep. The top was irregular, but only a few spots were rough. The entire countryside was visible for 360 degrees, absolutely the best view we had seen in Normandy. The spires of the great monastery at Mont Saint-Michel could be seen about twenty-five miles to the west, but they meant nothing to us. As we looked down on Mortain, more American troops entered the town and set up roadblocks on entry roads. In the event of a German attack, Mortain would be an obvious avenue to the west, but it could be a bottleneck because of the deep valley and topsy-turvy hills on the west and Hill 314 on the east. For the Germans to take Mortain and gain access to its road to the west, they would have to knock us off of Hill 314. That's what the coming battle boiled down to.

You can get a clear idea of the shape of Hill 314 if you visualize the letter Y on the ground. The base, or main axis, of the Y points almost due north, the right branch angles slightly to the southwest, and the left branch to the southeast. The town of Mortain is on the right side. However, there were roads around the Y, which, if taken by the enemy, would enable him to attack from any direction and isolate us on top. Most of the German attacks would come from the east and southeast against the left branch of the Y, which was held by Lt. Ralph A. Kerley's E Company. Lt. Ronal E. Woody's G Company defended the right (west) branch of the Y. It is significant that all company commanders on the hill were lieutenants rather than the captains stipulated by the army. The reason for this is very simple: the captains had been killed, wounded, or captured.

As the battle unfolded, I was usually in the base of the Y in the area defended by Lt. Joseph K. Reaser's K Company. At other times I was on the west branch. With help from Reaser's scouts, that first afternoon Bartz and I went around the hilltop, looking over the countryside, picking out roads, intersections, potential assembly areas, and likely routes for an attack by German infantry or tanks. I plotted locations on a map where we could request either an emergency barrage or a normal barrage. I assigned a number to each location. Emergency barrages were plotted on areas considered likely for an enemy attack. Normal barrages were planned for likely supply depots and support areas farther into enemy territory. If an attack came, we would only have to request "Emergency Barrage Number 3" or another number depending on the location, and the gunners would know where to fire.

By radio, Bartz and I contacted our fire direction center located near our firing batteries several miles behind us and transmitted the map coordinates for the batteries to aim their guns on the targets we selected. Then the batteries fired spotting rounds on those locations. We watched them impact and radioed adjustments to get them exactly on the target, using such terms as "Up 15" and "Right 20." Once that was done, the guns were presighted, and we could call down artillery fire on an enemy attack at any hour, day or night, by simply calling the fire direction center and specifying the target with a certain number, the urgency of our request, and the density of the barrage, like "concentration number five," and the type of rounds to be used, either antipersonnel or antitank. Immediately available to us were twelve 105-mm howitzers, but we could call on all Thirtieth Division artillery, as well as artillery from other divisions, which included numerous larger and more powerful guns.

Lieutenant Bartz had come to us as a replacement for Lieutenant Miller, and this would be his first combat. He seemed tense and worried. To Lieutenant Weiss, he had the "pale stamp of death on his face." Weiss suspected that Bartz "thought a great deal about death and dying." Bartz's first important decision was where our observation party—himself, Goldstein, and me—should bed down that first night. It was a question of where we should be if the Germans attacked. He decided the three of us should occupy the same foxhole and selected one on the western edge of the hill among riflemen of K Company; it was less a hole than a depression. I suggested that we should be close to their company commander, Lieutenant Reaser, at the north end of the ridge (the base of the Y), so he could tell us the artillery support he wanted, if the need arose. Reaser had scouts and listening posts from the base of the "Y" along the ridgeline that we did not have. Bartz rejected my advice, but he would soon change his mind.

Unknown to us, the Germans were about to launch an enormous attack, intended to smash through the American lines and push to sea at the town of Avranches, twenty miles west of Hill 314. On the orders of Adolf Hitler, their goal was to annihilate the Americans between Mortain and the coast, and cut a narrow corridor through to Avranches, where Patton's Third Army was pouring through German defenses, going ever deeper into France, before wheeling east to toward Paris and Germany. The German offensive, meant to split the American armies, would become known as the "Mortain counterattack"—and we were between the Germans and their objective—the sea.

MONDAY, AUGUST 7 (DAY 1)

At one o'clock in the morning on August 7, our first night on Hill 314, the Germans attacked. Our first clue was the unnerving sound of clanking tank tracks. Approaching from the south and southeast, they overran a roadblock and got into the outskirts of Mortain. Small groups got up on Hill 314, yelling "Heil Hitler" at the top of their voices, and penetrated our defensive perimeter where our guys beat them back, some in hand-to-hand fighting. An hour later they struck from the north—the other end of Mortain—having infiltrated past a roadblock and entered the town. Our position was like a balcony looking down on them, so close that Bartz could not use our radio because it would give away our position. I actually lay on top of the radio to keep the sound from the Germans. This convinced Bartz that we should move to Lieutenant Reaser's command post. The move was only a few hundred yards, but we had to find it in the darkness while lugging seventy-five pounds of radio and battery that we had removed from our jeep. The radio was an SCR 510, SCR abbreviating Signal Corps Radio. As we searched for the command post, Bartz told me that he could not carry on and that I'd have to take over. He then got in a foxhole, and I did not see him until our ordeal ended five days later.

By dawn—still August 7—the Germans had occupied most of Mortain with both troops and tanks, and we were completely surrounded. The fog that morning was so dense that we suspected the enemy was producing it artificially. After it burned off, we were surprised to see columns of German foot soldiers and tanks streaming from the east and around the right branch of the Y to enter Mortain. Seemingly oblivious to our presence on Hill 314, their compact columns were an artilleryman's dream, and we made the most of it. While Lieutenant Weiss called in artillery on the east and southeast, I called for it on the south and southwest. We laid a solid ring of fire on them. Their casualties and vehicle damage were incredible. The few undamaged German vehicles withdrew to the east, loaded with men fleeing from a killing ground.

Thus turned away, the enemy commanders realized the importance of controlling Hill 314. If they could take it away from us, they would eliminate our artillery fire and gain excellent observation of other American units and their movements for miles around. About 10:00 a.m. they began firing on us with everything imaginable in the way of artillery and mortar fire—even a bombing and strafing attack, a rare event, given the overwhelming American air-ground support. When the firing stopped, their infantry attacked up the hill, supported by tanks. Once again, we called down heavy concentrations of artillery on them and broke up their main attack, but not before some of them got on top of the hill, where they provoked a severe firefight and inflicted numerous casualties before being driven off. Wounded men, both German and American, were lying around in the open, being hit by steel fragments from exploding shells.

About two o'clock that afternoon, the Germans tried again, this time from the west, straight up the steep slopes from the town of Mortain. Although the attack was turned back in short order with accurate artillery fire, we had more casualties. About noon, we ate the last of our K-rations. Ammunition was dangerously low and, since we were surrounded, evacuation of the dead and wounded was impossible. Communications between Hill 314 and higher levels of command were entirely by the radios of our two forward observation teams, but the radios were unreliable because their batteries were playing out. So we used our radios as little as possible and found that, if we turned them off for a couple of hours, they came back with more power. We also placed spare batteries on rocks in the sun, hoping the heat would recharge them. I don't know if it worked, but it seemed to.

We needed food, ammunition, medical supplies, and batteries—desperately! Most men were hungry, but I hardly remember thinking about food. Maybe I was too scared or too busy. I used my bayonet to slice thin slivers from a chocolate D-bar and that is all I ate. Our saving grace was several water wells on the hill, although the Germans sometimes took them under sniper fire.

Above, American fighter planes, on this single day, flew 429 sorties over German forces in front of us to keep the Luftwaffe away. Ten squadrons of bomb-carrying Royal Air Force Typhoons flew 290 sorties and fired 2,088 rockets at German tanks and vehicles below, keeping the enemy at bay. I'll never forget the sound of those rockets fired from the British Typhoons. We had never heard anything like that before.

After dark, German infiltrators—singly and in small groups—stole up the hill, and they had to be rooted out, one by one. Our casualties for the day were reported as seventy-eight killed, wounded, or captured. And no relief was in sight.

TUESDAY, AUGUST 8 (DAY 2)

Our second full day on the hill was fairly quiet. The Germans made no serious attempt to take Hill 314. They tried to bypass it on minor roads and trails to continue their drive to the west, but, with good visibility, we harassed them with artillery fire. When we saw the muzzle blast of a German artillery piece or a tank gun, we called the location back to the fire direction center and watched with great satisfaction as our own rounds began hitting around the gun that had fired.

The dead—German and American—lay where they had fallen on the hilltop, their bodies deteriorating in the warm August heat. The odor was nauseating and demoralizing. The wounded were in numerous locations, and it was a problem for the three infantry company commanders to solve. They decided to assemble the wounded in three large slit trenches dug into the side of embankments to shield them from incoming mortar rounds, one trench within the area of each company. They would be made as comfortable as possible. No medical aid was available. The dead were placed out of sight in three other locations. We moved them that night. Later we were harassed by enemy patrols, got little or no sleep, and several of our wounded died.

WEDNESDAY, AUGUST 9 (DAY 3)

On the next day, other elements of our Thirtieth Division tried and failed to break through the enemy cordon and rescue us. We had almost no ammunition. Some men dug potatoes and cabbage or plucked apples from an abandoned farm. Our defense depended on supporting artillery fire. Morale declined when an attempt to resupply us using two small Piper Cub–type planes—ordinarily used as spotters for artillery—failed when enemy fire drove them off. Afterward we were told that a parachute drop by C-47s was planned for the next day, but given our experience with close air support in the breakout near Saint-Lô, we were skeptical about its success.

About 6:00 p.m., a German officer accompanied by an enlisted man carrying a white flag came part way up the hill and was met by our E Company commander, Lieutenant Kerley. The German explained that he was an SS officer and was authorized to offer us an honorable surrender. He said he admired the fight we had put up but our situation was hopeless. He coupled a promise of good medical treatment for our wounded with an ultimatum: if his offer was not accepted within two hours—by 8:00 p.m.—we would be annihilated in a forthcoming attack.

Kerley's rejection of the ultimatum is unprintable here, but he used the most vulgar words of the English language. The German officer may not have understood American obscenities, but there was no doubt when Kerley told him we would not "surrender until the last round of ammunition had been fired and the last bayonet broken off in a German belly." I didn't know about this at the time but true to the German officer's promise, they launched a major ground attack about 8:15 p.m. It was a test of our determination and unity. At first, our limited supply of ammunition allowed them to make easy progress. Could artillery suffice? When the Germans penetrated our inner defenses, Kerley called for artillery fire on his own company command post. We called in high explosive, antipersonnel rounds that detonated on contact, thus not penetrating the ground. Since the Americans knew the barrage was coming, they took cover, but the Germans were caught in the open and wiped out, literally blown to bits or vaporized. All these years I have tried to imagine what it must have been like to be a German soldier in that situation. Someone calculated that it was equivalent to being on a football field and having a twenty-pound package of TNT explode within a few feet of you about every five seconds. Those not killed or wounded withdrew, and morale soared on Hill 314. Artillery was truly the "King of the Battlefield."

Thursday, August 10 (Day 4)

The Germans didn't bother us much the next morning. About three-thirty in the afternoon several of our fighter planes dive-bombed German positions, setting off fires and explosions. Later, a flight of twelve C-47s came in, escorted by P-47s, and dropped beautiful multicolored parachutes with packages of food, ammo, and medical supplies. At the last moment, a strong breeze blew most of them within German positions, but we were better off than we had been. We quickly requested another drop, especially for medical supplies. Knowing the Germans were listening, we bragged in radio transmissions that we had plenty of food, water, and ammo.

Meanwhile, back at our 230th Artillery Battalion headquarters, someone had a novel idea to help us. Among the variety of artillery rounds available there was a nonexplosive "propaganda shell" used to put leaflets with demoralizing information in the hands of German soldiers. The bright idea was to fill the space for leaflets with bandages, dressings, sulfanilamide, and morphine syrettes and fire them into our positions on Hill 314. We got a message about how to open them and that the shells would have a red strip around their base. Usually they broke open on impact. Several were fired about dusk, but we could not find them because of ricochets and the darkness. However, the next morning six rounds were fired, and we recovered them. I understood this was the first time in history that this technique had ever been used, but it was only partially successful because the impact shattered the containers of plasma and morphine. Nonetheless, all wounded men got some penicillin. I can still see the smiles on their faces when they got that medicine and special attention.

Friday, August 11 (Day 5)

On the morning of August 11, we heard heavy firing behind us toward the American lines, and the Germans began withdrawing. As they did, we inflicted untold damage on them with artillery, aerial bombing, and strafing. The destruction was unmerciful with the slaughter continuing throughout the day. The view from Hill 314 gave us ringside seats to this horrible spectacle that the Germans had brought on themselves. When night came, their foot soldiers began walking out, and they too were cut down by artillery fire that plastered their routes of withdrawal, using the preregistered firing instructions our forward observer teams had provided. From atop the hill we could hear their screams and hysterical cries. Although we were still surrounded, we rested and listened to the constant rumbling boom of our guns firing from far behind us, followed by the swooshing roar of their projectiles passing overhead, and then the sights and sounds of their impact on enemy positions down range. The next day, August 12, men of the Thirty-fifth Infantry Division advanced into Mortain, and we could leave Hill 314 at last. After six days with little food, we looked like ghosts to the GIs who relieved us. Of the approximately 665 men who had taken up positions on Hill 314 on August 6, 277—two out of five—had been killed, wounded, or were missing.

When I got back to our 230th Artillery Battalion headquarters, I requested permission to meet with our battery commander, Capt. Merrill Alexander. I made an oral report of what we had done in the past week and described Lieutenant Bartz's conduct. Alexander thanked and dismissed me. Later a military policeman came into our bivouac area and took Bartz into custody. En route to Thirtieth Division headquarters, where legal officers would consider his case, their vehicle was strafed by a German plane, I was told, and they, with the driver, were killed. Ironically, Bartz would posthumously receive the same decorations as the rest of us for bravery and gallantry, because he had never been convicted of dereliction or neglect of duty.

Second Silver Star

Following review by our division commander, Maj. Gen. Leland S. Hobbs, I was awarded a second Silver Star, or more correctly, an Oak Leaf Cluster to wear on my previously awarded Silver Star. I do not know who recommended me or wrote the accompanying citation, but I was happy to receive it. By then I was a proud staff sergeant, still nineteen years old.

Staff Sergeant Franklin W. Denius, 38480234, 230th Field Artillery Battalion, United States Army, is awarded a bronze Oak Leaf Cluster for wear with the Silver Star previously awarded, for gallantry in action from 7 August 1944 to 12 August 1944, in France. When the enemy launched a determined counteroffensive in the vicinity of Mortain, France, designed to reach the sea and divide American armies in France, Sergeant Denius distinguished himself as a member of a forward observer party directing artillery fire in support of an infantry regiment. Despite intense enemy pressure, which included an attack by paratroopers, considerable armor, and large infantry forces, Sergeant Denius and his companions remained valiantly at their vulnerable post for seventy-two hours without rest, directing artillery fire which was a contributing factor in thwarting the German effort. In spite of direct tank, artillery, and small arms fire, which were directed on their positions, Sergeant Denius and his small group displayed gallantry.

The infantrymen of the 120th Regiment deserve most of the credit for holding Hill 314 and turning back the enemy's Mortain counterattack. At the same time, the battle demonstrated that the artillery was indispensable. Every day that we were isolated on the hill, my 230th Field Artillery Battalion fired an average of two thousand rounds. Even so, when the 120th Regiment was awarded the rare and prestigious Presidential Unit Citation for its heroic stand, the artillerymen were left out—but not wholly forgotten. In April 1945, near the end of the war, special orders came down authorizing us, the fourteen artillerymen who had been on Hill 314, to wear on our uniforms the coveted badge of a PUC, a solid blue ribbon within a gold frame. On a unit level, the PUC is equivalent to the Distinguished Service Cross, which is second only to the Medal of Honor as an award to individuals for valor and gallantry in the face of the enemy.

I don't think the Thirtieth Division's success in holding Hill 314 and repelling the enemy's "Mortain counterattack" has been properly appreciated by historians as one of the important battles of the war in Europe.

To support my point of view, I want to quote from the memoir of Gen. Omar N. Bradley, the American ground commander at the time: "In his reckless attack . . . at Mortain, the enemy challenged us to a decision, the most decisive of our French campaign. It was to cost the enemy an Army and gain us France. When the Germans first struck, only [the Thirtieth Infantry Division] stood between von Kluge's panzers and the sea."

CHAPTER 5

Vive l'Amerique to Aachen

After Mortain, the Jerries were pulling out fast, and we were in hot pursuit. We had trapped them, and they were desperate to escape from the noose that Hitler's foolhardy order to counterattack had forced on them. A quarter of a million Germans were now encircled by British, Canadian, and American armies, except for a narrow corridor to the east near the town of Falaise—which gave its name to the area where they were snared—the Falaise Pocket. My Thirtieth Division was on the south side of the pocket, moving north and east to help cut off the enemy's only remaining escape route.

Although we were still in combat, it was a peaceful time compared to the ordeal on Hill 314. By August 17, we were twenty miles east of Mortain near the village of St. Bomer les Forges. About this time, we learned that the Germans were calling the Thirtieth Division "Roosevelt's SS troops" for the fighting power and determination we had shown in blocking their counterattack. As we moved to the east, the hedgerows were fewer and smaller, but caution was still the watchword. Tipped off by a French farmer, we used a mine detector along hedgerows in our bivouac area and found eight camouflaged Bouncing Bettys, the enemy's spring-loaded land mine that launched up about three feet before exploding and projecting lethal bits of steel in all directions. We set up our howitzers to fire on the retreating Germans, but were denied permission by the British, who were advancing toward us from the north with the same objective—to block the narrow corridor to the east and trap the enemy in the Falaise Pocket. This helps explain why the Germans' escape route was never closed; Allied commanders were concerned about "friendly fire." They were afraid that their heavily armed forces advancing toward each other would mistake the other for the enemy and fire on them.

On August 19 we moved a phenomenal 112 miles. Passing through villages and towns, we were slowed down, almost overwhelmed by the rejoicing French people. Wine flowed, our vehicles were covered with flowers, and there would have been more kisses if we had stopped. Clouds of powdered dust rose as our trucks roared through towns shattered by recent bombing. We kept moving until almost midnight, and, shortly after daybreak, we moved again, augmented by a fourth battery of four 105-mm howitzers, giving our 230th Field Artillery Battalion an arsenal of sixteen guns.

With four batteries, we could cover the troops in front of us by advancing in two echelons with two batteries in each. Each echelon covered the other by leap-frogging it as we moved forward. This was good news for the troops we were trying to protect, but forward observers like myself were still expected to be out in front, finding the enemy before our advancing infantry encountered them. Each echelon had a forward observer team, and I was still in charge of my team because Lieutenant Bartz's replacement had not arrived.

We skirted Paris to the north, catching just a glimpse of the Eiffel Tower. When Paris was liberated on August 25, we were on the Seine River about thirty-five miles downstream. We crossed the Seine near Mantes-la-Jolie on a U.S. Army bridge laid over river barges. Although the Germans were still pulling out, most of the time they were in range of our guns and on August 27 we fired 397 rounds while coping with snipers they left behind; our infantrymen were reluctant to accept captured snipers as prisoners of war. We usually knew approximately where the Germans were by reports from our aerial observers flying Piper Cubs almost continuously above us and on our flanks. On the 28th, we did not move at all and, as enemy artillery fell around us, we fired 888 rounds in return. Advancing to new positions ahead of the infantry, we ran into a minefield marked with "Achtung Minen!" and skull-and-crossbones signs. We backed out gingerly, stepping in our own footsteps.

Vive l'Amerique

The Germans continued their retreat, and we pursued them toward Belgium. Village streets were full of cheering civilians crying, "Vive l'Amerique," and little boys yelling, "cigarette pour Papa," the French equivalent of "any gum chum," and we gave it to them. Several of us went swimming in a large pool on a private estate. The Madame told us how terrible the shelling had been. I did not know until later that our gunners had used her conspicuous home as a reference point to adjust the range and direction of their fire. Many civilians did not sleep in their homes, but in caves and wine cellars deep underground.

Bearing north, we passed through Pontoise, which the FFI (French Forces of the Interior) had cleared of Germans, after asking us not to fire on the town. The people hailed us with unrestrained joy; the squares were so packed with crowds that our trucks could barely move. Here we saw the humiliation heaped on women accused of being too cozy with the Germans. Forced to kneel in public squares, their heads were shaved, usually by men, but also by other women. I wondered what these "innocents," especially the men, did during the war. Then, the disgraced women, cropped and crying, were paraded through the streets past lines of jeering and spitting townspeople. However heartrending, they were not our concern. We were focused on the enemy, on ending the war, and we moved on to the east.

On the morning of September 1, our advance party moved out early to find and organize our assigned bivouac area in Belgium, but for reasons we could not immediately understand, the rest of our battalion did not move until late afternoon. We understood the delay when we caught up with a huge convoy strung out for miles. The whole U.S. Army seemed to be on the road, moving slowly, but steadily through shattered German vehicles and equipment. For hours, Sherman Goldstein and I sat in our jeep with driver Louis Sberna. We could do nothing else. Civilians lined the roads, waving and cheering, but many were busy carrying away abandoned equipment or carving up horses, killed by our planes when they strafed the retreating German columns. The Germans were heavily dependent on horses for transportation. That night two subsonic pilotless V-1 flying bombs—buzz bombs or doodlebugs—flew over our convoy, apparently heading toward England, the first we had heard or seen. The traffic was stop-and-go, and we slept in the trucks during the long halts. Cold and wet, we didn't feel like conquering heroes. For two days, our convoy jerked along as we passed through the battlefields of the First World War—the valley of the Somme, Cambrai, and Lille—which years later I visited with my friend Kerry Merritt. I have always been treated with utmost courtesy by the people of France, during the war and afterward. My family and friends know the affection I feel for the French people.

When we crossed the Belgium border, the hysterical joy of the people again overwhelmed us. Thousands of flags appeared as if by magic with great throngs of shouting, crying people throwing flowers and fruit, holding up babies to be kissed, or climbing up for real adult kisses. We were handed bottles or glasses of wine and cognac. Nuns blessed us, and priests opened their doors. It was like a carnival with lots of noise and color. "Vive l'Amerique—Vive la Belgique!" Yet under it all there was a tone of quiet sadness. An elderly lady, her tears streaming, reached into our jeep, gently touched Goldstein's face, and kissed him, saying, "We waited so long for you." They gave us their hearts, and we gave them their freedom.

It was getting dark when we entered the village of Bruyelles, only a couple of miles inside Belgium. Strung out for miles behind us, other units arrived throughout the night, the last at six in the morning after a road march of about 125 miles that required almost twenty-four hours. We were surprised at the number of German stragglers we took prisoner. One of our guys slept in a haystack with a German he did not see until he took him prisoner the next morning, when the German crawled out of the hay.

For the next few days, we stayed put, cleaning and repairing equipment, and most of all, resting. We were tired, and our vehicles needed maintenance or replacement. On September 3, I wrote to my mother stating that I was "Somewhere in Belgium" and had attended a memorial service in honor of a young Belgian man, who had worked in the underground for three years, only to be killed by a burst from a German machine gun when he appeared openly on the day of liberation.

Our unofficial rest period ended on September 7 when we moved fifty miles to Waterloo, where we bivouacked on the edge of the famous battlefield where Napoleon was finally defeated in 1815. The next day we advanced sixty miles to Tongeren, still in Belgium, but nearing the Dutch border. As we had skirted Paris on the north, we bypassed Brussels on the south. At last, we got a replacement for Lieutenant Bartz in the person of 1st Lt. John W. Jacobs Jr. of Gainesville, Georgia, a graduate of the University of Missouri's School of Journalism and the ROTC program. Although he had never been in combat, he was well trained and willing to learn from those who had. John Jacobs and I got along famously and became friends for life. I contributed to scholarships established in his name at Brenau University in his hometown.

On September 13 we advanced into the Netherlands, south of Maastricht, in the region known as the Maastricht Appendix, a narrow extension of Holland between Germany and Belgium that reached into metropolitan Aachen. We crossed the well-known Albert Canal without difficulty and occupied without casualties the famous Belgian fortress, Fort Eben Emael, once considered the most powerful in the world. My battery supported the advance of the infantrymen into the huge fortress and they returned with Nazi battle flags, which were given to our officers. When we set up positions near the Dutch town of Noorbeek, we were at last within range of German soil. We celebrated by firing one volley at no particular target in the Fatherland for no other reason than that we wanted to and we could.

Aachen

About ten o'clock on the night of September 15 we got an unexpected order to move immediately to a muddy hillside not far away. Our infantry was advancing rapidly toward Aachen and needed our support. We worked through the night, and we had our guns ready to fire at dawn. Later in the day, we moved again, still in Holland, and only ten miles from Aachen. Prisoners were streaming in by the thousands, and one of our men sketched a cartoon with the caption, "Hitler, count your men."

Our movement was around the northern perimeter of Aachen, while remaining in the Netherlands. It became clear that the army's plan was to encircle Aachen, and we would have a major role. Once encircled, the

Germans inside Aachen could not be reinforced from the outside. While terrible fighting and dying occurred in the city, it seemed strange that the people nearby in Holland literally danced with joy for their liberation, and little girls wore the bright orange ribbons of their country in their hair. Every Dutchman was carrying a radio, perhaps removed from a hidden place, or stolen from a German. During the night we heard the soft whistle of heavy shells as they passed overhead toward our rear area, probably from railroad guns in Germany. We were only a mile from the German frontier. Enemy planes were more active, coming over low but usually causing no trouble.

On the 18th we were within a half-mile of the German frontier, and could see the legendary concrete dragon's teeth of the Siegfried Line, which were hardly an obstacle when we crossed them a few days later. Our engineers just piled dirt on top of them and we drove over them. The real worry here was the increasingly active and accurate enemy artillery. Nonetheless, we liked this place for one good reason: hot showers! Not far away there was a small coal mine owned by the Dutch government called the Wilhelmina Mine with hot showers for miners that we used. After weeks, even months, of sleeping on the ground at night and traveling along dusty roads without bathing, except for a dip in streams or washing up with our helmet, hot showers were a luxury.

Although we had a good view of the Dutch town of Kerkade, it was still occupied by the Germans. For two days we watched the evacuation of the entire town, some thirty thousand people, presumably as ordered by the Germans. The roads leading out of Kerkade were thronged with long lines of civilians of all ages, plodding slowly along on foot, riding bicycles, pushing carts and baby buggies, and riding on every type of wheeled vehicle from fancy carriages to lumbering farm wagons. We did not know where they went, but a few came directly from their local hospital through the lines and into our care. Some were killed by enemy shelling. On the faces of the old, there was the passive acceptance of the hardships of yet another war in a region that had known so many. In contrast, the children smiled, bright-eyed with wonder and excitement. My forward observer team established an observation post in a slag-pile (waste from coal mines) near the German frontier and called in many firing missions, particularly against enemy artillery, which was becoming increasingly effective. One of our guns suffered a direct hit and an adjacent battery was heavily shelled twice, but nothing came my way.

On September 28 we moved a few hundred yards for better firing positions, but were still five miles north of Aachen and in Holland. Except for occasional enemy rounds impacting our area, all was peaceful. The direct attack into the center of the city by the "Big Red One" was about to begin, and the army brought in the heaviest artillery pieces yet, the 155-mm Long-Toms and 8-inch (203-mm) howitzers. (The Long-Toms were long-barreled cannon with a relatively flat trajectory in contrast to a howitzer, which was also a cannon, but had a comparatively short barrel, and was used especially for firing shells at a high angle of elevation, to reach a target behind a hill.) To a German soldier defending Aachen, this was almost point-blank range, as those guns could fire a 125-lb. shell about fifteen miles. When they let go, the ground shook and soil fell from our foxholes down on us. One of our sentries caught a German saboteur, dressed in a Dutch public employee's uniform, cutting barbed wire that we had erected around our area. The weather was turning cold, and the winter rains were beginning. We were issued overcoats, but they did not repel water; as a result, when they got wet, they were unusable. Longing for warm places to rest, we were motivated to advance by the sight of the fine homes ahead of us in Germany.

We had all heard about Hitler's fabled West Wall, which the Brits ridiculed as the Siegfried Line with the ditty, "We're going to hang out the washing on the Siegfried Line." But the joking ended when we learned that our Thirtieth Division had been selected to crack the Siegfried Line in support of the First Infantry Division, which was to attack Aachen head-on in about two weeks. (The actual date was October 13.) My forward observer team was to support the 120th, which was to feint an attack on Kerkade, then hold, while our other two regiments (the 117th and 119th) assaulted the Siegfried Line after a massive attack by aerial bombardment and artillery. We, the forward observers, were enthusiastic about the plan. The air show would be spectacular, and little was expected of us. We made ourselves comfortable in observation posts and settled down to watch the big show. But, some of us—now called "old-timers"—remembered the bombing shortfall in July near Saint-Lô that killed hundreds of Thirtieth Division men. We wanted a good view of the attack, but made sure there were no obstacles between ourselves and a refuge, ideally a deep cellar. To protect the hundreds of incoming Allied planes, we got orders to saturate enemy antiaircraft batteries and to fire at the slightest movement in enemy territory.

The air show to soften up enemy defenses began in mid-morning on October 2 with massive bombings by about three hundred P-38s and P-47s primarily on the perimeter of the city. They let loose more than sixty-two tons of bombs. In late morning, we began an artillery barrage to soften up the resistance. It was deafening. The combined artillery of several divisions hurled some five thousand rounds into the city, a total of 169 tons of high explosives. We wondered how the Jerries could stand it, but learned later that little damage had been done. Our plane losses appeared to be relatively light, although a twin-engine bomber, crippled by ack-ack, came down in flames not far behind us and sent up a great ring of black smoke. The attack continued on October 3, and we stayed busy, expending 1,173 rounds on targets of opportunity. Enemy artillery was troublesome, and we tried to locate their positions by observing the flash from their barrels at night, placing a man with a telescopic scope on a slag-pile. He gave us good calls, and we obliterated some of them. Meanwhile, the Luftwaffe was striking back stronger than ever, dropping antipersonnel bombs around us.

On October 6, the Thirtieth Division broke through the Siegfried Line and crossed the Wurm River at Rimburg, at last entering the Third Reich only four months after we had landed on Omaha Beach. The Siegfried Line was not impregnable, but the cost was heavy. German pillboxes were skillfully sited on the hillside or camouflaged in the woods, covering all approaches. Now they were silent and empty, marked with the impact of direct-fire guns and chipped by bullets. Most of us tried to ignore the extraordinary carnage, not because we were hardened by the sight of enemy dead and material destruction, but because we were concentrating on our jobs, on protecting our buddies and ourselves. Yet, I remember vividly the sprawling rows of young, dead German soldiers lying in open fields where they had been caught by our artillery. Not until decades later did I reflect on the fact that they looked much like me and I might have been responsible for their deaths by calling in the rounds that killed them. I went on a reconnaissance to the city of Palenberg, and it was a lifeless shell. Ubach, an adjoining town, was littered with burned-out vehicles with their crews also burned and twisted in death.

Having passed through the Siegfried Line, we veered to the right (south) and, on October 16, linked up with the First Division at Wuerselen, closing the Germans' escape corridor to the east from Aachen. However, the Germans outside the encirclement still fought desperately to relieve the garrison in the city by counterattacking toward us to break the siege. That's when the real fight for Aachen began. While desperate fighting ensued outside of Aachen, the German commander in the city refused a surrender ultimatum, compelling the First Infantry Division to launch a systematic assault on the city. Infantrymen of the "Big Red One" had to blast their way through the city—from street to street, house to house, even in sewers, to root out diehard resistance. Finally, on October 21, the Germans in Aachen surrendered, as we in the Thirtieth Division, already east of Aachen, continued to advance slowly to the east, village by village, toward the Roer River. Since the terrain was flat and devoid of vegetation, there were few places to hide; thus, forward observers were either easy targets or they sought protection in obvious places. Fortunately, the Germans had constructed numerous pillboxes in the area, and they were ideal protection for us, despite their conspicuousness and their doors being on the wrong side.

In villages like Wilhelmschacht and towns like Ubach, civilians began to emerge from the rubble, not a Nazi among them, of course. But they feared the return of the German army, because they had not left as they had been ordered to do. Several of us wandered from building to building through "mouseholes" knocked in basement walls by the Jerries for defensive purposes. We saw signs instructing German soldiers not to plunder homes and businesses.

The enemy continued to counterattack, and we fired day and night to break up their attacks. In four days we knocked out twenty-two tanks, firing a total of 8,557 rounds. Most of the time, I was up front with our 120th Infantry Regiment, which threw back one determined counterattack after another, advancing steadily with almost continuous artillery support. We—the forward observers and aerial liaison aviators—did our jobs and took our losses. Night-firing was especially dangerous around our guns because the Luftwaffe was often overhead and could see our muzzle blasts, which became their targets. Two of our batteries got hit and suffered casualties. At meal times our kitchens became prime targets as the enemy tried to catch the mess line in the open. Chow time was pushed ahead, and kitchens were moved frequently. At night we'd hear the soft swooshing of "boxcar" (for their size) shells fired by enemy railroad guns passing over us. Usually, most damage was to the nerves, but we avoided the airstrips for our little liaison spotter planes because they drew too much fire. Camouflage became more important. While these things were happening, a man stepped on a mine in an area where many of us had walked—and lost his foot.

In early November, the "brass" recognized that we needed a time and place to rest, relax, and recuperate, and we were pulled back to Visé, barely in Belgium on the Netherlands border, just west of Maastricht. We were housed in old Belgian barracks that had showers. I lucked out and got a five-day pass to Paris. It was my first visit. On November 5, I wrote to my mother, beginning with the usual reassuring line, which was not always the truth: "Dear Mother, I am fine and hope you and mama are all right. Just a note to let you know where I am. Got a short pass here to Paris and having a swell time. I know you and mama and Sha would enjoy all the shops here."

CHAPTER 6

The Battle of the Bulge to German Surrender

ECEMBER 16, 1944, WAS A QUIET DAY, considering that the enemy was only a few hundred yards away. We were east of Aachen, and the Germans were further east between us and the Roer River. In subjugating Aachen, the first major German city to fall, we had fought our way around its north side and linked up with the First Infantry Division, which came through the city after defeating the enemy within. We had fended off German attempts to break through the American encirclement of the city, while continuing to attack from village to village toward the Roer River. The enemy was on home ground and fighting bitterly to preserve the Fatherland. His supply lines became shorter as ours grew longer. It was tough going.

We had to cross the Roer to reach the Rhine, which we had to cross if we were to advance into the Reich, where the objective was to neutralize the heavily industrialized region known as the Ruhr, the region of Germany's principal steel and synthetic-fuel production. Our biggest problem was that the enemy could flood the Roer by releasing water from upstream dams, creating floods downstream at will. The floods were obstacles and, if we got men across the river, the Germans could release water and isolate them on the other side, creating a dilemma where their choice was between surrender and annihilation. The Germans had successfully defended the dams from our ground attacks, and our aerial bombing had failed to breach them. Meanwhile, we continued training, moving forward, and perfecting techniques of house-to-house fighting. Several infantry companies of our Thirtieth Division were praised for their effectiveness and used to train other units by demonstrating efficient ways of attacking sturdy German villages constructed with stones and bricks.

Late on December 16, scuttlebutt spread that the Germans were on the attack in Belgium, about fifty miles south of us in a hilly region known as the Ardennes, which I later learned the "brass" considered unlikely for an enemy offensive. However, rumors were the norm in the army and most of us had learned not to worry about hearsay or unverified stories. The daily diary of my 230th Field Artillery Battalion shows that we did not fire a single round on December 15 and only fourteen on the 16th as compared to 3,689 rounds on October 12 near the peak of the battle for Aachen. Things changed the morning of the 17th when we were placed on alert and told to get ready to move. The order was "Close station March order," which meant two things: notify everyone in your communications network that you were shutting down and prepare to relocate. It was the beginning of the Thirtieth Division's involvement in the enormous clash that came to be called the Battle of the Bulge. Most of us had no idea of where we were going and could not have imagined that we would be major participants in the largest head-to-head battle in U.S. Army history, a battle in which the Americans would absorb almost a hundred thousand casualties.

On the morning of December 17, Captain Alexander, our battery commander, called me to his command post and said, "Sergeant Denius, for this movement, I am putting you in charge of our advance quartering party and appointing you chief of detail." Our "battery," "C" Battery of the battalion, was made up of four 105-mm howitzers and about a hundred men, including five officers. As chief of the advance quartering party, my job was to precede the battery, find our assigned assembly area, and then lead the battery into it. As chief of detail, when I found our assembly area, I had three tasks: the first was to select the area to position the guns, the second was to lead them into their positions when they arrived, and the third was to "lay in the guns," align them so that they were all pointing in exactly the same direction. This third task involved surveying the land around them, a complex skill I had learned in the instrument and survey course at Camp Roberts, California, and later practiced at Fort Meade, Maryland, and in England. There was more to all this than drawing a goose egg on a map and telling the men to find a place to park their vehicles and artillery pieces. I was proud and confident of my new responsibilities.

The main body of our 230th Field Artillery Battalion was part of a long convoy that did not get organized and moving until almost midnight on December 17. However, I left that morning, traveling in a jeep driven, as usual, by the reliable Louis Sberna. I sat in the passenger seat, with radioman Sherman Goldstein on the bench seat behind us. Each of us had the same weapon: a lightweight M-1 carbine that was standard for most artillerymen. Our convoy was composed of other advance quartering parties from the Thirtieth Division with similar assignments to ours. While we were waiting to pull out, a lieutenant came along the line of vehicles and told us that we'd have air cover, and we did, but not what we expected. It was the Luftwaffe keeping an eye on us from high up, while staying out of range. Our route was around the south side of Aachen, then southwest into Belgium. We had no maps, only the lieutenant's descriptions, and, oddly enough, the radio voice of "Axis Sally," the GI's nickname for a couple of American women employed by Nazi Germany to broadcast propaganda to us. Axis Sally announced that the Germans had attacked in the Ardennes and "remnants of the Thirtieth Infantry Division, defeated at Aachen," were on the way there to rescue the Seventh Armored Division. None of this was taken seriously. We had not been defeated at Aachen, but the most interesting thing about it was how we were able to hear it. Few American military vehicles had radios that could pick up civilian frequencies. We liked to listen to music, but couldn't on our army radios. So when we went into a village, we always looked for radios to "liberate." When we got one, it had to be adapted from alternating current to the six-volt direct-current battery in our jeep, and Goldstein was expert at rigging them.

Amused as we were by Axis Sally, we were cold and miserable in the open jeep. The skies were murky, and a brisk wind blew from the north. On today's modern highway our route is N 68 from Aachen into Belgium, through Eynatten, Eupen, and Bévercé. After about forty miles, we pulled into an overnight bivouac area a few miles north of Malmedy to await further orders. On the way, considerable U.S. Army traffic passed us going helter-skelter in the opposite direction. Identification markings on the vehicles' bumpers indicated they were mostly medical units, probably carrying hospital staff, like nurses, technicians, orderlies, and doctors. There were also ambulances with injured men. We didn't know they were fleeing from a powerful German counterattack that we would soon confront. We heard heavy shelling a few miles in front of us, but did not yet know the Germans had broken through our lines there. Occasionally a V-1 buzz bomb passed overhead, and we thought the firing might have been at them. Several days later we learned that some of the gunfire that day—December 17, 1944—might have been the infamous slaughter of eighty-six American POWs standing in a field with their hands over their heads. The atrocity came to be called the Malmedy Massacre, although it actually occurred three miles south of Malmedy at the Baugnez Crossroads. It was the largest mass murder of Americans by Germans during the war. A few of the victims escaped and, although the killings quickly became known, fresh snow covered many of the bodies and concealed the full scale of the crime until the snow melted in January.

Leaving our overnight bivouac on the morning of December 18, an officer briefed me on the likely direction of the enemy and approximately where to locate the battery's designated assembly area. Sberna, Goldstein, and I drove on to find it and scout the area. We were entering the high-forested hills of the northern Ardennes, where the snow was already deep in the fields and accumulating on the Douglas firs and spruce trees. Fortunately, the road was firm, and we made good time. We proceeded with caution. Although Americans had been in the vicinity since September, we knew Germans were not far away, and there were reports that they had dropped paratroopers wearing U.S. Army uniforms into the area. When we found the area, we made a quick reconnaissance around the perimeter with our weapons at the ready before deciding we were safe. Down long firebreaks in the forest we heard the rattle of occasional rapid gunfire, but we did not yet know that an entire evacuation hospital had just withdrawn from Malmedy, probably in the vehicles that passed our convoy going the opposite direction.

"C" Battery's new area was on the north side of a high ridge about a half-mile north of Malmedy, opposite the southerly direction from which I'd been told the enemy would probably approach. If we were correct in this estimate, and subsequent events would prove that we were, the Germans could not get a fix on us by seeing the muzzle blasts from our guns, even at night, except from the air. We had to be concerned about them locating and firing on us, as they were experts at counter-battery fire and we were always a high priority because our big guns could put enormous destructive power on them. Within the assembly area, I selected the site for each of the four howitzers and for the battery command post. There was enough space along the base of the ridge for the entire battery and for the truck drivers to get in and out from the main road. Goldstein combined good judgment with a quick mind and we discussed these decisions, which were actually recommendations for Captain Alexander. From early afternoon, I waited for him on the main road to show him the area. When he arrived about four o'clock, he was composed but obviously harried. German fighters had strafed his convoy on the road, but the battalion suffered no losses. He concurred in my recommendations, which prompts me to comment on the qualifications of artillery officers that I encountered. Most of them were highly skilled, and some were graduates of academies like West Point, Virginia Military Institute, the Citadel, and rigorous college training programs. They were well trained and proficient in mathematics and trigonometry, on which accurate artillery fire depends. At the same time, I can say that I was well prepared to do my job. By late 1944 I had been in military training for six straight years, including one year as a Citadel cadet, followed by six months of rigorous field training, and more recently, by six months of almost continuous combat.

By the time our battalion's main body arrived, the road was teeming with trucks and armored vehicles, steadily moving southward. A long column of tanks, half-tracks, and trucks of the Seventh Armored Division passed through. Assisted by other enlisted men, I began laying in the guns, positioning them for aiming both in deflection—that's the horizontal direction—and in elevation, the vertical angle of the gun barrels. It was a technical job, and the tools for it were range finders, steel tapes, surveyor's chains, and aiming circles. An "aiming circle" is the proper term for a piece of optical equipment that measures the angular distance between true north and magnetic north, which we had to know to align the four guns so they would shoot parallel with each other.

When the guns were positioned and their wheels dug in up to the hubs, Lieutenant Jacobs, Goldstein, and I went up on the ridge to get an overview of the countryside. As usual, we were supporting the 120th Infantry Regiment of some two thousand fighting soldiers and another thousand support personnel. They were closer to Malmedy than we were because their orders were to defend it, as well as us. Other than the 120th Regiment, we did not know the location of friends or foes, but the rumor about German paratroopers in the area gave us a spooky feeling. We would have been more concerned if we had known the Germans had penetrated into Malmedy earlier in the day, threatened the local people, and then withdrawn. The next day (December 19) Lieutenant Jacobs and I went to the 120th's regimental command post for instructions about where we should post our forward observer team. We saw considerable abandoned American equipment in Malmedy. Looking into an empty schoolhouse, I discovered medical supplies and clothing from the abandoned hospital. I asked Captain Alexander what to do with them, and he said, "Get what you can." Goldstein and I liberated the clothing storeroom and got the first clean uniforms we'd had in weeks, as well as supplies of sugar, flour, canned goods, and medical supplies.

In the next few days, the American Armed Forces Radio and the *Stars and Stripes* newspaper mistakenly described Malmedy as in enemy hands, probably misled because the Germans were not far away, and continuing to threaten the town. In this period, the Americans bombed the town three times, virtually destroying it. However, Malmedy's electrical power plant was intact and not far from our area. Burning coal, the power plant became a warm refuge just when temperatures were falling and winds were rising. Northwest Europe's harshest winter in decades was setting in. Any hour of the day or night you could go to the power plant and search for a place to lie down among your buddies, who looked like bundles of dirty clothes in their sleeping bags, around the generators and pumps, in the corridors, and under stairways. I usually slept in an abandoned house. Since most local people had fled, our medics salvaged medications from pharmacies and homes, while some of the boys thoughtfully moved the contents of wine cellars to higher ground. While prowling through the power station one day, I liberated a coveted U.S. Army automatic Colt pistol that someone, presumably one of our officers, had left unattended for a few minutes. It was one of two things that I have stolen in my life. The other was a fancy rearview mirror from a car at the Dairy Queen in Athens, just before I left for overseas. I regret stealing the mirror, but not the pistol, which, incidentally, I did not bring home.

We remained in the same assembly area just north of Malmedy until January 16, a full month, and our longest time in one place during the entire war, but we were active the whole time. Although our firing batteries did not move, almost daily my forward observer team was two to four miles in front of them, looking for targets in areas held by the Germans. On December 21, the third day after laying in the guns, our battalion fired 1,973 rounds. Before daylight on the next day, Goldstein and I were positioned about three miles from our battery, overlooking the highway between Malmedy and Stavelot and reporting the location of enemy forces attempting to continue their advance toward Liege. In hard fighting along this road the previous day, the 120th had not yielded and now the Germans had renewed the attack. As an indication of the hard fighting, on both December 21 and 22, an infantryman from the 120th earned the Medal of Honor. Goldstein and I were awarded Silver Stars because when German tanks fired on our position, we stayed our post, and continued to call down fire on them. Neither of us thought much about the incident, but someone behind us reported what we had done and both of us were eventually awarded another Silver Star "for gallantry" in the face of the enemy.

The citation for this, my third, stated that it was "for gallantry in action on 22 December 1944, near Malmedy in Belgium."

Sergeant Denius was an instrument operator with a forward observer party rendering artillery support to an infantry battalion occupying defensive positions. During an attack by the enemy, when the observation post was discovered and direct fire from enemy tanks began to fall around him, Sergeant Denius refused to withdraw and courageously remained in the hazardous location until the attack had been repulsed. The heroic devotion to duty exhibited by Sergeant Denius reflects great credit upon himself and is in keeping with the highest traditions of the Armed Forces.

The Luftwaffe attempted to bomb and strafe our battalion's bivouac behind the ridge but inaccurately, probably because newly installed anti-aircraft guns near us bounced them around up there, shooting down several planes. One of our defenses was a new all-purpose 90-mm gun that could fire vertically at airplanes or horizontally at tanks. We set up this new gun—the first we had seen—in front of Captain Alexander's command post to take care of the Germans' formidable Panther and Tiger tanks, which never came. Despite the rumors of Germans infiltrating our lines, I never saw one that I know of. However, a German officer, who had been living as a civilian in a house near our battalion commander's command post, came out and turned himself in. He wisely surrendered to an intelligence specialist, rather than confront face-to-face combat foot soldiers, who might not observe the rules of war.

Because of our position on the back side of the ridge, we were almost free of shelling, although Malmedy was heavily hit with shells and rockets. One night, three rounds whistled in, one landing near the medics, and another in front of Captain Alexander's command post. When the rounds came in, one of our men was sleeping—for the first time in combat—in his undershorts rather than his combat gear. After the shelling, he swore he would not take off his clothes again until the war was over. For once, our air force and the German air force were bombing the same target—Malmedy. Not all bombs fell in the intended locations. Some dropped behind and in front of us, and tore up a hillside to the east. On New Year's Day the Luftwaffe was up in force with planes of all types. Several were shot down, and one crashed on the hill behind the power plant. The pilot bailed out but was dead when we found him. Another German plane flew the length of the valley, a few hundred feet off the ground, escaping from P-47s. During the clear winter days the skies were a pattern of vapor trails left by dog-fighting planes and bombers. At night, too, the planes were up, but they did not bother us. V-1s frequently came over us from Germany on flight paths to Liege or Antwerp. From the hillsides we had grandstand seats, and if I had no other combat duty, I went there and watched the heavy action. Some V-1s were sputtering as they passed over us, barely clearing the ridges, but only one came down in our vicinity.

Christmas Day was peaceful in our valley, and that night it was bathed white in the moonlight. Even the deadly howitzers had been whitewashed to camouflage them. The chaplains conducted church services, and we had a turkey dinner with all the trimmings. Some men decorated small fir trees with bits of bright paper and the tinfoil of chewing gum wrappers. Others collected candy and food from us for the homeless children of Malmedy and for sick and wounded civilians in the hospitals. As the winter became increasingly bitter, ice formed on blankets and our uniforms at night. Since the ground was frozen, we were sometimes issued small packets of TNT for use when we needed to blast a new hole. We celebrated the New Year at the stroke of midnight on January 1 by simultaneously firing three salvoes from all artillery pieces. They were not wasted—the targets were selected with the usual care.

By late December, it was obvious that the Germans were pulling back in a fighting withdrawal. Most of our firing was to repel their counterattacks, which were methodical and determined. On January 14 we fired the most rounds of any day of the war: 4,629! The next day, in a company of the 120th Infantry, I went forward as chief of detail with an instruments and survey team to lay in the guns in new positions near the notorious Baugnez Crossroads, about four miles closer to the enemy. The battalion diary says the guns "were surveyed in under heavy artillery fire," but I think it was sporadic, or "interdictory" in an artilleryman's lingo. Whatever the concentration, we focused on our assignment, keenly aware of an "Off Limits" sign on the edge of a nearby field. There, under the snow, lay the bodies of American soldiers, captured by an SS Panzer Division and shot down in cold blood on December 17 as they stood helplessly, with their arms raised. At this crossroads the main German force of tanks—*Kampfgruppe Peiper*—had then turned to the west, thus sparing Malmedy the hardship of reoccupation, but for their infamous deed, many of our infantrymen vowed not to take any more prisoners, regardless of the laws of war. *Kampfgruppe Peiper*, literally "Battle Group Peiper," was named for its commander, Waffen-SS colonel Joachim Peiper, who was tried as a war criminal by an army tribunal in 1946, released from prison in 1956, and mysteriously murdered in France in 1976.

Three miles further on (southeast), the battle raged around the small town of Thirimont. Our foot soldiers slugging it out at close quarters with the enemy called for a forward observer, specifically for me. When I heard someone shout, "Sergeant Denius, needed up front," it was the highest compliment of my life. I heard it the first time in the hedgerows of Normandy after I took Lieutenant Miller's place. Our trigger pullers wanted me with them to help find the enemy and bring down artillery on him. We were desperate for white camouflage. Our olive drab uniforms were easy targets on the white landscape, and forward observers were expected to slip into enemy territory. It was risky. Two members of forward observer teams had recently been captured and two others wounded. Local people began coming out of their homes with bed sheets, tablecloths, and nightshirts, anything that was white. We were grateful, but frankly, if they hadn't brought them, we'd have gone in for them. It was potentially a matter of life and death. While I was preparing to go forward, I paused to watch the questioning of six German prisoners who might reveal useful information about where I was going. They didn't, but they were filthy. All had body lice, and they smelled as though they had wrestled in a barnyard.

When Thirimont was retaken, we pushed on into an unfamiliar area of small farms and villages scattered across the hills. Shelter from the elements was hard to find. We had many men with frostbitten and frozen feet and hands. Ahead of us in the snow-filled woods GIs were freezing and, we heard, dying in their shallow foxholes. Ordinarily we could get occasional warmth, but with so few houses and barns, it was more difficult. Against the rule, many men put wood-burning stoves in the truck beds and huddled or slept around them.

On January 17, we moved again to the badly battered village of Ligneuville to help hold a vital bridge crossing. A monstrous sixty-ton King Tiger tank sat abandoned on the main street, and the boys found an enemy battery of 150-mm guns still in position to fire on nearby hills. We found a booby-trapped truck in a garage, and a German with maps was flushed from a nearby house. He may have been an artillery observer.

The main effort of the American army now was to flatten the Bulge and force the Germans to withdraw back to the lines as they existed before the attack on December 16. Like a football team that plays well at the beginning of a game and then collapses, they had shot their bolt. We were on the north side and pushing south toward the strategic town of St. Vith to help cut off the last remaining enemy forces in what had been the Bulge. Apparently, the Germans were holding on to St. Vith as a withdrawal route. On January 20, I went farther south with a reconnaissance party to select a position for our guns near the village of Recht, about five miles from St. Vith. On January 28, the last trace of the Bulge was gone, but I would not be around to celebrate it, because I was wounded on the 25th. I also had frozen feet and hands that came from several days' exposure to the elements. With only a field jacket and gloves for outer clothing, there was no way to stay warm or dry. We'd dig a deep foxhole and pull something over it to keep out the snow, usually a sheet of tin, planks, or logs. Then, our body heat would melt the snow above us, which dripped on us. Our extremities were especially vulnerable.

Thus I became a casualty, and it happened this way. When we went toward the village of Recht, I was the lone forward observer with a company-sized combat patrol of nearly two hundred infantrymen of the Second Battalion of the 120th Regiment that was to penetrate into German-held territory and put pressure on them to continue to withdraw. Halting near the edge of a dense forest, we faced a road that ran parallel to our positions. As we lay concealed in the forest, a motorized German patrol passed back and forth along the road in front of us. Our commander determined that the patrol passed at intervals of about eight minutes. He decided that we—all two hundred of us—should cross the road, in squad-sized groups of about twelve men, in the intervals between the passing German patrol. Our movement was coordinated with a squadron of about five Sherman tanks that were to advance in parallel with us on a narrow hard-surface road to our right. We got across our road, but the lead tank on the road on our right was knocked out and blocked their road, thus preventing the other tanks from moving forward with us. As a result, we found ourselves in enemy territory without the supportive firepower of the tanks. By now, the Germans realized we were in the area, but did not know exactly where we were. Since we were on the latitude of Montreal in the dead of winter, by mid-afternoon the sun was already low in the sky. Darkness would come quickly.

Our captain organized us a 360-degree perimeter defense, and we dug in for the night. Sure enough, shortly before dark the Germans began attacking our outposts and dropping artillery rounds in the vicinity of our tanks. I was in a foxhole with my radioman on the leading edge of the perimeter. Our CO, in an adjacent foxhole, told me to begin calling in artillery on the German positions, but I could not see them. I did not know where they were, but I studied my map with a flashlight in the bottom of the foxhole and began calling coordinates of their estimated positions to the radioman, who, at this crucial moment, was not up to the task. For some reason, when Captain Alexander selected me for this mission, he did not also send the experienced Sherman Goldstein as my radioman. Goldstein and I were almost intuitive in understanding each other. He was my best friend in the army. However, Captain Alexander sent a new man that we were breaking in. In the foxhole that night, the fellow got the jitters and was not adept with the radio in the dim light. With me holding the flashlight and reassuring him that we were going to be okay, he got the radio messages through to the fire direction center and our artillery rounds began falling a few hundred yards in front of us.

My strongest recollection is the noise, incredible and unceasing. Both enemy and friendly high-explosive artillery rounds were impacting in our vicinity as the Germans engaged the whole area with rifles, machine guns, and the short-ranged rockets called *Nebelwerfers* that made a shrill howling noise as they came in. We had two nicknames for *Nebelwerfers*—"Screaming Mimi" and "Moaning Minnie." They were not very accurate, but the sound was probably terrifying to my rookie radioman, who—poor fellow—was declared unfit for combat when we got back to our battery.

The next morning (January 23) we maintained our position, and I called in artillery fire to support the advance of our tanks, which had gotten around the one blocking the road, but still lagged behind us. This continued for most of the day while our CO sent out patrols to find the enemy. We remained in the same perimeter defense the next day, January 24. On the fourth day, January 25, our tanks caught up with us and we began advancing again. The Germans were withdrawing, but their artillery fire continued and they left behind pockets of defenders to delay our advance. When they surrendered, our infantrymen were tempted not to accept them as prisoners of war. The Malmedy Massacre had aroused strong passions in many American soldiers. To this was added the fact that the defending Germans would fight bitterly, killing and wounding many of our comrades, knowing all the while that they would be overcome. Then, when they surrendered, they expected to be treated humanely. Some were disappointed, I am sure, but I witnessed no abuse of them.

At some point in our advance, I was struck in the right thigh by shell fragments, probably from a *Nebelwerfer*. I did not realize I'd been hit until I saw red stains on the white sheet I was wearing as camouflage. I treated myself with penicillin and bandages, and became one of the "walking wounded." When I returned to my battery, a medic drove me to the battalion aid station where the diagnosis was more serious than I thought. In addition to the shell fragments in my thigh, my feet and legs were swollen from having been frozen.

Eventually, I was awarded a fourth Silver Star for actions around Recht, but I never got a written citation stating exactly what it was for. However, it could only have been for staying close with the company and calling in artillery fire almost on top of us, because that's where the Germans were. I was grateful for the recognition, but the way I look at it, I could not have fled from my post without exposing myself to enemy fire and endangering others. The events around Recht were another experience that convinced me that managing fear is an essential quality for a successful life.

From the aid station, I was taken to an evacuation hospital some fifteen to twenty miles behind our lines near Spa, Belgium. The hospital was in a schoolhouse where many of the wounded lay on the floor covered by blankets. Since I could walk, I helped out by carrying urinals to them. Two days later, I was among many wounded men placed on a hospital train to Paris in cars that were adapted for patients from the notorious French "40 and 8" boxcars, so-called because they were designed in the early 1900s to carry forty men or eight horses. Each car accommodated about twenty-five men in hammocks suspended from the ceiling. When the train went around a curve, you slung from side to side. We arrived in the Orsay railway station, later the Musée d'Orsay art museum, from where we were transported to a local general hospital (which I think is the current Grand Hotel) for a few days before being transported in more "40 and 8" boxcars to Cherbourg, where we transferred to a hospital ship bound for Southampton. I was a litter patient on the hospital ship, presumably to conserve the limited space available. From Southampton, I was taken by ambulance to a general hospital in Cheltenham, England, west of London in the Cotswolds. The hospital was just rows and rows of Quonset huts. Although I remained there about three weeks, I was ambulatory, and helped with the physical therapy of men who had difficulty moving their arms and legs. At other times, I went with other recuperating soldiers on walks across the countryside.

During the second week of March, I rejoined my battery in the German town of Süsterseel, north of Aachen and near the boundary with Holland. The Dutch towns in this vicinity were more home to us than any other place on the continent. We had spent so much time around Heerlen, Vise, and Maastricht, that many men had formed friendships in the towns, friendships that have withstood the test of time in the postwar era.

On March 7 the U.S. Ninth Armored Division had crossed the Rhine at Remagen about eighty-five miles south of us, and we were preparing to cross it in our area. On the night of March 17, with no lights showing, we moved to new positions within a thousand yards of the Rhine near Ossenburg, a town that could be seen by the enemy. We were in place by three o'clock on the morning of March 18, and then waited, remaining under strict camouflage discipline for the entire day. Although the German civilians had fled, the Wehrmacht on the east bank knew we were there, but could not get a fix on us, so they fired randomly toward us, and several men were wounded. When night came we went to work and dug in. Then, for almost a week we waited in hiding for the attack order, known as *Operation Flashpoint,* to cross the Rhine.

Preparations were similar to those for *Operation Cobra* the previous July in Normandy. As security measures, we ripped off our shoulder patches and painted over truck bumper markings. Fires were verboten if the stovepipe was visible to the enemy. German families had chickens, and some had chicken farms, but whole flocks began disappearing. Some of our units posted guards on hen houses near them to ward off predators—other GIs like themselves. We were amazed at the foodstuffs stored or hidden throughout the area. Our men learned to hunt for souvenirs by examining the surface of the ground for indications of recent digging. GIs brought up jewelry, silverware, pistols, and swords that had been buried by the fleeing families.

On March 25 at two o'clock in the morning, our 230th Field Artillery Battalion began crossing the Rhine in deuce-and-a-half trucks on a rubber pontoon bridge through a heavy smokescreen that covered the river. The army was taking no chances. For the next two weeks we moved constantly, laying in the guns again and again to provide fire support for the advancing infantrymen. We thought we were in a race for Berlin, and morale was high. On April 10 we got an unusual message from Colonel Vieman, our battalion commander: "Do not fire unless fired upon. Negotiations for surrender are underway." By April 16, we reached the city of Magdeburg on the Elbe River, more than 250 miles since crossing the Rhine, and only a hundred miles from Berlin. After Magdeburg, German defenses disintegrated, and German soldiers began surrendering wholesale. After we cleared a small German fighting force on the west bank of the river, our fighting days were over. On April 25 the Russians and Americans linked up at Torgau, also on the Elbe River about 110 miles southeast of Magdeburg. A week later Russians appeared across the river, and some of our men went over to meet them.

At nine o'clock on the morning of May 7, 1945, this message came down from our division headquarters: "As of 0001 on the 8th of May 1945 hostilities will cease in Europe. VE Day begins 0001 on the 9th of May 1945." "0001" means one minute after midnight. I do not remember the rejoicing on May 8 so much as the great turmoil on the roads, as massive numbers of German refugees fled west, hoping to come under the control of the Americans, British, or Canadians, instead of the Russians. They were a pitiful sight, in miserable condition, ill fed, ill clothed, and carrying, pulling, or pushing their belongings in every conceivable kind of buggy or wagon. The children were the most pathetic, but there was little we could do, given their extraordinary numbers. Likewise,

Athens, Texas, in 1928 when I was three years old.

1938, my first year at the Schreiner Institute in Kerrville, Texas.

Schreiner Institute, 1941.

A cadet at the Citadel,
the Military College of
South Carolina, 1943.

January 1944. I had just completed basic training and was home in Athens before going to Boston from where I shipped out for Europe.

Late August 1944, northern France, between Paris and the English Channel. The device I am sighting through is an aiming circle, used by artillerymen to measure the difference between magnetic north and true north.

Fall–winter 1945. Probably in Belgium. L-R: radio operator Sherman Goldstein, me, driver Louis Sberna, and Capt. Merrill Alexander, our battery commander.

Spring 1945. Captain Alexander, somewhere in Germany.

Sherman Goldstein was awarded four Silver Stars for gallantry in action. I have always believed he saved my life in Normandy.

The ten most decorated men of the Thirtieth Infantry Division on the deck of the *Queen Mary*, August 14, 1945. I am fourth from the left. In the center is our outstanding division commander, Maj. Gen. Leland S. Hobbs.

August 21, 1945. The *Queen Mary* arrives in New York Harbor carrying 15,000 men of the Thirtieth Infantry Division, me among them.

September 1945. My last photograph before I was discharged from the army.

1946. A new initiate in the Kappa Alpha social fraternity and a full-time student at the University of Texas.

Kappa Alpha fraternity. I am on the far left in the front row. I was the chapter's alumni adviser from 1949 to 1988.

I returned from the war with enough money for a down payment on a new 1946 Ford convertible.

A formal dance sponsored by Kappa Alpha in 1947.

Our wedding at the First Presbyterian Church in Athens, Texas. November 19, 1949.

The three most important women of my life, Easter 1951: Grandmother Cain, Charmaine, and my mother in front of my grandparents' home in Athens.

At the Highland Park Country Club in Dallas, Friday night before the OU game, early 1950s.

A family scene from when the children were small.

Christmas 1960. Woffie was eight and Little Charmaine was four.

With Charmaine in the foyer of our home, mid-1970s.

The Seton Hospital Gala, 1992, with our daughter, Charmaine, and her husband, Gordon McGill. The two Charmaines were co-chairs of the event.

With my son, Wofford "Woffie" Denius, at a game in DKR–Texas Memorial Stadium, 2009.

Wofford Cain, my kind and benevolent uncle, co-founder of Southern Union Gas with Clint Murchison Sr., in 1929 and founder of the Cain Foundation in 1952.

In the Oval Office with President Johnson in 1964 discussing KTBC-Channel 7 and television service in Austin.

To Frank Denius with appreciation — Lyndon B. Johnson

Delhi International's executive committee, 1977. Edward Clark, my senior law partner, is on the left and chairman John Dabney Murchison is at the head of the table.

most German soldiers were desperate to surrender to us. Eventually, our Thirtieth Division would capture a total of 50,126 German military personnel, according to the army's records, and help tens of thousands of civilian refugees. Even maintaining order among them was virtually impossible. I cannot explain why we were so calm, but I can suggest several possibilities. To begin with, we were worn down. Since the previous June 10—some 330 days—our battalion had been on battlefields confronting the enemy for a total of 287 days. Our days of "R and R" were usually brief, although I was better rested than most men, having been hospitalized in England in February and March. We were also sobered by our losses. The record shows that the division had taken 26,038 casualties, more than its authorized strength of around 17,000. Of this number, 3,003 had been killed in action, and 506 had died of wounds. Of the approximate 500 men in my battalion, 38 had been killed. Underlying these reflective influences on our conduct was the usual, consistent discipline in our division. Like our division commander, Maj. Gen. Leland S. Hobbs, we were workingmen.

In the fall of 1945, some six months after the end of the war in Europe, General Eisenhower, the supreme allied commander, was considering which U.S. Army divisions should be awarded the coveted Presidential Unit Citation. He asked the chief military historian in the European theater of operations, Col. S. L. A. "Sam" Marshall, to help him by evaluating the performance of all divisions to determine those that had been the most efficient and consistent in battle. With thirty-five other historical officers, Marshall reviewed records and decided to recommend our Thirtieth Infantry Division for the PUC. The historians found that the division had never performed discreditably, had never carried less than its share of the burden, or looked bad in comparison with the forces on its flanks. The historians were especially impressed with the fact that the division had consistently achieved results without undue wastage of its men. Marshall concluded that on "balance of things, the 30th was the outstanding infantry division in the ETO." Despite this recommendation, the division was not awarded the Presidential Unit Citation, but I am still working for it.

CHAPTER 7

The Good Soil of Texas

Shortly after VE Day, we moved to Saalsfeld, Germany, a railway junction and garrison town about 150 miles east of Frankfurt, near the Czechoslovakian border. The best thing about Saalsfeld was that a bunch of us bivouacked in a fine home. I never saw the owners and assumed they had fled to escape the Russians. The army's point system for determining who was eligible to return home and be discharged now came into play. The general principle was that those who had fought longest and hardest should be returned home first. A soldier's total number of points took into account several factors. One point was awarded for each month of service, one point for each month overseas, and five points for each battle star. A battle star was earned for each major campaign (defined geographically by the army) in which a soldier had fought, and I had been in five: Normandy, Northern France, Rhineland, Central Europe, and Ardennes-Alsace. A decoration counted for additional points, and I had a Purple Heart, a Presidential Unit Citation, and three Silver Stars. A fourth Silver Star and a second Purple Heart would be awarded later.

Sherman Goldstein was one of the first to leave, going home to Toledo, Ohio, to make his career in the jewelry business. I owed him a lot and did not want to see him go, but he deserved it. Decades would pass before I saw him again. Those of us who remained got maps of Japan and lectures on its geography, its armed forces and Japanese culture.

No explanation was needed. The war with Japan still raged in Asia and the Pacific. We also began firing artillery pieces in practice for the short ranges that would be required for fighting on small islands, perhaps two hundred or three hundred yards rather than the three to seven miles we were accustomed to. The shorter the distance from the gun to the target, the more nearly vertical the barrel must be when the projectile is fired.

In early July, the entire Thirtieth Division was transported in U.S. Army trucks some five hundred miles from central Germany to a "tent city" called Camp Oklahoma City in the countryside southwest of Reims, where the army had laid out eighteen assembly areas, each named after an American city. This was where we turned in our trucks, guns, and equipment and waited for the next step in the long journey home. We anticipated that after a furlough—leave from duty—in the States, we would go to an island in the Pacific that would be the staging area for an amphibious invasion of Japan. I do not recall hearing men complain about this prospect, although the thought of more combat was worrisome. The war was not over, and we expected to continue the fight until Japan was subdued. Vigorous young men often misbehave, but there were no problem soldiers at Camp Oklahoma City. Only a fool would cause trouble now.

On August 2, we moved across the channel to a British army post—another tent city—near Southampton, our port of embarkation for the United States. This was the beginning of a period that I consider the "glory days" of my life. I was alive! After all the dangers and close calls, I had survived and would see home again. The weather was perfect and it was a glorious summer in southern England. Everyone was at ease. Our time was our own. We played baseball and I was the center fielder on one of the Thirtieth Division teams. Orchestras came from nearby towns to soothe our memories of battle and entertain us, filling the air with the great songs that had lifted our hearts through the war—like "Boogie Woogie Bugle Boy" and "I'll Be Seeing You." It was marvelous therapy. News about the war with Japan was sketchy. I recall hearing about the bombing of Hiroshima and Nagasaki with an awesome new weapon, but nothing about the scale of destruction, or anything definite that Japan might surrender. What could be worse than the cities we had seen laid to waste, particularly Aachen, a great city almost totally destroyed.

When the ship that would take us home docked in Southampton, it was the *Queen Mary*—surpassed in size only by her sister ship, the *Queen Elizabeth*—still camouflaged in the steel gray that blended with the North Atlantic sea and sky. Several days were required for loading, but when it was done, some 15,000 GIs were aboard, along with 58 civilians and about 1,100 crewmembers. For me, the best part was when our headquarters issued special orders and a press release recognizing the ten most decorated men in the division. I was one of the ten. It was the apex of my military career. I was extremely proud, yet humble, because I knew that many highly decorated men were dead, hospitalized, or had already gone home. Each of the ten most decorated was issued an armband marked "General's Party," referring to the division commander, Maj. Gen. Leland S. Hobbs, and given special privileges. I was assigned a stateroom with a private bath. The ship's British crew served our meals on fine china with silverware, in a dining room in the company of only a dozen other men, and at normal times during the day. By comparison, the other soldiers took turns sleeping in bunk beds built wherever there was space in the twelve decks that extended far below the water level, and they were fed twice a day around the clock. However thrilling this recognition and comfort was, the greatest joy was going home.

We sailed from Southampton on August 15. On the previous day, Japan declared its intention to surrender, but I recall nothing about it, maybe because I was so excited about being aboard the *Queen Mary*, or maybe enemy intentions did not count, only what the enemy did. At the time, I was probably thinking more about being one the most decorated men in the division. I cherish a photograph of the ten most decorated with our division commander, General Hobbs. We were so proud of him. He was more than the top-ranking soldier in the division, he personified the division in spirit and in deeds—steadfast in devotion to duty, steady in times of stress, fair in his judgment, and generous with his compliments.

The historic crossing required six days. Approaching New York, I don't know what the other GIs were thinking, but I was thinking about a girl—just one, that feminine figure on an island in the center of the harbor. On August 21st, I got up at three o'clock in the morning to catch the first glimpse of the Statue of Liberty emerging through the mist of

New York harbor. A huge Thirtieth Division banner was draped over the side of the ship. Thousands of us hung on the rails or peered through portholes as tugboats blew whistles and spewed streams of water high in the sky. An Associated Press story described our arrival as the "greatest and noisiest celebration since V-E Day." After docking at Pier Ninety-four, we marched to a railroad siding on Forty-ninth Street, only two blocks from the Hudson River, and boarded a train for Camp Kilmer, New Jersey, where for two days we were "processed" yet again. We got new khaki uniforms to replace our woolens, and were granted thirty-day furloughs, after which we were to report to Fort Lewis, Washington. I do not know what the army had in mind for us. Maybe it was to prepare for occupation duty in Japan. The Japanese committed to surrender on August 14, but did not sign until September 2.

When the processing done, several hundred of us boarded a train destined for Fort Sam Houston in San Antonio, with countless stops on the way. Since trains are my hobby, I want to tell you about this one. Remember that I am describing, not complaining. We were all so happy to be back in the United States of America and going home that any transportation that rolled was welcome. Our train had about seventy-five boxcars, and each was dropped off in a predetermined town on a meandering route across the continent. The boxcars were of three types: hammock cars, kitchen cars, and latrine cars. About twenty-five men were assigned to each hammock car, so called because a hammock was suspended from the ceiling for each man. There were no windows, only the standard doors for loading and unloading freight, which were normally open. We stashed our duffel bags around the edges of the car and lay in the hammocks most of the time, day and night, jolted by the rocking of the car and lulled by the constant clicking on the rails. During the day several men usually sat in the open doors, their legs dangling over the side. The train's three coal-burning locomotives spewed cinders that sometimes swirled back into our boxcars. Even the smoke smelled good, and the whistle was reminiscent of unhurried days in Athens. We were going home at a steady clip.

As a staff sergeant, I was appointed to maintain order and make announcements in my car. There were no problems. We could only go to a kitchen car or latrine car when the train stopped, which was at irregular intervals, usually on a siding off the main track. Our meals were cooked in the kitchen cars. We'd jump off, dash to the kitchen car with our mess kits, and be served by the cooks from their door. We were always hungry.

Leaving Camp Kilmer, we went north to upstate New York, dropped off a few cars, then turned south, passing through Pittsburgh, Louisville, and St. Louis on our route. Our spirits had never been higher, and we got tremendous receptions along the way. When the train slowed or stopped and people saw that we were GIs, they shouted and waved, and we waved back. As I said, these were the "glory days" of my life.

We got to Texarkana about noon, our first stop in Texas. Believe me, when the train stopped, I jumped from the boxcar, ran to the railroad station flagpole, saluted, kneeled down, and kissed the good soil of Texas. When we got to Fort Sam Houston in San Antonio, I called my mother in Athens and told her I could catch a bus to arrive in Austin about eleven o'clock that night. She and my grandmother began driving and met me at the Greyhound station at Fourth and Congress in Austin about one o'clock in the morning. We could have stayed overnight, but I wanted to be home in Athens, and we drove through the night to get there. A fellow soldier traveling with me was going to Fort Worth. We dropped him off at the bus station in Waco, continued on, and at last got home about six in the morning.

Later that day, Aunt Sha and Uncle Chick had us to their home for lunch, a wonderful gesture that was typical of them. Aunt Sha served my favorite dessert—angel food cake with ice cream and strawberries. A check for one thousand dollars was taped to the bottom of my plate, the gift that Uncle Chick had promised when I left, if I did not smoke or drink until I was twenty-one years old. I was still twenty, but he gave it to me anyway, and I put it to good use by ordering a new black Ford convertible, the first one seen on the streets of Athens. My mother had put up a deposit on the order before I got home, and the total cost was $1,518.00! My part of it was a little easier because I got home with a couple of hundred dollars from my share of Howie Young's winnings onboard the USS *Wakefield* between Boston and Liverpool. However, I had to wait until July of the next year for delivery. During the war, there were no new car sales to civilians, except to doctors, police and fire departments, critical war workers, and traveling salesmen. This created a backlog of demand that car manufacturers could not meet in the immediate postwar period, hence the delay of ten months for my car. Film and car buffs may be interested to know that my black 1946 Ford convertible was just like Biff Tannen's car in the movie *Back to the Future*.

In Athens, I went to all the old familiar places, ambled around the town square, talking with old-timers, friends, and acquaintances, exuberant to be among them again. I went to Stirman's Drug Store where businessmen came for coffee, to the Safeway whose manager always had a job for me, to the Dixie Theater, and to the courthouse to see anyone I might know. Sitting silently, I rejoiced listening to the voices of people I did not know talking in familiar accents about cattle, cotton, oil, black-eyed peas, hunting, and fishing. I had to remind myself that this was not a dream. One encounter was immeasurably important. Those who know me will not be surprised that it happened at a football game. I went to Athens High School's first game of the season and saw an attractive young lady sitting in the bleachers below me. She was obviously a student at Athens High School, and I thought I knew about everyone in Athens, but I had never seen her before. She was the prettiest girl I had ever seen. The next morning I described her to my mother, who said, "That's Charmaine Hooper. You don't know her because her family moved here about when you went into the service." I replied, "Mom, I sure would like to meet her." So my mother called her mother and asked if she could bring me down to meet her. That afternoon, my mother and I went to Charmaine's home and our mothers introduced us. I asked Charmaine if she would like to go to the Dairy Queen for a coke, and that was our first date.

Our romance was old-fashioned and evolved slowly. We dated occasionally as she finished her last year of high school and during the year she went to Fairfax College in Virginia. In the fall of 1947, Charmaine transferred to the University of Texas, pledged Kappa Kappa Gamma, and we began dating steadily. Before long, we were pinned, as fraternity boys and sorority girls say, and in June of 1949, we became engaged. We decided that I should complete law school before we married. The grand event finally occurred at the First Presbyterian Church in Athens on November 19, 1949, four years after we met for the first time. Uncle Wofford was my best man, and his best friend, Clint Murchison, came with him.

On September 2, 1945, Japan surrendered, and a few days later I got a letter from the army that I could be discharged immediately, but I had to return to Fort Sam Houston for it. When I got there, the officer in charge said, "Sergeant, you have accumulated leave time for two more thirty-day furloughs. If you stay in the army, and take the furloughs rather than the discharge, you'll be paid for the time?" I did not have to think twice before I said, "Major, not on your life. If I can be discharged this week, I can return to the University of Texas." I knew about fall enrollment only because my mother had called a friend in Austin, who inquired at the university and learned that classes would resume on October 30. There was no secret about the schedule, but the change from wartime exigencies to peacetime routines was occurring rapidly, and disseminating the latest information to every high school and community in Texas was difficult. The university was still on its wartime year-round academic calendar of three four-month "trimesters." Unless I got an early discharge, I would have to wait until March 1946 to enroll. "Too bad," the major said, "you will never make it. Your records are across the street in that barracks with about a million-and-a-half others. You can't find yours in time." I asked if I could try, and he said, "Okay. Good luck!" Within forty-five minutes, I had located my file and reported back. He was astonished, but he signed my papers for the discharge. Two days later, on October 2, I was discharged from the United States Army, a date that I will never forget.

I drove straight to Austin to search for a place to live. Housing was tight, but, as often happened in my early life, my mother intervened in a very positive way. Her friend, Emma Campbell, helped me locate a room with a family in West Austin where I would live for more than three years while I attended the university. I went home to Athens and returned to Austin on October 25, bought my books, got myself organized, and began classes on October 30, 1945. Looking back, I am amazed that, although I had been in the army for three years and had been "To Hell and Back," as Audie Murphy said, I was in my third year of college, and still only twenty years old. The GI Bill of Rights was a boost for me, as it was for millions of other veterans. The benefits included cash payments of tuition and living expenses to attend college. I got an additional allowance on my monthly stipend because I had been wounded. The stated purpose of the extra money was "rehabilitation," but I called it "walk around money," and it came in handy to buy civilian clothes, which I needed.

When I went to class that fall of 1945, no one could have been happier than I was. In all the stressful times of the war, two thoughts—call them hopes and prayers—were constantly on my mind. One was to come home alive and the other was to return to the University of Texas. After everything that had happened, I was there, walking on a cloud, living a dream. I cannot explain the irresistible appeal of the university. The war quickly became a distant memory that I hardly thought about for years. I knew what I wanted to do, and I was in a hurry. Walking across the campus, I'd look up at the Tower as though to say, "Here I am." My classes in Waggener Hall were virtually in the shadow of the Tower, and the law school was nearby in Pearce Hall, a building on Twenty-first Street, torn down in 1974 to make space to expand the business school.

By enrolling in October 1945, I was in the first group of veterans on the campus. They came in even greater numbers in the spring of 1946 and especially that fall. Their extraordinary numbers dramatically changed the university culture, most obviously by the crowded conditions, but the changes were also social and environmental. Enrollment went from 8,794 in the fall of 1944 to 17,242 in 1946. Classroom, dormitory, and office space was augmented with surplus military barracks, which were disassembled on army posts, and hauled to the campus, where they were reassembled. Cold in winter, hot in summer, and unsightly, they nonetheless dotted the campus, especially along Waller Creek. One large former barracks called "V-Hall" was staffed by university employees who dealt only with issues presented by returning veterans, like negotiating and clarifying their benefits with the Veterans Administration. V-Hall was conveniently located where the Harry Ransom Humanities Research Center was later built. However, the size of these temporary structures was dwarfed by those on Lake Austin Boulevard, which were remodeled as apartments for married students and faculty, including two future presidents of the university, Peter T. Flawn and William S. Livingston.

Battle-hardened veterans—like fighter pilot Olin White, who had escorted B-17s over Berlin, and Bob Green, a much decorated army sergeant who had survived the horrific battle of Okinawa—dated and married coeds just out of high school. Bob Bearden returned from a German prisoner-of-war camp determined to be a Longhorn cheerleader and was elected, with the help of his Sigma Nu fraternity brothers. There has never been another cheerleader like him. As a parachutist in the Eighty-second Airborne Division, he had jumped into nighttime Normandy on D-Day, been wounded twice, and finally captured when he was surrounded, out of ammunition and food. The 1946 yearbook, the *Cactus,* included an incomplete list of 1,663 former UT students who had been killed in the war. Hundreds were still unaccounted for, and two—Neel E. Kearby and John C. Morgan—had been decorated with the Medal of Honor. Both were pilots in the Army Air Corps. A graduate of the business school, fighter pilot Kearby had risen to the rank of colonel and was credited with twenty-one Japanese planes downed before he crashed in the jungle on the north shore of New Guinea, where he died of wounds. His remains were found two years later. Morgan visited the campus after the war. The feat for which he was awarded the Medal of Honor is the basis for a scene in *Twelve O'Clock High,* the 1949 Academy Award–winning movie.

The campus atmosphere was serious and purposeful. My generation of young men was uniquely mature as well as impatient to make up for lost time, and I was typical. We wanted to get on with our lives. We did not wear a hat or cap to class. Like many, I instinctively answered professors with "sir." If a professor said, "Remember, you're not in the army anymore," I'd reply, "Yes, sir." Some men wore a tie to class, at least occasionally; it was a custom that persisted until the 1960s. When you have lived a life of discipline and regimentation, it's difficult to give it up overnight. I studied hard and did my best to make good grades. Every course was interesting—some more than others, of course—and I soaked up whatever my professors offered. I cannot say the university was easy for me, but I was diligent and enthusiastic. I enjoyed being a student again and getting to know the younger students. I tried to be a worthy example for them, as in the two government courses that were required for a degree. The professors assigned outside readings that were available only in books that could not be removed from the library. When I did the readings, I made legible notes by hand that another student took to an off-campus blueprint shop and made mimeographed copies that he gave to other students. This time-consuming effort was necessary before the advent of copy machines. For years my notes occasionally surfaced in course files kept by student organizations.

Later generations can be grateful that the method of registering has improved immeasurably since my days on the campus. When I registered in September 1947, registration took place at fifteen to twenty tables on the south side of the Main Building. By nine in the morning, about seventeen thousand students were standing in lines between Nineteenth Street (now Martin Luther King Jr. Blvd.) and the Main Building. The first step in the process was to get a registration form, and you waited in line for it. Registration went on all day and into the evening. I remember getting in line about 6:00 a.m. and finishing up about noon, while there were still masses of students trying to sign up for courses. That's difficult to imagine with the current ability to register online from anywhere in the world.

Returning veterans formed many new clubs to continue the comradeship of the war. I helped organize the Former Servicemen's Club. The marines had their own club, aptly labeled the *Semper Fi*. Even a Texas A&M Club was organized for the stated purpose of "uniting the exes of Texas A&M College." My social life revolved around the Kappa Alpha social fraternity. I pledged in the fall of 1945 and was soon elected to an office. After three years in the army and eleven months of almost continuous combat duty, I am still amazed that I enjoyed Kappa Alpha fraternity as I did, socializing and playing intramural sports. It was a lighthearted contrast with the war. Happily, though fraternities can promote scholarship, they are not classrooms. Fraternities are about companionship and having fun—good clean fun, we must insist. I made lifelong friends through Kappa Alpha, and I have seen many young men become better adults by living in fraternal communities—which, as another positive, are becoming more diverse over the course of time. In

1949, I became the chapter's alumni advisor and served in that capacity until 1988, a mere thirty-nine years! Consistent positive alumni influence is essential for a beneficial culture in an active chapter.

I attended the first home football game played after I returned to the campus that fall of 1945. It was Texas against Rice on October 27, and Texas lost 7 to 6. Two weeks later, Texas beat Baylor 21 to 14 in Memorial Stadium. Since 1945, I have missed only two home games. I attend many out-of-town games, and I have not missed an OU game since 1946. Texas won the A&M game in College Station on Thanksgiving Day by a score of 20 to 10. Three other KAs and I drove to the game, not in the best car we had, but in the car with the best tires. Tires were rationed and difficult to come by during the war and for a while after the war.

I have often been asked if my affinity for Longhorn football was love at first sight. "Love at first sound" is more accurate. Grandfather Cain's enthusiasm for Athens High School football infected me with a passion for the game at a tender age. Remember, too, that my fourth grade classroom teacher played a recording of the school song whose words are easy to hum and sing "all the live long day." Then came Kern Tips on the radio broadcasting Southwest Conference games in the 1930s under the sponsorship of the Humble Oil and Refining Company. Kern Tips's voice, his colorful language, and cadence were magnetic. He made you want to listen, and he was still broadcasting when I returned from the war. Football, especially Longhorn football, was part of my life even before I enrolled in the University of Texas, but it would rise to new heights once I was there.

CHAPTER 8

Everett Looney and Edward Clark

W HILE A THIRD-YEAR LAW STUDENT IN 1948, I got a job clerking in the Austin law firm of Looney & Clark. My uncle,
Wofford Cain, helped me get the job through his friend
and business partner, Clint Murchison. Mr. Murchison had retained the
firm to represent his considerable business and governmental interests
in Austin. Uncle Wofford mentioned my situation to Mr. Murchison,
who asked Mr. Looney, the firm's managing partner, if the firm could
use another clerk. Murchison—Uncle Clint to me—had known me
since childhood and, in a surprising twist of fate, his business interests
became a major factor in my law practice and in my role as director on
numerous corporate boards.

By the time I joined Looney & Clark, Clint Murchison was a widely
known celebrity in the oil industry, especially in Texas. He made his
initial fortune in the 1920s as a wildcatter with a keen understanding of
banking and finance. By the 1940s he needed a well-connected law firm
to represent him, because in the thirties he had diversified his investments into life insurance companies, banks, bus lines, publishing firms,
industrial building materials, and an assortment of companies serving
leisure activities—even a fishing tackle company in Minnesota and the
Daisy Rifle Company, which he explained by saying his hobbies were
hunting and fishing. One of his bus lines was the public transportation

system in the capital city of Texas, the Austin Transit Company, which became one of my first clients.

When I interviewed with Mr. Looney, he asked, "When would you like to start?" I said, "As soon as you'll let me," and I went to work the next day. There were several other clerks, and we called ourselves the *pistoleros,* slang for a gunman or anyone who does what the boss says without question. The *pistoleros* did anything the lawyers or their secretaries wanted: we made coffee, delivered documents around town, and ran errands to the courthouse. Since this was before high-speed copy machines, one of our tedious tasks was copying documents by hand in the courthouse, and some of them were long. We organized and maintained files. Attention to detail was important when we filed and retrieved documents. Clerking was good training, and I learned about the firm from the inside.

Everett L. Looney and Edward A. Clark formed the firm in 1938 on the strength of a retainer fee from the Houston construction company of Brown and Root. The two young lawyers became acquainted when they were both assistants to James Allred while he was state attorney general from 1931 to 1935. When Allred was elected governor in 1935, Mr. Clark went with him, and, two years later, Allred appointed him secretary of state. Ed Clark was only thirty years old, and the appointment made him responsible for overseeing elections in all 254 counties in Texas and keeping all business records required by the state. It positioned him to know people across the state, especially elected officials and businessmen, and greatly enhanced his knowledge of Texas government at all levels, particularly the governor's office and the legislature. Ed Clark had a fine legal mind, great common sense, and excellent political judgment Politics was always his primary interest; his second major interest was banking, and he was very successful at that too.

Another senior member of the firm was R. Dean Moorhead. He had joined the firm in 1948 and was made a partner the next year. Originally from Kansas, he had graduated from Columbia University Law School and had come to Texas as an assistant to Texas attorney general Gerald Mann. Unlike the rest of us, Mr. Moorhead never dictated to a secretary or machine. He was a stylist who crafted marvelously concise and lucid briefs and appeals on his manual typewriter, as all typewriters were in those days.

Everett Looney was the finest lawyer I have ever known. He had extraordinarily good judgment about the law and people, and he could dictate a perfect brief, not a draft, but a finished document. When he and Ed Clark formed the firm in 1938, Clark resigned as secretary of state to devote his political talents full-time to helping Herman Brown, CEO of Brown and Root. At the time, Herman Brown desperately needed the kind of political and legal help that Ed Clark could provide. Brown and Root was threatened by the questionable legality of a contract awarded in 1936 to construct the Marshall Ford Dam (now Mansfield Dam) on the Colorado River about eighteen miles upstream from Austin. (A second construction company had a minority interest in the contract.) It was far and away the biggest project ever for Brown and Root, until then mostly a road-paving and bridge-building operation. In addition to contractual issues, funding for the dam was snarled in political infighting in Congress, and jurisdictional conflict between the federal Bureau of Reclamation and the Lower Colorado River Authority, a regional entity created by the Texas Legislature in 1934 for flood control, water supply, and hydroelectric power generation.

Uncertainty about the completion of the dam increased when Congressman James P. Buchanan, powerful chairman of the Committee on Appropriations, and in whose district the dam was located, died suddenly on February 22, 1937. Buchanan was succeeded by Mr. Clark's close friend, Lyndon B. Johnson, who campaigned as an all-out supporter of President Roosevelt and the "New Deal" at a time when the president was widely criticized for attempting to "pack" the Supreme Court. By winning the election, Johnson went to Washington as a favorite of the president, an "insider," sometimes called FDR's protégé. This prominence gave Lyndon unique access to seats of power in the nation's capital, and he put his whole heart in the Marshall Ford project. Nothing was more important to him, to the Brown brothers, or to Ed Clark, who absolutely relished that kind of politic-legal involvement. Eventually, the problems were resolved, and the dam was completed. Although many people were involved in the effort, Johnson rightly got the lion's share of the credit for it. Brown and Root made huge profits from the project and henceforth would go all-out for Johnson. In 1940, with Lyndon pulling levers of power, the Roosevelt administration awarded Brown and Root the contract to build the mammoth Corpus Christi Naval Air Station, which redounded to the benefit of the Looney & Clark law firm. The historic consequences of LBJ's alliance with Brown and Root would have profound ramifications for Texas, and for the political history of our country, especially during LBJ's presidential years, 1963–1969. I have always doubted whether Lyndon could have ascended from member of Congress representing the Tenth District of Texas to president of the United States without the support he got along the way from George and Herman Brown in terms of money, transportation, and influence. Aided by Johnson's political skill, they were wealthy and had airplanes and lobbyists as well as other officeholders they could call on. Keep in mind that from his election to the House in 1937, LBJ had to win election every other year beginning in 1938 until he was elected to the Senate in 1948 and again in 1954.

In my job clerking for the law firm in 1948 and 1949, I worked almost exclusively with Mr. Looney. I took the bar examination in February 1949 and received notice that I had passed it on May 10. When I went to the office the next morning, I encountered Mr. Looney in the library drinking coffee and told him the good news. His immediate reaction was to say, "Welcome to the profession. We'd like to invite you to join the firm as an associate." I accepted, and he raised my salary to $175 a month. Thus, I became the sixth member of the firm. The other associates were Donald Thomas and Martin Harris. In 1956 I was made partner in the firm.

Although Mr. Looney managed the firm, Mr. Clark brought us important clients, and his philosophy about our firm prevailed. He said we should have close ties to a congressman, own a bank, and have a friendly relationship with the news media. Lyndon Johnson, of course, outperformed the Clark formula. As for the firm owning a bank, Mr. Clark and several other men owned the controlling interest in the Capital National Bank, and he became chairman of the board of directors. Rounding out Mr. Clark's philosophy about having close contact with the news media, we represented the local newspaper, the *Austin American-Statesman*, and several radio stations, notably the Johnson family's station KTBC, which acquired the television license in 1952 and was the only commercial network station until 1965.

The financial underpinning of Looney & Clark came from a number of prominent clients who had the firm on permanent retainer. By "permanent retainer," I mean they sent us a check every month, whether we did anything for them or not. This revenue stream sustained the firm. All other business was gravy—more than was required for a viable firm. The retainer clients included the Capital National Bank, the *American-Statesman* newspaper, the American General Insurance Company, the Metropolitan Life Insurance Company, Southland Insurance Company, Brown and Root, the Associated General Contractors of Texas (the trade association of companies that build roads), the commercial trucking industry, and the Texas Restaurant Association. Other retainer clients were most of the public utilities, including Texas Utilities; Dallas Power and Light; Central and Southwest Power and Light; the Texas Army National Guard, which we helped to sell revenue bonds to construct new armories; and the Pedernales Electric Cooperative, the first nonprofit rural electric cooperative in the nation as well as the largest. Strange as it seems today, a number of law firms outside of Austin had our firm on retainer, because few, if any, of them had an office in Austin staffed with lawyers. Instead, they contracted with Looney & Clark to assist them with their clients' needs before state agencies and in appellate proceedings before state courts. The large and venerable firm of Vinson & Elkins in Houston retained our firm. Eventually, many such firms established their own offices in Austin. Underlying the influence of our firm was the unique web of relationships that Mr. Looney, and especially Mr. Clark, had cultivated over the years. We were capable of helping individuals and organizations, whether the issues were regulatory, legislative, public relations, or political campaigns.

Most of my initial practice was with companies that had Looney & Clark on retainer. One that became increasingly important to me was the Capital National Bank in Austin. My work with the bank illustrates how the law firm set me up for a wide-ranging legal practice in both banking and corporate governance. However, make no mistake that I had to provide high quality service to maintain the confidence of clients. The Capital National Bank became my client in a straightforward way. Not long after I passed the bar, Mr. Looney took me to the bank and introduced me to the president, Mr. Walter Bremond. He told Mr. Bremond that I was on call to help him on whatever issue he needed an attorney. This began my forty-five-year relationship with the bank. The relationship between the Capital National Bank and Looney & Clark was mutually beneficial. The law firm's offices were near the bank, and Ed Clark was, or became, chairman of its board of directors. If a bank customer wanted to create a trust or prepare a will or deed, a bank officer sent the customer to our firm. When Everett Looney told Mr. Bremond I was available to help the bank on any issue, it meant that I did the low and the high, the rudimentary and the challenging tasks. I reviewed the bank's business forms and prepared new forms, collected delinquent notes, drew up trusts and wills, briefed the directors on their responsibilities and liabilities, inspected properties taken as collateral, and foreclosed on properties. When I was elected to the board of directors in 1960, I knew the bank inside out. I remained a director until 2005, when after a series of mergers, the once proudly freestanding Capital National Bank had disappeared, wholly absorbed into JP Morgan Chase, a global holding company.

In the same way that Everett Looney had introduced me to Walter Bremond, I met Clyde "Bama" Malone, the general manager and claims adjuster for the Austin Transit Company, which was then owned, as I stated earlier, by Clint Murchison. Inevitably, a fleet of urban buses will have numerous accidents that must be investigated, which I did by reenacting what happened, with the driver and managers of the company in the bus, at the scene of the accident. I represented the company in court and before the Austin City Council, which fixed their rates. I also mediated wage disputes between the management and bus drivers, usually to the satisfaction of both, I think. You can be sure that a smile spread across my face when a driver waved or shouted "Hi Mr. Denius" as I walked in downtown Austin. Similarly, I represented Roy's Taxis, owned by Roy Velasquez. Early in my practice, Mr. Velasquez applied to the city council for approval to add more taxis to his fleet. His application was staunchly opposed by his main competitor, Yellow Cabs, whose attorney was Trueman E. O'Quinn, a respected public figure in Austin. Mr. O'Quinn was a former member of the legislature, and interestingly enough, a published scholar on the subject of William Sidney Porter, the short story writer who wrote under the pen name O. Henry. Mr. O'Quinn, whom I liked and admired, had also been Austin city attorney from 1936 until 1950, except for war service when he rose to the rank of lieutenant colonel in the 101st Airborne Division. After we argued for our clients before the city council, the council voted in favor of allowing Roy Velasquez to enlarge his fleet of taxicabs. When I got back to the office, Mr. Looney told me how proud he was and how important my success was for our firm. From then on, he assigned me most of our cases before the city council, unless he took them himself.

About the time I was starting my practice, Ed Clark referred to me as the firm's "civic ambassador" to Austin. He had sized up the situation correctly and that is how my law practice evolved. In a parallel way, he was our firm's "ambassador to the legislature," although neither role was official or exclusive to Mr. Clark and me. Charmaine and I thought it was perfect casting for us. She had a host of old friends in the city, and an ever-expanding circle of new friends. We enjoyed the social life, and we had decided that Austin was where we wanted to live and raise our family. I could have gone to a law firm in Dallas favored by Uncle Wofford or back to Athens. Several influential people in Athens asked me to return and run for district attorney, but that was never anything I wanted to do. That would have removed me from Longhorn Country!

Lawyers in the firm of Looney & Clark were not accountable for their time. Neither did we bill our clients by the hour. This was possible because, as I mentioned earlier, we were sustained by our monthly retainer income. This easygoing style lasted until the firm had about eight members. Within the firm, Mr. Looney assigned cases to us as they came in. If it was an appellate matter, he gave it to Dean Moorhead. Mary Jo Carroll came to the firm to help Mr. Moorhead with his briefings. If a case required in-depth legal study and perhaps a trial, Mr. Looney usually gave it to Donald Thomas or took it himself, in which case I helped him, especially in the first few years, when he was virtually my mentor. State and federal cases that involved lobbying and legislation went to Mr. Clark. Sam Winters came to the firm as a specialist on insurance issues. If the case was a local commercial or governmental issue, Mr. Looney often assigned it to me. Sander Shapiro came to the firm as a tax authority and was joined by Mike Cook, who specialized in the same area.

As a rule, the firm encouraged civic activities and pro bono legal work (without monetary compensation). For instance, my services were volunteered to the United Way, and I became chairman in 1968, with two goals. The first was to consolidate the fundraising goals of numerous charitable organizations under the umbrella of the United Way; and the second was to raise a million dollars, an extraordinary amount at the time. We exceeded our goal! While these activities absorbed time that would have been applied to legal cases, Mr. Clark liked to point out that pro bono work brought us more clients. I can still hear him saying, "Frank, "all those people serve on juries. And lots of them will need our lawyerly help." Mr. Clark was a treasure of folksy advice and taught me more about people than anyone. Once over lunch when I was still a novice, he counseled, "Frank, I want to tell you something. 'Never get in a pissing contest with a skunk.'" He liked to say, "Honest men rejoice when thieves fall out." Mrs. Clark understood him and often remarked, "Ed wants to be the corpse at every funeral and the bride at every wedding."

Ed Clark was forever volunteering my services or suggesting that I help an organization. When the Better Business Bureau needed a new general counsel, he volunteered me, and I represented the BBB for thirty years at no cost to them. I was rewarded with many new friends, like Nancy and Kerry Merritt, with whom Charmaine and I dined and traveled extensively. Similarly, I worked with the Young Men's Business League and became its president in 1955. We helped the Salvation Army, and I solicited donations by ringing a bell on Congress Avenue at Christmas time. When the Headliners Club was chartered in 1954 under Mr. Looney's direction, I drew the articles of incorporation and bylaws in collaboration with Mr. Looney, and made sure that the membership included four categories: journalists, businessmen, academics, and also the military, as Bergstrom Air Force Base was important to the city. I was a founding trustee of the club, filed the application for charter, and was president in 1961 and 1962. The three founders were Charles E. Green, Everett Looney, and KTBC news announcer Paul Bolton. Mr. Green, editor of the *American-Statesman* and a very good friend of mine, was really the founder of the Headliners Club.

As a result of doing so much in the community, I developed a diverse portfolio and a wide variety of clients. As I had enjoyed walking around the town square in Athens and talking to people, I enjoyed my clients. Most were just folks, down-to-earth and open-hearted. They were more than cases to me. I was interested in them and their life stories. By having cases in wide-ranging fields, I got to participate in projects that were important to the growth and development of Austin, an increasingly dynamic city.

My first jury trial was significant for my career because I worked directly with Mr. Looney. The case involved an automobile accident on the old U.S. Highway 81 north of Austin. Under Mr. Looney's tutelage, I investigated the case, wrote a trial brief for him, and otherwise did anything he asked. It was a wonderful experience. He was marvelous with juries and all of the strategizing that's necessary in a jury trial. Our client was the defendant, a man named Utz, who was in the rose-growing business in Tyler, Texas. He had delivered a truckload of rose bushes to San Antonio and, on the way back, had loaded his truck with cedar posts that he bought west of San Marcos. The plaintiff was the estate of the driver of the other vehicle, who was killed in the accident. Utz thought he had seen a third man who had witnessed the accident and then left the scene. Mr. Looney said we needed to find this potential witness. I scoured the state, especially Central Texas, and found him at Pflugerville High School, where he was a janitor known as "Nervous" Hinson.

The case was tried over a period of about fifteen months. After settling a venue question, it was conducted in Travis County and went to a full jury trial on the merits for damages. The lawyers for the other side were Frank Erwin and Jack Sparks, both friends of mine. By sitting right behind Mr. Looney for the entire trial of about ten days, I learned a lot about people, about juries, and about the law. When the case ended in 1951, the jury found in favor of our client, and no damages were assessed against Mr. Utz. In his argument, Mr. Looney used a relatively new legal theory called the doctrine of the "last clear chance." He persuaded the jury that the plaintiff had the last clear chance to avoid the accident and that, therefore, our client—the defendant, Mr. Utz—should not be liable. Many people thought we took the case because Utz had a hefty insurance policy, but he had no insurance. This was before a state law was enacted that required motorists to have insurance.

In a humorous sidelight of the case, Mr. Looney instructed me to go to the restroom any time the jury left the jury box for deliberations. The jury room was next to the men's restroom, and the Travis County Courthouse was not air-conditioned. By listening carefully and occasionally putting my head out the window (for fresh air, if anyone asked), I overheard what the jurors were saying to each other. I also bought Mr. Hinson a new pair of overalls that emphasized his belly to wear in the courtroom. The idea was to undermine the credibility of our opposition's witness to the accident, who said that Hinson was tall and slender.

Mr. Looney taught me things about the practice of law that guided me from then on. The first is that you must investigate and learn the facts of a case to the nth degree. Second, you must understand your client and know his or her objectives. Third, you must study and know the case law. You must spend time briefing and reading. Fourth, be aware of the consequences of the lawsuit or case. Finally, Everett Looney taught me that you had to be devoted to the practice of law and the case you were handling. "The law," he liked to say, "is a jealous mistress." You had to be devoted and honorable. To him, the law was a beautiful chorus, if properly expressed. He encouraged me to think of the law rhythmically or lyrically and to express it with personal feeling whether orally in courtrooms or in written briefs. With that in mind, he once bought the latest-model dictating machines for several of us in the firm, and insisted that we use them rather than write in longhand or hunt-and-peck on typewriters. Occasionally, he'd come into my office and ask, "Are you using your dictating machine?" After we'd finished a case, whether we'd won or lost, Mr. Looney sent me to interview the jurors who would talk about it. He wanted to know what jurors had understood about the facts, their opinions or trust in the lawyers who had held forth before them, the effect of the lawyers' mannerisms, or anything that had influenced jurors. Naturally, I applied the same principles in other venues, like the Austin City Council, the Railroad Commission, the Appellate Court, even tax cases.

To my great distress, Mr. Looney suffered a stroke in January 1958 and was never able to resume his practice of law. What I learned from him as a young lawyer was important to my future career. He was my mentor for the practice of law.

Only a few months before I began clerking at the firm, both Mr. Looney and Mr. Clark were deeply involved in the controversial Democratic Party primary of 1948 when Lyndon Johnson beat Coke Stevenson, a popular former governor, for a U.S. Senate seat by the official margin of eighty-seven votes. In those days, the Democratic primary decided the outcome of the general election, and the runoff was for the Democratic Party nomination. During the campaign Ed Clark hustled to get favorable votes into the record on election day. He told me about flying down to South Texas in an unmarked Brown and Root plane, landing on the airstrip of a ranch in a remote location, meeting with political bosses—with plenty of cash in his pockets—and flying back to Austin that night. Amid charges of ballot-box stuffing and other fraudulent practices, Johnson was declared the Democratic nominee only after extended legal battles, during which Mr. Looney was one of his advisors.

It may not have been a coincidence that there was a second law firm with similar political alignment was on the same floor of the Brown Building as Looney & Clark. It was the firm of Powell, Wirtz, Raubut & Gideon. State senator Alvin Wirtz joined the firm in 1934, the same year he wrote the statute that created the Lower Colorado River Authority. He was an advocate of public power, and as an undersecretary of the U.S. Department of the Interior (1940–1941), he helped Johnson get grants and loans that enabled Brown and Root to complete the Marshall Ford Dam. When the State Democratic Executive Committee canvassed the votes of the contested Johnson-Stevenson election, Alvin Wirtz represented Johnson before the committee, and Everett Looney advised him. Our future governor, John Connally, was with the Wirtz firm, or closely associated with it, for three or four years after Johnson's 1948 campaign, which he ran. Since his office was near mine, we got acquainted.

Mainly on Ed Clark's initiatives, our firm was involved in political campaigns. He brought me into several, usually as a sponsor of fundraising events for candidates running for statewide office. For example, during the gubernatorial campaigns of 1952, 1954, and 1956, I traveled from Galveston north to Tyler and into East Texas calling on publishers and editors of small town and county newspapers. Paying cash, I took out advertisements in the newspapers for Allan Shivers in his campaigns against Ralph Yarborough. I did the same thing for Price Daniel in 1956, and several times for Ben Ramsey in his six consecutive successful campaigns for lieutenant governor from 1950 to 1960.

It was amazing how much a fifteen-dollar cash payment in advance would affect a newspaper's editorial policy for the candidates, who were my clients. In 1957, Lieutenant Governor Ramsey appointed me to a constitutional review committee. I was one of his six appointments to a citizens' committee created by the legislature to study the constitution and make recommendations related to ethics. The governor and the speaker also had six appointments each. Our committee made recommendations, and the legislature enacted a code of ethics, one of only a few in the nation at the time, and a statute requiring lobbyists to register, the first for Texas.

CHAPTER 9

Mayor Tom Miller and Jake Pickle

I N 1955, I BECAME INVOLVED in an important city council election in
Austin on behalf of the legendary mayor Tom Miller (1893–1962).
Tom Miller was popular from the onset of his political career. When
he was first elected to the city council in 1933, the other four council-
men immediately voted him mayor, which is how the office was filled in
those days. He remained as mayor until 1949, when he chose not to run
for reelection. Although no longer in office, everyone still called him
Mayor Miller. He personified the kind of mayor most people wanted.
By popular demand in 1955, he was elected to the city council again, and
was again selected mayor by the other members.

Tom Miller's only ambition was for Austin to develop as a great city.
He loved Austin, all of it, passionately. Watching him in action was
an education in citizenship and leadership. He reached out to include
minorities in important decisions, before law or political realities
required it. His first years as mayor coincided with those of President
Roosevelt's presidency and the New Deal programs. Seeking benefits for
Austin, Mayor Miller traveled often to Washington, D.C., always paying his own expenses. Under his leadership, Austin got the first federal
housing project in the nation. He tapped New Deal coffers to support
cultural and recreational facilities, which helped develop numerous city
parks, and revived the Austin Symphony Orchestra in 1938 with financial
support through the Parks and Recreation Department. In fact, Austin

got more New Deal dollars for unemployment relief and public works than any other city in Texas, although it ranked seventh in population, just below Beaumont and barely above Galveston. With Tom Miller's vision, this investment resulted in lasting changes to Austin, changes that created the ambience and built many features that today symbolize Austin to the world.

Mayor Miller was the guiding light behind the purchase of three thousand acres of farmland southeast of the city in 1942 for construction of the Del Valle Airfield that fifty years later became the Austin-Bergstrom International Airport. The land was donated to the federal government during the war, with the stipulation that it would revert to the city if the government abandoned it, which came to pass in the early 1990s. Knowing the geography of Austin like the back of his hand, he envisioned thoroughfares like MoPac and the interregional highway on the east side that became Interstate 35, as well as the widening of Lamar Boulevard and Fifteenth Street decades before their construction. By chance, I was in his office on a day in 1957 when executives of the Missouri-Pacific Railroad came to talk about the use of their right-of-way through the west side of Austin for a major highway. Mayor Miller told them that Austin would grow north and south, and that a major traffic artery through the area was necessary. At the time, few people could imagine a highway on the Missouri-Pacific roadway or how vital it would be to the city. In Mayor Miller's office that day, the Missouri-Pacific people wanted assurance that the city would name any highway built on their right-of-way the "MoPac" boulevard or expressway. Miller agreed and it was a deal. He had laid the groundwork for construction, which did not begin for twenty years.

Mayor Tom Miller called me often and said something like, "Come on over. I want to go look at some property. The city needs to expand some streets and buy right-of-ways." I'd go to his office and, as we drove around Austin, he'd point out historical buildings and monuments, all the while talking about the people of Austin, about their needs, and how the city could evolve in a way that enhanced life for everyone. He bargained and flattered to advance his goals, which explains, for example, how Ben White Boulevard got its name. Ben White was a member of the city council. An important project was coming up for a vote, and

Mayor Miller wanted Mr. White to support it. Looking down the road under construction, Miller told me, "We're going to name this big South Austin street the Ben White Boulevard." Mr. White liked Mayor Miller and voted for his proposition.

As I drove him mile after mile around the city, he described his visions of new streets and how various properties could be developed to improve the city. He desperately wanted Austin to grow into a big fine city. I marveled that any one person could have such ambitions for a city and as much sensitivity to its people as Mayor Miller did. One winter night in 1957 or 1958 my phone rang and it was him. "Frank, get dressed," he said. "I'm going to pick you up and we're going to take an electric heater out to a couple whose gas has been disconnected because of a leak. They have a newborn baby and it's cold." Somebody in the same apartment complex, annoyed by a work crew nearby, had called the gas company and told the dispatcher, "I'm Mayor Tom Miller and I want that drill stopped out in front of my apartment until in the morning because it's keeping people awake all night." Of course, it wasn't Tom Miller, but the dispatcher thought it was and stopped repair work on a gas line. We took an electric heater to this couple. There wasn't anything that Tom Miller wouldn't do for Austin and the people of Austin. He taught me more about responsible and constructive politics than anyone.

Austin prospered under Tom Miller's leadership because he was a practical visionary, always thinking of a future that was vastly different and better than the present. He combined his imagination with the capacity to communicate his visions of a better future in ways that were exciting to people and convinced them to support his goals. As we became close, our friendship extended to our families, and I would have done anything for him. He was one of the most inspiring influences of my life. Eventually, he became as nearly my personal mentor as anyone has ever been. In him I could see that a useful life involves continuous improvement of self, family, and community. The people of Austin today and those in the future are the direct beneficiaries of Mayor Tom Miller.

Since Tom Miller was such an important person in my life, I want to tell you some things we did together that involved his great friend,

Lyndon Johnson. My friendship with Mayor Miller was founded on his friendship with my senior partner, Ed Clark, a complete politician. Clark's original home was San Augustine and the mayor liked to imitate his high-pitched, lyrical East Texas dialect. He'd say, "Ed Clark is an honest man; that is, a reasonably honest man." When I was very junior in the law firm and hardly thirty years old, Mr. Clark would take me along as a driver to pick up Tom Miller and go to civic events. That's how I first got to know the mayor. Some of my greatest experiences with him occurred between 1954 and 1961 when Eisenhower was president, Sam Rayburn was Speaker of the House, and Lyndon Johnson was the majority leader of the United States Senate. Johnson would call the mayor and say he was arriving at the Robert Mueller Municipal Airport around noon, usually in a Brown and Root plane, and say, "Call Ed Clark, tell Frank to get your car, and the three of y'all meet me at the airport." The mayor would call me. I knew where he parked his car at the old city hall. I'd go over there, get the key, drive around to the front and pick him up. He always stood on the front steps of the city hall, wearing a suit and a vest. In warm weather he didn't have the coat on, but he'd have it folded over his left arm. Then we'd drive to the Brown Building, pick up Mr. Clark, and go on to the airport.

Johnson's plane was usually late. While we sat there waiting, the mayor inspected the old airport terminal, which was just a renovated army barracks left over from the war. When Lyndon came in, he'd get in the car and say, "Okay, Randy's Circle R Barbeque." It was down on Trinity and Fourth. Randy was popular and the Circle R Barbeque was widely known. Randy didn't have plates. He had brown paper and a back room that was private. That's where we'd go, the four of us. Randy would bring us drinks, all kinds of barbecue, tomatoes, onions, pickles, beans, all the trimmings—spread on paper. For a couple of hours, maybe longer, Senator Johnson would regale the mayor and Mr. Clark about his latest meetings with President Eisenhower and Speaker Rayburn, about legislative strategies, about world affairs, about what was going on in Washington. I would listen to them talk about the issues and business that affected the people of our country. It was an education you don't get in a college course. These were tremendous experiences for a young lawyer. I thoroughly enjoyed learning about world politics and matters of political significance to our country, and our people. We got together like this until Senator Johnson ran for president in 1960, which is another story that deserves to be told.

Mayor Miller was a delegate to the 1960 Democratic National Convention in Los Angeles. His son, Tom Jr., and I were alternate delegates, which in practical terms meant we were to do what we could to help him and his favored candidate, Lyndon Johnson. The trip began when the mayor hired a driver to take us about fifty-five miles south to Luling, where we caught the Southern Pacific Railroad's *Sunset Limited,* the famous train that came from New Orleans through Houston, to El Paso, and on to Los Angeles. It was loaded with delegates to the convention from across the South and there were fiery differences among them. Some were for JFK, others for LBJ, still others for Senator Stuart Symington of Missouri, or Adlai Stevenson, former governor of Illinois, and the party's nominee in 1952 and 1956. Former president Harry Truman was for Symington, and the Kennedy and Johnson camps were hardly on speaking terms.

Tom Jr. and I had bedroom compartments, and Mayor Miller had a suite. The morning before we got to Los Angeles, Tom Jr. and I were sitting in the diner when the mayor came in and said, "Boys, I had a vision last night. Senator Kennedy will be nominated. He will ask Lyndon to be his vice president and he will accept it." We didn't believe it. You could feel the hostility between the two groups. The mayor's vision seemed so improbable that we didn't even discuss it. But, as everyone knows, that's exactly what happened. It was another demonstration of Mayor Miller's extraordinary foresight.

Arriving in Los Angeles, I had flashbacks to 1943 when I passed through the same train station on the way home after training at Camp Roberts. Mayor Miller, Tom, and I took a taxi to the New Clark Hotel. The hotel had been assigned to the Texas delegation by Democratic Party operatives, who were predominantly for Kennedy. Well, it may have been called the New Clark Hotel, but it was new in name only. If you were walking along a street looking for a room and came to the New Clark Hotel, you would not have gone in. It was a flophouse. The political hacks of the party had deliberately assigned us to very undesirable quarters. While we were standing outside considering whether to find another hotel, out of the hotel comes Dr. Everett Givens, a well-known African American dentist in Austin, a member of our delegation. Dr. Givens was an extrovert, a man with flair, and expressive with his ideas. He and Mayor Miller were great friends. In the spring and summer, Dr. Givens always wore a white western suit, a cowboy outfit. He greeted us wearing white ostrich skin boots, a ten-gallon white hat, and a black bowtie. We shook hands. He says, "Mayor, I don't know about you white folks, but we black folks are not staying in this hotel. I'm getting an apartment. I will not stay in this hotel."

We laughed, but we decided to stay and learned right quick what he meant. The mayor took a double room, and Tom and I got a small room with twin beds. It was Tuesday, and that night we went to a special Democratic Party banquet for all of the candidates. Adlai Stevenson got the big press, and LBJ got the second-best coverage. I do not remember Kennedy at all. We got back to the hotel late and slept well. The next morning, Tom and I took showers, and we just threw our towels on the floor. When we came back in late afternoon, the towels were still on the floor, and the beds had not been made. The second morning, we took the sheets off the beds and put them out in the hall with our wet towels, but the housekeepers just hung the towels back in the bathroom and put the sheets back on the beds. They never changed the linens in the New Clark Hotel.

Governor Price Daniel, the head of the Texas delegation, also had a "suite" at the same hotel, but not like any suite I'd ever seen. There was a so-called ballroom where our delegation had meetings; it did not have enough chairs to seat all of us. Fortunately, we spent little time in the hotel. Tom Jr. and I got a rental car and toured around Los Angeles, like I did in 1943 with three buddies from Camp Roberts. On Wednesday morning, Tom and I went over to LBJ's suite in the Biltmore Hotel in downtown Los Angeles. It was large, well-appointed, and had several rooms. Sitting there were LBJ, Speaker Rayburn, Mayor Miller, and John Connally. Jake Pickle may have been there too. Tom and I stood around, saying little unless asked. In a while, Senator Kennedy came in and asked to meet with Senator Johnson. They went to another room, and that's when he asked LBJ to be his vice presidential candidate. As most everyone knows, LBJ did not accept then. I should explain here that my recollection of events during the convention is not the same as accounts in other books, notably not as in Robert A. Caro's biography of President Johnson—but Mr. Caro did not interview me for his book.

The convention was held in the Los Angeles Memorial Sports Arena next to the coliseum. Anticipating the nominations, Jake Pickle asked me to help him organize the demonstration for LBJ on the floor of the convention. The demonstration began right after John Connally placed Senator Johnson's name in nomination for president. Basically, a demonstration meant having a lot of people come into the convention hall and make a lot of noise for your nominee. Jake and I rented a vacant theater nearby as a place for our demonstrators to gather. Under the convention rules, each nominee was given fifty admission badges that would allow that many, and only that many, demonstrators onto the floor of the convention. Well, we managed to get a lot more demonstrators for LBJ into the convention hall. I'd give fifty demonstrators an admission badge, and lead them in. Then I'd collect their badges, go back to the theater, and get another fifty demonstrators. By repeating this several times, we were able to get four hundred demonstrators in there to celebrate and make a lot of noise for LBJ.

There's another interesting story that parallels this one. Knowing that Senator Johnson was behind in the polls, Jake Pickle and I and several others devised a debate between Senator Kennedy and Senator Johnson in the hotel where the Johnsons were staying. We rented a ballroom and set up the chairs. The debate was to give Senator Johnson and Senator Kennedy a chance to challenge each other publicly and, of course, in the press. I never will forget the words of Senator Kennedy. He said, "Senator Johnson is the greatest majority leader the country's ever had and we need to keep him in the Senate." Referring to the controversial 27.5 percent of oil revenue—the so-called oil depletion allowance—that was tax free by federal law, Kennedy declared, "I come from a consuming state and Senator Johnson comes from a producing state and therefore our interests will never be exactly the same." For his entire career, Johnson had supported the oil depletion allowance, and during the campaign, Kennedy supported it too. Lots of people, including the press, came and listened to that debate, and most of the publicity went to Senator Kennedy. Senator Johnson did extremely well, but the political fallout from it was that Kennedy—through his great command of the English language—overshadowed the debate.

From then on, I think most of us accepted the reality that Kennedy would be the presidential nominee. Mayor Miller's attitude probably mirrored what most of us thought. He felt that Senator Johnson would make a better president than Senator Kennedy, but the politics of the time wouldn't permit it. And he fully supported the Kennedy-Johnson ticket, as did I. I attended the precinct, county, and state conventions and was the chairman of the resolutions committee at the county convention. I do not contend that I had a major role in the campaign of 1960, other than to participate and be supportive at all levels of the Democratic Party.

An important benefit of the convention for me was that Jake Pickle and I gained mutual confidence in each other. We had fun together and moved quickly to get things done. In the coming years, our friendship had positive consequences for both of us. A small group of his admirers persuaded him to run for Congress for the first time in 1963. Joe Kilgore and I cochaired the meeting in the Driskill Hotel when Pickle finally yielded to our persuasion. Joe and I then ran his winning campaign. He served thirty-three years, rising to leadership positions in the House of Representatives, particularly on the Ways and Means Committee. Jake became one of the dearest friends of my life, and we remained close until his death in 2005.

CHAPTER 10

LBJ and Television in Austin

THE REGULATION OF COMMERCIAL TELEVISION during its early years in Austin was a hot political issue, the most volatile ever over a public utility. It began in 1952 when the first station was licensed to broadcast in the city. The fact that the license was awarded to Mrs. Lyndon B. Johnson would be a factor in the controversy, which did not end until the mid-1960s. The station, KTBC-TV, commonly referred to as Channel 7, was a property of the Texas Broadcasting Company, which was privately owned by the family of U.S. Senator Lyndon Johnson. Our firm did the legal work for the Johnson family's business interests, and I had responsibility for some of those interests, including KTBC-TV and the radio station KTBC-AM. KTBC-TV was an affiliate of the CBS network, but had contracts with the other two major networks, NBC and ABC, for their programs. Sports fans will be interested to know that the first television program broadcast live in Austin was KTBC's airing of the football game between the University of Texas and Texas A&M on Thanksgiving Day 1952.

The issue of Austin having only one television outlet began to heat up in 1956 when a group from Little Rock, Arkansas, filed an application to establish and operate a cable TV system in the city. The law firm of John McClellan, Arkansas's senior United States senator, represented the group. It was a collision of political titans. McClellan was prominent nationally, well known for chairing the Senate's investigations of corruption and subversion, while Johnson was Senate majority leader, a position he would hold until he became vice president in 1961. Both McClellan and Johnson were Democrats.

When the Arkansas group's application was filed, I immediately filed a similar application on behalf of KTBC-TV for a cable contract with the city. This occurred before the advent of open meeting laws, and for five years, all negotiations were behind closed doors. In late 1961, the city council held its first public hearings on the competing applications. Probably no other dispute sparked as much public interest as the competition for that contract. At the urging of Mayor Miller, the Arkansas group and the Lyndon Johnson group merged their application into one corporation named Capital Cable Company, with each party owning 50 percent. Capital Cable Company became my client. During the five-year interim, other groups filed applications to provide cable service in the city, further complicating the situation and delaying the award of the contract. Other applicants included the owners of a prominent chain of movie houses called the Interstate Theater Group, and Newspapers, Inc., the publisher of the *Austin American-Statesman*. Both the applications and the process for selecting the winner were highly publicized. Finally, on January 28, 1963, my client—the Capital Cable Company— was awarded the contract and began building a cable system in Austin. No one should be surprised that the first home in Austin to receive a cable television connection was mine at 2521 Tanglewood Trail.

When LBJ became president, I was still our firm's lawyer for the Johnsons' radio and television stations KTBC-TV, KTBC-AM and KTBC-FM as well as cable television, which was in its infancy. KTBC, Channel 7, was the only commercially viable broadcasting television station in Central Texas. I say that because KTBC-TV's signal was transmitted in a frequency range officially termed Very High Frequency, or VHF, which included Channels 2 to 13. VHF channels had greater strength and range than Ultra High Frequency (UHF), Channels 14 to 83, whose signals usually do not travel well over long distances or rugged terrain. Few television sets were able receive UHF signals until after 1964, when Congress began requiring manufacturers to include both VHF and UHF tuners in all new sets. And then, years were required for VHF/UHF combo sets to reach a critical mass in the U.S. market. Thus, KTBC-TV, broadcasting on VHF Channel 7, was the only commercially viable television station in Central Texas from 1952 until well into the 1960s.

This is how the situation evolved: Mrs. Lyndon Johnson had acquired KTBC-AM radio in 1943. In 1951 she applied to the FCC for the one VHF television broadcast license that the FCC had allocated for Austin. Her application was approved on July 11, 1952, while about the same time, the FCC approved three VHF broadcast licenses each for Houston, Dallas–Fort Worth, and San Antonio. Small town Austin got only one VHF station, carefully spaced between the channel frequencies of stations in the three major metropolitan areas to assure that none overlapped and interfered with others. Meanwhile, anyone could have applied to the FCC for a UHF license in Austin from the early 1950s forward, but until manufacturers included a UHF tuner in new sets and a critical mass of people had them, a UHF station was virtually worthless, as only those with a clumsy, ineffective tuner, called a "converter," purchased separately could receive its signal. In this way, KTBC remained the only game in town.

There was considerable acrimony across Central Texas about President Johnson's private business dominating the television market. As his profile rose, KTBC became a lightning rod for his critics, who said it was a monopoly, enabled by the FCC, and manipulated politically by Johnson for his financial benefit. There was more to the story, and the economics of VHF and UHF channels was a major part of it. Although KTBC's basic affiliation was with CBS, ABC and NBC worked out agreements with KTBC to also carry their programs. KTBC's program director, Cactus Pryor, bragged that his viewers got the best TV viewing in the nation because he selected the best and highest-rated programs of all three networks and broadcast them on KTBC. He accomplished this by putting competing shows on the air at different times. As a result, KTBC's viewers did not have to choose between *Gunsmoke* on CBS and *The Rifleman* on ABC, or between two highly popular newscasts, Walter Cronkite on the *CBS Evening News* and the *Huntley-Brinkley Report* on NBC. When a youthful Neal Spelce became the anchor of KTBC's evening news telecast, he was on the air at eleven o'clock instead of ten o'clock as other central time zone stations were, in order to allow more time to air ABC and NBC programs in "prime time."

By sheer numbers, KTBC's audience gradually became larger than those of any San Antonio station. CBS executives were enthusiastic about KTBC, while ABC and NBC executives were reluctant to transfer their programming away from KTBC's big VHF audiences to a weaker, start-up UHF station. As Austin's population grew, and the number of UHF-equipped TV sets increased, it was evident that a second station could go on the air with a reasonable chance of success. Yet investor groups, particularly those with critics of President Johnson, were hesitant to file an application with the FCC, which they may have assumed he controlled.

It was no secret that I represented the Johnson family's television interests. One day in early summer 1964, I was conducting some personal business in the lobby of the Capital National Bank, when two acquaintances—John and E. C. Kingsbury—approached me and asked if we could talk privately for a few minutes. In a nearby conference room not then in use, they explained in a very cordial way that they were interested in making application for a second television station in Austin. I don't think they had a definite action plan, but I saw immediately that their application would have political implications for President Johnson and for KTBC's business. Don't forget that 1964 was a presidential election year. If their application created the slightest controversy, it would have a negative affect on LBJ's campaign and could undermine his agenda with Congress. It was a serious matter, and I promptly let President Johnson know through his local station manager, Jesse Kellam. A few days later, Charmaine and I received an invitation to a state dinner at the White House. We accepted the invitation and stayed in the White House as guests of President and Mrs. Johnson. The next morning, I briefed the president privately in the Oval Office. Within a fairly short period of time, the FCC approved the Kingsbury family's application with minor attention from the news media, which were more interested in sensational events that occurred about the same time, especially the escalation of the war in Vietnam after attacks on American ships by North Vietnamese torpedo boats in the Gulf of Tonkin in early August, and the Chinese Communists exploding their first nuclear weapon in mid-October. Johnson coasted to victory with the largest proportion of the popular vote ever, 61.2 percent. In February 1965, the Kingsbury station went on the air as KHFI-TV broadcasting on UHF Channel 42.

I was invited to the White House and the LBJ Ranch several times during President Johnson's tenure in office. Charmaine and I attended the White House wedding of Lynda Johnson and marine captain Charles S. Robb on December 9, 1967. Several times I was sitting with President Johnson at two or three in the morning when he spoke with Gen. William C. Westmoreland in Vietnam. Once at a state dinner, I was seated next to Thomas J. Watson Jr., president of IBM Corporation (1952–1971). Mr. Watson wanted to talk about the business climate in Texas, particularly the workforce in Austin. It was evident that he was considering a corporate investment in the vicinity. I was as positive as I could possibly be about Central Texas and remain credible. In 1967, three years later, IBM set up a manufacturing plant in north Austin, arguably the beginning of high-tech development in Austin. It was evident to me that President Johnson and his associates were thinking about the future when they decided on seating arrangements at the White House events.

CHAPTER 11

School Trustee and White House Liaison

I N 1964 AND 1969, THE BOARD OF TRUSTEES of the Austin Independent School District (AISD) asked me to run campaigns to pass
school bond issues. Despite some opposition, especially for bonds
that paid for installing air conditioning in schools, both campaigns were
successful. After the 1969 bond issue passed, friends began telling me
that I should put my name on the ballot for election to the board of
trustees. Over the years I had recruited people to run for the board and
for the city council. Now they said, "Frank, it's your turn." So, I filed my
application and in April 1970 was elected to the school board, where I
served for three years. The responsibilities were demanding, and I was
grateful to have dedicated, high quality fellow members in Roy Butler
(soon to be elected mayor), Will Davis, Mrs. Wilhemina Delco, Mrs.
Marjorie "Sitty" Wilkes, Desmond Kidd, Carole Keeton, and M. K. Hage.

Unexpectedly, I became personally involved in the lawsuit that eventually brought about the complete integration of public schools in Austin. The statute of limitations has expired, so it is okay to talk about
how this happened. Officially, Austin schools had been desegregated
since 1955, the year after the landmark *Brown vs. Board of Education* case
decided by the U.S. Supreme Court. In this decision, the Court ordered
the states to end segregation with "all deliberate speed." This vagueness
allowed for time to phase in integration and, obviously, for others to
organize resistance to it. In 1955, the Austin school board decided to

integrate "from the top down," beginning with the twelfth grade, integrating one additional grade level each year. When, by the late 1960s, Austin schools were still not integrated, the U.S. Department of Justice took an interest in the situation. After President Nixon succeeded Johnson to become president in January 1969, the executive branch of the federal government became even more interested in the Austin case.

In 1971, President Nixon appointed former Texas governor John B. Connally as his secretary of the treasury. Governor Connally and I knew each other very well. In 1961 I had nominated him for the Texas Exes' Distinguished Alumnus Award. In 1962 I had raised money for his first gubernatorial campaign, campaigned for him, and cochaired his inaugural committee the next year. Connally called me not long after he became treasury secretary, and said, "Frank, when will you be in Washington the next time?" I told him I'd be up there next week. He said, "Several of the president's assistants would like to talk with you about the Austin school situation." I agreed to visit with them, but I told him that I had reservations about going to the White House. I was just one of seven members on the board. Will Davis was president of the board. Governor Connally was also close to Will, and I suspect he called Will before he called me, and that Will referred him to me because I traveled frequently to Washington. I told Governor Connally when to expect me.

I stayed at the old Statler Hilton Hotel. The morning after my arrival the White House sent a car with a lawyer and an administrative assistant from Nixon's staff to pick me up. The important point is that they were not from the Department of Justice, but from the White House. We went to the exclusive Jockey Club, and they talked about achieving a better system to mix black and white students. I remember this clearly because they drew a sketch of Austin on the table cloth, with north-south lines across the city, dividing Austin into four quarters with north and south lines. This was different from the school board's plan that presumed east-west integration. They thought we'd do better by integrating north-south, and they asked me why we did not integrate the schools in this way. I told them that a west-to-east river runs right through the middle of town, and we only have three bridges across it. That fundamental fact made north-south integration more difficult than east-west.

The White House officials agreed that AISD was already desegregated in terms of school board policy, but they said the new regime in the Justice Department's civil rights division wanted a quota system. "We are trying," they told me, "to stop the pure quota system." Talking from eleven in the morning until about six in the evening, we really messed up that tablecloth. When they took me back to the hotel, they said they'd be in contact for further information. My "take" on the meeting was that the White House officials were interested in developing a plan that furthered integration in Austin without disrupting the educational process, and they wanted me to help them access local decision-makers.

When I got back to Austin I made a personal visit to each school board trustee. Accompanied by school superintendent Jack Davidson, I told them about the contact from Governor Connally and my subsequent meeting with the White House staff. Then certain White House officials began coming regularly to Austin. For about five weeks they flew down to Austin in a government plane for night meetings with school administrators, Will Davis, Davidson, and Jay Patterson, the school district's lawyer. Mr. Patterson was transitioning into retirement and his successor, Bill Bingham, was included. Occasionally, I was there as an interface between the parties because my meeting in Washington had started this informal interaction between the White House and school district officials. A room in the basement of the school district's administrative offices at 6100 Guadalupe was set aside for these meetings, to display maps and data from which to refine proposals for integrating schools. My law partner, Don Thomas, a fine trial lawyer, and I were brought in because we knew how to use the evidence to buffer the school district against the Justice Department's civil rights division. As expected, at some point in this sequence of events, the Department of Justice filed suit on the Austin Independent School District in federal court to compel desegregation on a quota system, which could only mean massive busing.

The case was heard before federal judge Jack Roberts, whom I knew very well. Before President Johnson appointed him to the federal bench in 1966, he had been the district attorney in Travis County from 1946 to 1948 and a judge on the 126th State District Court from 1948 to 1966. I had actually tried my first case before him and once, in oral argument, argued a gas company case before him for fourteen hours in two consecutive days. In this situation, Judge Roberts called me and said, "I want you to come to my house and tell me the complete history of integration in the Austin Independent School District." I told him, "Judge, I'll be happy to do that, although it may be a violation of ethics. But I need to bring our school superintendent, Jack Davidson, because you're going to ask me questions for which I will not know the answers with particularity." I picked up Jack at the school board offices and we went to Judge Roberts's home about one o'clock in the afternoon. I spread the maps out on his living room floor, and we went over the entire case. As a result, when we went to trial, Judge Roberts knew more about the Austin Independent School District than the Justice Department lawyers did.

In the litigation, my law partner, Don Thomas, and I represented the school board against the lawyers from the Department of Justice civil rights division who were insisting on a quota system. One of our arguments was the effectiveness of the school board's majority-to-minority transfer rule. Under that rule, if you were a student in, for example, the previously all-black Anderson High School and you wanted to transfer to the mostly white Austin High School, all you had to do was request the transfer and it was approved. We had other flexible rules that permitted students to transfer. Later, such transfers became known as freedom of school choice.

When our case came to trial, Austin was just one of the high profile cases around the country that were pending at the Department of Justice. My impression is that the Justice Department was trying to use those cases to force quota systems in other cities. One was the Charlotte Mecklenburg (city-county) School System in North Carolina, where massive busing was imposed. I want to be clear that the Austin school board was not resisting integration but trying to delay forced busing by the Department of Justice until the U.S. Supreme Court rendered a quota system unnecessary. As far as I knew, no one in Austin favored massive busing of students across the city.

With some modifications, Judge Roberts ruled in our favor. He basically upheld that we were desegregated and that because of the geographical boundaries of the school attendance zones, coupled with the geography of Austin, the district as a whole was making satisfactory progress. The Justice Department appealed his ruling to the Fifth Circuit, which made more modifications, but did not order the massive busing that would have been required under a quota system.

While all this was going on, the Austin schools actually made considerable progress. We built new schools in different parts of the city, which improved education and helped accommodate the further integration of the population. By effective negotiation, we converted a potential adversity into a positive. I think we helped prepare Austin for the tremendous growth that began a few years later and made it the internationally renowned city that it became, truly one of the great cities of the world. I believe we did the right thing for society and our community.

CHAPTER 12

Oscar Wyatt Jr. and Natural Gas for Austin

MUCH OF MY EARLY PRACTICE was representing public utility companies that had contracts with the City of Austin—companies that had retained my law firm of Looney & Clark to represent them. The City of Austin provided water and electricity to its service area, but contracted with private companies to provide transportation, communications, and natural gas. Our firm's clients included Southwestern Bell Telephone, Southern Union Gas, the local bus company, and one of the taxicab companies. Since I was the firm's point man for these companies, I was in frequent contact with the city attorney, the mayor's office, and the city council. As a result, I became highly involved in regulatory issues because the city council was the approval authority for all public utilities that served Austin. This changed in 1975 when the Texas Public Utilities Commission was created, but in the intervening years I became one of the most experienced attorneys in Texas in the field of public utility law.

My initiation to regulatory law and public utilities occurred in the early 1950s, during my first years with the firm, when Southwestern Bell proposed several adjustments in prices and services. It was the company's first request since the war. During the war, federal law had imposed restraints on rate increases, and expansion of services had been limited because copper and other materials were prioritized for the military. Southwestern Bell now proposed an increase in the monthly charge for basic business and residential service, limiting the number of two- and four-party lines by converting them to single, or private lines, and increasing the cost of calling from a pay telephone. Certain areas of Austin only had party lines and some people in those areas wanted a single-line service, while others wanted to continue multiparty line service because it was much cheaper. The most publicized part of the proposal seems incredulous today—the increase in charge from a nickel to a dime for a local call from pay phones. You can see that I was negotiating for both an increase in the cost of the service and for an increase in charges to improve service by the telephone company. Although the rate increase was small by today's standards, the city council held numerous public hearings on the proposed changes over a two-year period. The opposition was vocal, loud, and widely publicized in the *American-Statesman*. Often accompanied by Everett Looney and Dean Moorhead, I participated in the hearings and eventually negotiated an agreed-to rate increase with the city attorney, Mr. Doren Eskew, that was passed by the city council. In this case, I learned more about practical negotiating skills than about law. Rather than intellectually demanding, it was an exercise in local politics—maneuvering and persuading.

For a regulatory case that had gravity, was prolonged, and was ultimately very expensive to the public, I want to tell you about my battles with Oscar S. Wyatt Jr., who founded Coastal States Gas Producing Company in 1951 and was the CEO for the entire time that I dealt with him, from 1961 until the early 1970s. As background, you need to know that having an adequate supply of natural gas was one the most contentious and widely publicized issues in Austin and San Antonio from the late 1950s until the mid-1970s. Mr. Wyatt caused much of the difficulty by political manipulation that enabled him to win improvident contracts to provide gas to both cities. By boldness and an astute understanding of political processes, he got long-term contracts to provide gas that he could not deliver.

In Austin, the main concern was a reliable contract to buy gas, which the city then sold to businesses and individuals and allocated to two electrical power-generating plants owned and operated by the City of Austin. A third power plant was in the planning stages. The Seaholm Power Plant, now the art deco anchor of the Seaholm Development

District, was west of Congress Avenue on the north shore of Lady Bird
Lake, and the Holly Street Plant was downstream, east of the interstate,
also on the shore of the lake. Each power plant required vast amounts
of natural gas and water. Natural gas was burned to heat water and produce steam that then turned turbines to generate electricity, and water
was required both to produce steam and to cool the turbines. Water for
the power plants was obtained by building the Longhorn Dam, which
retained water in the Colorado River streambed to form the reservoir
now called Lady Bird Lake. Ironically, Lady Bird Lake, admired for its
beauty by visitors from around the world, was not created for aesthetic
or recreational reasons, but to supply water to the two power plants then
located on its shoreline. The lake has existed since the dam was completed in 1960.

For the lake to have the necessary capacity, it had to be enlarged by
removing sandbars and islands, particularly toward the lower end. Until
then, people hunted ducks around those islands. To be exact, the lake
had to be enlarged to an average width of four hundred feet, cut bank
to cut bank; and to an average depth of fifteen feet for the entire length
of the lake. I was involved in the project because the contractor who
excavated the lake was my client, the H. B. Zachary Company of San
Antonio. I well remember the day that Mayor Tom Miller, City Manager
Bill Williams, and I got in a small boat with two firemen, who rowed us
around the lake as we discussed the work that would be required. For
months in the early 1960s, Mr. Zachary had a tugboat and two barges
in the lake, dredging to meet those dimensions. The sand and gravel
removed had monetary value that was split between the state and the
city. The state claimed a share because the Colorado River is a navigable
stream.

Gas for the power plants was received in accordance with contracts
approved by the Austin City Council with the United Gas Pipeline
Company and Southern Union Gas. United delivered gas from distant
sources by large transmission pipelines to the Austin city-gate, where
Southern Union Gas took ownership for the city. (A city-gate is the
measuring station where a local gas utility company receives natural gas
from a pipeline company.) Southern Union Gas, Austin's local gas utility, distributed the gas through a network of smaller diameter pipes to

the meter of each individual customer and to the city's electric power plants. Southern Union was my client, but I often represented the interests of United Gas because of the contractual relationship between the two companies.

In 1960, the Austin City Council awarded contracts based on competitive bids to United Gas Pipeline and Southern Union Gas. Two years later, the city solicited bids for new contracts to supply only its three power plants. There were several bidders for this contract. One was Oscar Wyatt's Coastal States Gas Producing Company, which collected and distributed natural gas from the South Texas oil and gas fields. Oscar Wyatt Jr., a mechanical engineering graduate of Texas A&M, was a very aggressive personality with a good understanding of Texas politics. Previously, Coastal States and United Gas had battled for the contract to supply gas to San Antonio, whose contracting entity, the City Public Service Board, had awarded the contract to Coastal States. United Gas had appealed the decision to the state regulatory agency, the Texas Railroad Commission, but the commission disclaimed jurisdiction over the contract. United Gas then appealed the commission's denial of jurisdiction to the 126th District Court in Austin, arguing that the Texas Railroad Commission, in fact, did have jurisdiction.

San Antonio's award of the contract to Coastal States was highly controversial because Coastal States had bid a fixed-price contract to last for twenty years. Twenty years! By contrast, United had bid the actual cost (called "weighted average cost") of gas delivered to San Antonio, which could be changed within the terms of the contract as the price of gas fluctuated, which it was bound to do over a twenty-year period. However, Coastal States was awarded the contract. Many of us familiar with the natural gas business did not believe Coastal States had sufficient reserves or the pipeline network to fulfill the contract at the fixed price that Oscar Wyatt proposed.

Almost the same thing happened in Austin in late 1962, when the Austin City Council rejected its previous contractors, Southern Union and United Gas, and granted a twenty-year contract to Coastal States to supply gas at a fixed price to its three electrical power generating plants, beginning April 1, 1964. This was a big issue because, as I told the city council in public session, Coastal States did not have sufficient gas reserves at known prices to meet its commitment to maintain a fixed price for twenty years. As would be borne out, Coastal States had proposed an improvident contract that did not anticipate its future consequences, at least not in a reasonable way. Coastal States was "kiting gas"—overstating the amount of gas available—by exaggerating the size of its reserves, thus committing the company to sell the same gas reserves to both San Antonio and Austin and possibly other customers. Sure enough, within two years, Coastal States filed an application with the Texas Railroad Commission to modify its contract with the City of Austin by increasing the price that the city would pay Coastal States for its gas. The best that can be said is that Oscar Wyatt had based his contract on the assumption that he could buy gas in the future at a sufficiently low price to make money on the fixed-price contract. When he could not do so without placing Coastal States in jeopardy, he sought relief from the fixed-price contract. The outcome of the commission's ruling on this application was important to all public utility companies and gas providers. The integrity of their contracts was fundamental to the conduct of their businesses and, ultimately, to their solvency. The case became widely known in the industry as "Docket 500," which was the number for the application assigned by the Texas Railroad Commission on the list of cases awaiting action by the commission. In the following narrative, I will refer to the case as Docket 500.

I believe Mr. Wyatt knew exactly what he was doing when his company, Coastal States, proposed unrealistic long-term fixed-price contracts. He and his advisors understood, as the rest of us in the industry did, the fluctuations in the price and the availability of natural gas and their effect on its market value. Wyatt may have thought he could control the price of gas, but he could not. A cold winter in the Northeast, for example, could drive up the price in Texas. Mr. Wyatt recognized and exploited the political vulnerability of members of the Austin City Council and the San Antonio City Public Service Board. They could not resist the temptation to accept his irresponsible and imprudent proposal. Later, they could not permit Mr. Wyatt's company, Coastal States, to default on the contracts because every person living in both cities would suffer from the lack of natural gas. In Austin the members of the city council would be embarrassed personally and damaged politically, which illustrates that the difficulties with the Coastal States contracts were both political and legal. That's why I say Oscar Wyatt understood politics and used that knowledge to gain unfair advantages over his competitors and to negotiate lucrative contracts.

When the price of gas increased, Wyatt could not buy gas at the prices required to fulfill the terms of his contract without placing Coastal States in jeopardy. Then he sought to revise the contracts, forcing Austin and San Antonio to pay more to Coastal States for their gas. If the Texas Railroad Commission did not permit an increase in the rates for Coastal States, the company would go into bankruptcy or receivership and be unable to perform. Over time, it became clear to me that Oscar Wyatt selected the public utility industry for his unethical schemes because regulatory law, bankruptcy, and receivership jurisprudence are more lenient for public utilities than for private enterprise companies. The law takes into account the necessity of public utilities continuing to serve the public interest while undergoing difficulties.

This process that I have described had ramifications beyond Austin and San Antonio. Every gas utility across the state—including my client, Southern Union Gas—had a vested interest in the railroad commission's decision on United Gas's appeal on the validity of the contract that San Antonio's City Public Service Board (CPSB) had awarded to Coastal States. They had to be interested because they had contracts for the purchase of natural gas from companies like Coastal States. When the case came before the commission's hearing examiner, I was the first speaker. Lawyers for other public utilities companies in Texas were in attendance to hear my presentation. Then, a number of them went to the microphone, identified themselves and their respective clients, and said they agreed with my argument. In effect, I became their spokesman in proceedings before the Railroad Commission for Docket 500.

Not only was the case on the docket of the Texas Railroad Commission, but it was in the courts. In an earlier parallel case, United Gas had appealed to the 126th District Court in Austin for assurance that the Railroad Commission had the authority to rule on the validity of the contract that San Antonio's CPSB had awarded to Coastal States. Attorneys from across the state eagerly followed the proceedings, and there was considerable publicity about the case in the news media. With lawyers from the Vinson & Elkins law firm in Houston, I argued the case on behalf of United Gas—and we won when the district court found that the Railroad Commission had jurisdiction. Then Coastal States appealed the case to the Court of Civil Appeals, which overruled the district court. We appealed to the Supreme Court of Texas, but the court declined to hear our appeal, which had the practical effect of causing us to lose. In a later case in which I did not participate, the Texas Supreme Court ruled that the Texas Railroad Commission, in fact, did have the final say over these types of gas contracts. Then, the commission held hearings on the case. Thus, our argument was eventually upheld, although the practical effect was nil because the ruling came too late. However, in the long run, Docket 500 was important to all parties—sellers, buyers, and transmitters of natural gas—because it clarified the authority of the Texas Railroad Commission to rule on natural gas contracts when cases were appealed from a city like Austin or an agency such as San Antonio's City Public Service Board. I cannot resist adding a personal note here that one of our problems in trying this case was taking Mr. Wyatt's deposition; he was both an expert witness and an expert in avoiding us.

The controversy about which government entity had jurisdiction over gas contracts had implications at the federal level as well as the state. If the Texas Railroad Commission did not have jurisdiction, as Oscar Wyatt and Coastal States maintained, the only other possibility was the Federal Power Commission (predecessor of the Federal Energy Regulatory Commission). However, there was the possibility that Coastal States was also exempt from federal jurisdiction by an act of Congress called the Hinshaw Amendment, which exempted gas pipeline companies from federal jurisdiction if they were under the jurisdiction of a state commission. The intention of the Hinshaw Amendment was to lessen the regulatory burden on gas pipeline companies, but it created an ambiguity that Oscar Wyatt attempted to exploit. He confused the issue by arguing in Washington, D.C., that the Texas Railroad Commission had jurisdiction over Coastal States, yet when he was in Texas, he maintained that the Railroad Commission did not have jurisdiction. If the Railroad Commission had jurisdiction, the effect was to deny Federal Power Commission jurisdiction, and, if the Federal Power Commission had jurisdiction, then the Texas Railroad Commission did not. Thus, if the arguments of Coastal States prevailed in both venues, neither the state of Texas nor the federal government had jurisdiction over Coastal States's contracts. To understand how these contradictory arguments by the same advocates could be taken seriously and not exposed, keep in mind that communication was not as easy and complete then as it would become a few years later. There were no next-day deliveries, fax machines, or e-mail. These highly controversial issues became entwined with governmental bureaucracies and permeated the gas utility jurisdiction law in Texas for years, raising questions about integrity in contracting.

What was the effect of the entanglement with Oscar Wyatt and Coastal States for the cities of Austin, San Antonio, and other customers? After the Texas Supreme Court affirmed the authority of the Railroad Commission over gas contracts, the commission permitted an upward adjustment in the price of gas that Coastal States sold to Austin and San Antonio, which resulted in a substantial increase in the price of gas for consumers. The City of Austin went further and paid Coastal States substantially more than actual construction costs to build a new pipeline to supply gas to the power plant on Long Lake. This extra money apparently helped Mr. Wyatt and his company to weather their immediate crisis, if there was one. Later the Railroad Commission revised the rates again in order to prevent Coastal States from going into bankruptcy or receivership or being unable to perform.

In the early 1960s, Coastal States established a subsidiary called Lo-Vaca Gathering to fulfill its contract to supply natural gas to Texas cities and utilities. Then came the energy crisis of the early 1970s. During the crisis Lo-Vaca raised prices, and customers sued Coastal, the parent company. Regulators ordered Lo-Vaca to refund $1.6 billion in 1977, and Coastal spun off Lo-Vaca as Valero Energy to finance the settlement. The settlement was a long time in coming. In the meantime, hundreds of thousands of people were hurt by Mr. Wyatt kiting gas and proposing improvident contracts.

Since these proceedings, I have followed him only in the newspapers. According to one media report, in 2007 he pleaded guilty to conspiring to make illegal payments to Saddam Hussein's Iraq in the United Nations' Oil-for-Food Program and was sentenced to serve one year in the minimum-security camp of the Federal Correctional Complex in Beaumont, Texas. Mr. Wyatt was then eighty-two years old.

CHAPTER 13

ERCOT: *Present at the Creation*

IN RECENT YEARS, THE TEXAS NEWS MEDIA have made frequent references to an entity called ERCOT, the acronym for the Electric Reliability Council of Texas. This is because ERCOT manages the flow of electric power to about twenty-five million users in the state, whose demands are increasing exponentially as Texas grows, both in economic activity and in population. I want to explain what ERCOT is, how it came to be, and the role that my clients and I played in its creation in the mid-1960s. The events surrounding the creation of ERCOT was one of the most protracted and fascinating episodes of my legal career.

It is easy to mistake ERCOT as an abstraction that does not concern us. That's because very few of us have ever lived without electricity. We take it for granted, like oxygen, until something goes wrong, and we find ourselves fumbling in the dark for flashlights and candles and worrying about food spoiling in the fridge, or how to recharge our smart phones or cars. By flicking a switch, we expect the lights to come on at all times and in all places, except when camping out in the boonies. Not having electricity can be the difference between life and death. Public order depends on it. That is why ERCOT's function is important.

The series of events that led to the creation of ERCOT began with a huge electrical blackout in the Northeast in late 1965. The blackout started about dusk on November 9 and quickly spread from Ontario in

Canada down to New York City and into New Jersey, plunging over thirty million people into darkness. It was the biggest power failure in U.S. history. In Manhattan, the disruption in electrical power began at the height of rush hour, delaying millions of commuters, trapping 800,000 people in subways, and stranding thousands more in office buildings, elevators, and trains. Ten thousand National Guardsmen and five thousand off-duty policemen were called into service to prevent looting and maintain public order. Never before had a power outage occurred on such an immense scale and impacted such immense populations.

Since the availability of electricity in the Great Northeast Blackout involved the flow of electricity across state lines, primary jurisdiction to investigate and recommend remedies was with the federal government under the interstate commerce clause of the U.S. Constitution. Within hours after the blackout, President Lyndon Johnson directed the chairman of the Federal Power Commission "to launch a thorough study of the causes of this failure" and to "recommend steps to be taken to prevent a recurrence." Created in 1935, the FPC was charged with overseeing interstate electricity sales, among other things. The FPC study was nationwide, delving into issues of electrical generation and its regulation across the forty-eight contiguous states. Unexpectedly, I became a prominent participant in the inquiries and negotiations that followed, especially as they pertained to Texas. The proceedings went on for several years and eventually led to the creation of ERCOT.

The Federal Power Commission held hearings on the power outages and about the extent of its own jurisdiction and authority. An important part of the FPC's study was to analyze electrical grid systems. Here I should explain that an electrical "grid" is the network that synchronizes or balances the distribution of electricity from many generators in many locations to consumers, wherever they are. The generators are connected to back each other up when the capacity of one or more declines and when consumer demand rises. It requires constant attention and coordination because the demand for electricity varies by location and time.

After analyzing grid systems and the possibilities for future power outages in the lower forty-eight states, the Federal Power Commission concluded there was less likelihood of outages in the future if Congress gave the commission jurisdiction over all grid systems, with the authority and technical ability to exchange or switch power between them. The commission's study revealed that Texas was unique in comparison to other contiguous states. Except for El Paso, the Panhandle, and a sliver of East Texas, the Texas grid system was entirely within the state. By not crossing state lines, utilities generating electricity in Texas were not subject to federal rules. All major utilities in Texas, including municipalities, the Lower Colorado River Authority, electric cooperatives, and private companies were interconnected, but their electricity did not cross over the boundaries of the state, with the exception of those previously noted. Nonetheless, the Federal Power Commission was determined to have its way, arguing that having Texas in the national grid would enhance efficiency and reliability across the nation. But my clients, the Texas utilities, insisted on maintaining their independence by serving customers only within Texas, as they had always done, with two limited exceptions during World War II to benefit the war effort. One had permitted the transfer of electric power into Louisiana, from the Orange/Port Arthur area and the other into Oklahoma in the area around Lake Texoma, north of Dallas. Neither permit conferred jurisdiction on the Federal Power Commission.

Legal conflict was inevitable because there were lots of powerful and influential stakeholders invested in the outcome, especially the electricity generating companies and their owners. Some owners had companies that generated electricity in Texas as well as in other states and wanted all of them connected. But most owners wanted no part of federal regulations, and this conflict contributed to what one federal judge called "The Second Battle of the Alamo" and an "embarrassing bonanza for litigators." It was a defining moment in the Texas electric power industry's struggle to remain clear of federal regulation. Platoons of lawyers descended on regulatory and administrative agencies as well as the courts—and I am not embarrassed to say I was one of them!

The lawyers for the utility companies that generated most of the electricity in Texas asked me to represent them in hearings before the Federal Power Commission and congressional committees. Looking back, I can see that I was a "natural" for the selection. The companies they represented used huge quantities of natural gas to fire their turbines, and I had an extensive practice in natural gas law. Another consideration was that my firm—now called Clark, Thomas, Harris, Denius & Winters—had long represented some of these same companies, including the former Texas Utilities Company (which served Dallas, Fort Worth, most of North Texas, and Northeast Texas); a holding company called Central and Southwest (which had subsidiaries known as West Texas Utilities); and the Central Power and Light (which served most of South Texas and some of West Texas), and Houston Power and Light. Therefore, as a firm looking out for its clients, we were necessarily interested in the regulation of electric utility prices in Texas, particularly who would do the regulating and with what authority.

In addition, my close relationship with Austin's Congressman Jake Pickle may have been decisive when the other attorneys considered asking me to represent them. As mentioned earlier, Mr. Pickle was a member of the House Committee on Interstate Commerce, and he was well positioned to influence other members of the committee, particularly when they met in executive session, which they often did. I made certain he was properly informed about the issues.

Litigation in the dispute heated up when a holding company based in Shreveport and owning stock in companies serving Arkansas, Louisiana, and Texas decided it would benefit by interconnecting all of its companies with those in Texas. The Shreveport holding company filed suit in federal court complaining that Texas companies, by refusing to interconnect across the state boundary, were conspiring to restrict the transmission of electric energy in violation of the Sherman Antitrust Act. In an attack on our defense of ERCOT as a stand-alone grid in Texas, an anonymous person abetted the Shreveport holding company by surreptitiously sending electricity from Texas across the Red River in a shenanigan that became known as the "Midnight Connection." Like one of Admiral McRaven's special forces in enemy territory, someone in a station in Vernon, Texas, threw a switch that sent electricity from deep in the heart of Texas into Oklahoma for several hours, potentially placing Texas and all its utilities under federal jurisdiction.

When the incident was brought before the Federal Power Commission, I argued that this involuntary connection was not a legitimate basis for establishing federal jurisdiction. Congressman Pickle helped us by introducing a bill that exempted Texas from a national grid. He took the position that if Hawaii and Alaska were not in the national grid, which they obviously were not, then Texas should also be able to remain out of it. We never expected Jake's bill to pass, but it was a good defensive tactic, and the FPC eventually decided that the Midnight Connection did not justify federal jurisdiction. Since the dispute between the Shreveport holding company and electricity providers in Texas could affect so many producers, the dispute spawned other litigation. The entire industry had questions about forced interconnection and power transmission. My clients, the electric utility companies in Texas, were so wary of connections beyond Texas that we hired helicopters to fly the entire perimeter of the Texas grid, studying the surface of the ground to be sure there were no power lines across them.

Why? Because Texas had a surplus of power, and we thought the people of Texas would need that surplus. There was no compelling need for us to be regulated by the Federal Power Commission (or Federal Energy Regulatory System). Lest I seem not to appreciate the national necessity of having a stable flow of electricity, ERCOT cooperates with seven similar regional organizations to assure the flow of electricity to users across the United States.

With lessons from the Great Northeast Blackout and the Federal Power Commission's recognition that Texas was beyond their jurisdiction, my clients realized they should form their own grid, which they did in 1970, building on an informal organization that did business on a cooperative or handshake basis. And that's how ERCOT operated, regulated only by local governments until the Texas Public Utility Commission was created by the Texas Legislature in 1975.

ERCOT's mission was, and continues to be, important and demanding because, unlike the days when the sun controlled our lives, now we can decide when to turn off the lights, thanks to ERCOT regulating the grid. When generators are taken off line for mechanical reasons, the temporary loss of their capacity must be compensated for, or consumers will suffer an outage, which can vary from an inconvenience to life-threatening peril. A hurricane may disrupt power along the Gulf Coast while normal production continues in Central Texas. ERCOT balances supply and demand, while keeping the frequency at a constant 60 hertz (cycles per second). By "directing traffic" on the grid, ERCOT maintains reliability and ensures an adequate supply of electricity to consumers across Texas.

CHAPTER 14

Corporate Ventures with Clint Murchison and George Lindeman

S HORTLY AFTER I JOINED the Looney & Clark law firm in 1949, Mr. Looney called me to his office and said, "Frank, I am drawing up gas franchise contracts with the cities of Austin, Port Arthur, and Galveston for a company that Clint Murchison has acquired through a merger with Southern Union, but I am putting your name on them. From now on, he is your client." And from then on, that's the way it was.

An outsider looking at our firm might have considered my assignment as only professional, simply that the manager of the firm had made an internal decision to assign Murchison's account to me. However, Mr. Looney's decision was very personal and based on boyhood friendships formed in Athens, Texas, between Clint and my uncle, Wofford Cain. In adulthood, they partnered in business ventures, one of which was the founding of Southern Union Gas in 1929, which would be a bellwether of their fortunes for decades—and for mine as well. Sid Richardson was another Athens boy who achieved great success in the oil "bidness," and, in some ways, he mentored both men. As I said earlier, when I was a child, Mr. Murchison was often in our home, and it was only natural that I would call him "Uncle Clint," as he and "Uncle Wofford" usually came together.

The effective collaboration between Wofford Cain and Clint Murchison is well illustrated by the story of how they got the natural gas franchise contracts for Santa Fe and Albuquerque, which was the foundation of Southern Union Gas. It happened this way. In the spring of 1929, they went on a fishing vacation to New Mexico. After they got there, they learned that neither city had natural gas, but both wanted it. They knew that gas had been discovered in the San Juan Mountains near the Four Corners, about two hundred miles northwest of Albuquerque. They decided to cut bait and bid on the contracts. First, they had to own the gas that would be required. They got it by purchasing the small oil company that owned rights to the gas field. Next they had to win the bids with the city councils of Albuquerque and Santa Fe and negotiate the contracts. Then they had to build a pipeline over the Continental Divide to reach both cities. Lesser men would not have taken on this mammoth and complex project. They easily got the franchise for Santa Fe because there was virtually no competition, Santa Fe being then a town of only about eleven thousand people. But Albuquerque, population twenty-seven thousand, was another story. They got the franchise there by virtue of fast thinking, bold action, and Murchison's understanding of the banking system. They had two obstacles: competition from other bidders and the mayor, who wanted an unusually high deposit, or bond, not for himself, but to build a zoo for the city. Unlike today, there was no formal bidding procedure, just the mayor presiding over a meeting of the city council and asking for bids from the audience, which were then ratified or rejected by the council.

When the mayor asked for a show of hands by those interested in the franchise and who could put up a cash bond of $25,000 to insure financial viability, several hands went up, including Murchison's. The mayor then asked who could provide a $50,000 bond and only two hands went up, and Murchison's was one of them. The mayor then asked for a bond of $100,000, and only Uncle Clint raised his hand. He wrote out the check, and they were awarded the franchise. But it was a "hot" check; neither he nor Uncle Wofford had $100,000 cash. The solution to the problem was to drive all night to get back to Dallas, where the next morning they met with Nathan Adams, president of the First National Bank, a close friend of Clint's father. Adams agreed to cover their check. Clint told Wofford, "If you are honest and are trying, your creditors will play ball." Murchison's instinctive understanding of banking and finance set him apart from other early oilmen. It was knowledge acquired from his father, who owned and operated the First National Bank in Athens.

Now the physical work began: they still had to supply the gas to the two cities. Murchison chartered a plane and flew over the route, dropping small bags of flour tipped with flags to mark the right-of-way. Uncle Wofford, a civil engineering graduate of Texas A&M, supervised the construction, which required building roads across canyons and mountains, digging trenches, and hauling large sections of pipe that weighed hundreds of tons to remote locations. The project was under construction when the stock market crashed in October of 1929, but they did not stop. They ran out of money several times, only to be rescued by their creditors. Seven miles from Albuquerque, the project was out of money, on its last legs. Clint could not wrangle any more money from Dallas banks. The problem was solved when Uncle Wofford appealed to the mayor for a return of a portion of their cash bond. The mayor agreed, and it was enough to complete the project.

Although this was in the depths of the Great Depression, Clint Murchison continued to negotiate more gas franchises for Southern Union Gas. By late 1931, two years after Cain and Murchison founded the company, they were providing gas to forty-three towns in six states as far north as Ohio, despite the weekly struggle to meet their payroll. As a nine-year-old I watched the trenching for Southern Union's gas pipeline from a newly discovered field near Cayuga, Texas, into Athens, initially on the strength of only one customer, Uncle Chick's brick factory. As Uncle Wofford was the steady manager of the company, Uncle Clint was the bold, financial genius behind the operation, who got money out of banks when no one else could. Completion of the Albuquerque pipeline left them three million dollars in debt, and although the debt soared, they continued operating. In 1932, Murchison's personal debt was estimated at four million dollars, far more than his net worth, but he did not calculate it in the conventional way. Asked how much he was worth, he once replied, "About three times what I owe." He advised, "If you are going to owe money, owe more than you can pay. Then the banks cannot afford to foreclose on you."

After focusing his efforts on building Southern Union Gas for several years after its founding in 1929, Murchison began diversifying his investments from oil and gas, as I mentioned earlier. However, Uncle Wofford, ever a rock of earnest endeavor, stuck with Southern Union Gas, chairing its board of directors for forty years. More than once, he rescued Clint from financial ventures that had not panned out. Clint needed Wofford to help support his prolific spending. Clint said, "Cash makes a man sterile."

Almost immediately after Mr. Looney put my name on those gas franchise contracts for Port Arthur, Austin, and Galveston, I began negotiating rates with their city officials for Murchison's company. Most rate adjustments were reviewed annually. Right away, I was representing the company before the Texas Railroad Commission when a municipality contested a rate increase proposed by Southern Union. By law, the Railroad Commission was the arbiter. Such disputes were not unusual and involved the complex determination of a reasonable rate of return on our company's investment, which is what public utilities are legally entitled to. This was the beginning of my extensive experience in regulatory law and natural gas law, two fields in which I became very knowledgeable. It was not a bad start for an ambitious young lawyer.

My association with Mr. Murchison also got me heavily involved with other corporations, initially with his companies, and gradually with others. I served on their boards as a director or officer, as chairman and CEO, as well as an attorney, often in Austin and Washington. I was a handmaiden to their business transactions and represented them before state and national regulatory agencies. My first responsibility was always to assure that the corporation operated within the law. This part of my practice required knowledge of statutes and the regulations that were adopted by government agencies to implement them. I studied a lot, and I was extensively briefed on the laws concerning contracts, taxes, mergers, liquidations, accounting, securities, bankruptcies, environmental issues, licensing, zoning, and many other issues. I found the work demanding, usually interesting, occasionally exciting, and always rewarding.

My initiation to the world of corporate governance began as director and a lawyer (an acceptable combination at the time), for the Delhi Oil Corporation in 1952, which Murchison had spun out of Southern Union

Gas in 1946. He had quickly made it one of the largest integrated, independent oil companies in the country. My main tasks were to negotiate pipeline easements, litigate when necessary, and deal with the IRS. These assignments furthered my understanding of the law, and I learned much about the commercial world by associating with top-level businessmen. Mr. Murchison was president and CEO of Delhi Oil. Other directors were his son, John Dabney Murchison, Wofford Cain, Lee Moore from El Paso, and Moore's son-in-law, John T. MacGuire.

Delhi achieved international attention because of the great gas reserves developed by its subsidiary, Canadian Delhi, in western Canada. Mr. Murchison conceived of an all-Canadian pipeline to deliver natural gas from the fields of Alberta to the eastern seaboard and persuaded Canadian bankers to finance it to completion in 1958 as the 2,100-mile Trans-Canada Pipe Lines. As another indication of Murchison's foresight, in the 1950s he began buying mineral rights in North Dakota, which in the early twenty-first century became one of the most productive regions in the United States.

Shortly after I passed the bar, Murchison asked me to take responsibility for the construction of two natural gas pipelines in Texas, one from Rio Grande City in South Texas (Starr County) more than a hundred miles up the Rio Grande to a new power plant in Laredo, and the other from Blessing in Matagorda County, a distance of some sixty miles to Victoria, completed in 1952. Murchison's company for the project was Utilities Natural Gas, and the user in both Laredo and Victoria was Central Power and Light Company. I represented the company in that pipeline. My job was to coordinate both projects with the help of an engineer and a right-of-way specialist. I had fun with both projects. In South Texas, I learned a lot about early Texas history while negotiating easements across Spanish land grants dating from the mid-1750s. Land titles south of Laredo are different than any other in my experience, because the Spaniards subdivided it into tracts called *Porciones*, or portions.

Most grants combined a narrow frontage on the Rio Grande with long narrow strips that ran considerable distances into the interior of Texas. In this assignment, I learned a lot about negotiating because there were so many tracts, and most had a different owner. I did all the right-of-way purchasing and, when I was unable to negotiate with a landowner for the easement, I asserted the company's right of eminent domain and condemned his property to get it. The pipeline was completed in 1951. Five years later Laredo required additional gas, and we had to build another pipeline that would cross about a hundred tracts. I dreaded the negotiations, until the mayor of the small town of Roma volunteered, "Poncho, I'll help you." He invited the landowners to a barbecue at his ranch. A mariachi band played. I got a notary public there and set up several tables for the landowners to sign the easements. The mayor signed first, and after that no one declined. They all signed with hardly any negotiating. Later Murchison gave the City of Roma the internal distribution system for natural gas that his company had constructed. Thus it was a trade-off, and the mayor got something of value for his city.

In 1964, I became a director of Delhi Australia Corporation, which Murchison had spun out of Delhi Oil, to develop oil and gas reserves in the state of South Australia. With Adelaide as its capital, South Australia occupies most of the south central section of the continent. Murchison had obtained a concession for the entire state, some 380,000 square miles, an area almost one-and-a-half times the size of Texas. He paid for the concession by selling a portion of it and fulfilled his obligation to the Australian government by drilling and producing on the rest of it, yielding a profit for the company. When his son, John Dabney Murchison, succeeded him as CEO and chairman of Delhi Australia, he kept Perry Bass and me on his executive committee. We changed the name to Delhi International because the company owned interests in other countries besides Australia and the United States.

Delhi merged with Taylor Oil and Gas Company in 1955 to form the Delhi-Taylor Oil Corporation, which made me a board member of that corporation. The company owned a refinery in Taylor, Texas, and a bigger one in Corpus Christi. The most memorable aspect of my involvement with Delhi-Taylor occurred when it was liquidated in 1964. In negotiations with the Internal Revenue Service, I obtained a ruling that permitted its complete liquidation with no tax liability for the shareholders on the appreciated value of the corporation's assets; the shareholders received cash, Delhi contract units, and stock in Delhi Australia. Of all my negotiations with the IRS, this was probably the most outstanding achievement. The negotiations were complicated and the settlement was one of the biggest in the history of liquidations under Section 337 of the Internal Revenue Code. The fact that the liquidation was accomplished with no tax liability on the appreciated value for the shareholders may have been a factor in Congress abolishing Section 337 when the Revenue Code was revised in 1986.

In 1954, I became a director on the board of Aztec Oil and Gas, another entity spun off from Southern Union Gas as an exploration and production company. It was a public company with thousands of stockholders. Mr. Cain was chairman of the board and president of the company. This arrangement continued until 1972, when he retired, and I succeeded him. I remained chairman until April 1976, when another company acquired Aztec. Similarly, in 1955, I became one of nine directors on the board of Southern Union Gas. Upon Uncle Wofford's death in 1977, John T. MacGuire assumed the chairman's gavel, which he kept until 1985, when I became president, CEO, and chairman of the board. So that gives you a little history of some of the representations of various industries that I've had.

In 1958, I was one of the incorporators of a company called the First Small Business Investment Company of Texas, founded under the Small Business Investment Company Act of 1958. My good friend, Gordon Lord, and I, and the presidents of several banks in Austin, became directors of the company. Each bank owned 10 percent of the corporation. Its name was changed to Texas Capital Corporation when we went public in 1960; it was changed again to Telecom Corporation when the company became heavily involved in cable TV during the 1970s. In 1975, as my activities in corporate management and governance expanded, I phased out of the law firm that had been so important to me and set up my own law office.

By a remarkable coincidence, my corporate involvement began and ended with Southern Union Gas. When I assumed responsibility as CEO and chairman in 1985, the historic company was in decline, having lost a demoralizing and costly lawsuit that required refinancing, which was accomplished with the help of Goldman Sachs in 1987. Despite its troubles, the company still had valuable assets, including gas franchises in several Texas cities and their surrounding areas, such as El Paso, Austin, and Port Arthur, as well as across the Texas Panhandle and northern Arizona. Nonetheless, the company then went into play—became vulnerable to a hostile takeover—especially after we sold a subsidiary savings and loan company in Midland, Texas. This divestiture enhanced the market appeal of Southern Union to oil and gas executives, who wanted nothing to do with a financial institution burdened with cumbersome state and federal regulations. Although it gave me no pleasure to preside over the sale and potentially the demise of the company founded by Uncle Wofford and Clint Murchison Sr., the company was for sale. The highest and best offer came from George Lindeman, CEO and chairman of Metro Mobile, a cellular phone company. I did not know Mr. Lindeman before we began negotiating, but by the time we shook hands on the deal at the 21 Club in New York we had developed strong bonds of friendship and mutual confidence. When the sale was consummated on February 6, 1990, I expected to terminate my connection with the company that had been an important part of my entire adult life. Mr. Lindeman had other plans and kept me heavily involved in the company. It was the beginning of one of the most surprising and satisfying periods of my life, professionally and personally. And I owe it all to George Lindeman.

When George became chairman and CEO of the company created by the merger, he retained Southern Union Gas as its corporate name and designated me chairman emeritus. He asked me to remain a director and appointed me chairman of the audit committee with important responsibilities, especially to implement requirements of the Sarbanes-Oxley Act, a federal law that set new or expanded requirements for all publically traded company boards, management, and public accounting firms. It was a complex endeavor that required me to work closely with the other directors, corporate executives, company staff, and consultants, bringing to bear on the problem my half-century's experience in both law and corporate decision-making. I liked it. It was good for me, and George Lindeman made it possible. Later, he asked me to take on a project with similar challenges—to implement company-wide the Affordable Care Act, otherwise known as Obamacare. In time, our friendship extended to our families. He and his wife, Frayda, invited Charmaine and me to their daughter's wedding reception in their home in Greenwich, Connecticut.

When I revolved off the board of directors' audit committee, George created a finance committee and put me on it. Eventually, I became chairman and cochaired the board committee that negotiated the sale of the company in 2011 for more than fourteen billion dollars. In one of the great ironies of my life, this sale ended my association with Southern Union Gas, an extraordinary relationship in every way that began in 1938 when Uncle Wofford "borrowed" the savings I had accumulated as a Safeway bag boy to buy stock for me in the company.

CHAPTER 15

Changing the Aggie Culture

M Y EFFORTS ON BEHALF OF TEXAS A&M are not as well known as those for the University of Texas, but they are similar. My commitments to both institutions has been long-term and significant, both monetarily and morally. The teaching, research, and public service missions of both A&M and UT are important to the people of Texas and therefore to me. I believe in educating all the people. To that end, I have been an advocate for public education across the entire state. If we do not educate all of our people, we endanger not only our economic base but our culture and society as a whole. As a positive and contributing citizen of Texas, that has been my guidepost. When I have directed gifts to Texas A&M, I have also been mindful that my benevolent uncle, Wofford Cain, earned a degree from A&M in civil engineering in 1913.

Having a special interest in A&M's Corps of Cadets, I have been responsible for funding more than one hundred scholarships to its members, both personally and through the Effie and Wofford Cain Foundation. As president, or as an executive of the foundation since Uncle Wofford died in 1977, I have tried to treat Texas A&M and UT Austin equitably, and A&M's regents have named several facilities for Mr. Cain in recognition of Cain Foundation gifts. Until certain renovations, A&M's varsity athletes took their meals in the Cain Dining Hall and students swam in the Cain Pool. The Cain Park is next door to Cain

Hall, now a counseling center for students on Gene Stallings Drive across the street from Kyle Field. I also saw to the creation of a two million-dollar endowment in the name of Wofford Cain for the unrestricted use of Texas A&M's president. Other million-dollar endowments have been made to the schools of business and engineering. I have taken particular pride in assisting low-income and deserving students enrolled in the Corps of Cadets with numerous annual donations known as James Earl Rudder Scholarships in honor of A&M's most distinguished president.

Beyond these gifts, I want to tell you about three instances of pro bono legal service that I have provided to Texas A&M. In 1965, I was the sole attorney involved in legal work that led to the admission of women on the same basis as men, an event that quickly transformed the all-male traditional Aggie culture. The second was a minor effort that thwarted the publication of materials considered derogatory by members of the A&M governing board. And the third was a protracted and complex legal case involving numerous lawyers to defend a client's assets and to eventually direct them to Texas A&M as a major foundation bequest.

The Admission of Women

In a subsequent chapter, I will describe how Leon Jaworski and I handled a case styled *Sanders vs. Ransom* for the UT Board of Regents that prompted the board to order complete racial integration at the University of Texas. The case had hardly been settled when I was surprised by a visit from two well-known Aggies: Earl Rudder, the president of Texas A&M, and Sterling Evans, the chairman of the Texas A&M Board of Directors (it became the Texas A&M Board of Regents in 1975). It was the spring of 1965, and they wanted me to help them remove the legal barriers that kept women from being admitted to A&M on the same basis as men.

I was always curious to know the reason a client came to me for legal assistance. In this case, my work on the UT case mentioned above was probably a factor, but I had other connections to both men. I had first seen Rudder in England in early 1944 during the buildup for the Normandy invasion and, since then, I had been with him at a number of state and political functions. Mr. Evans was a business partner of Gus Wortham, founder of the American General Insurance Company, who was a close friend of my firm's senior partner, Ed Clark. American General had our firm on retainer.

The crux of Evans's and Rudder's concern was that, in terms of enrollment, A&M was not keeping up with the three other largest public universities in Texas. Texas Tech, the University of Houston, and UT Austin were fully coeducational and growing rapidly. A&M was stable with about eight thousand students, of whom fewer than two hundred were women—about one-fourth of 1 percent—who were admitted under exceptions to the general admissions policy of men only. The A&M Board of Directors had nine members, and Evans, the chairman, wanted me to represent him and four others—five in all—who favored the admission of women on the same basis as men. The other four wanted to continue admitting women in selected categories, like the wives and daughters of students and employees, and to the vet school and graduate programs that were not available in other state colleges. They were considering a proposal to admit women residing in Brazos County, where A&M was located. The four dissenting members opposed dormitories for women on the campus. My uncle, Wofford Cain, was one of the four. He and the other three apparently believed women's dorms would fundamentally change the character of Texas A&M, which they were determined to preserve, even if women were admitted. The split in A&M's governing board paralleled divisions in the Aggie "family" over the issue.

For at least twenty-five years the issue had periodically embroiled A&M in lawsuits, judgments and appeals, and legislative posturing. Rudder and Evans wanted to resolve the issue and get on with developing the institution, which they aptly called a "sleeping giant." I have always been a strong supporter of Texas A&M in its academic programs and military training—except for about three hours a year, until they bolted to the Southeastern Conference.

After listening to Rudder and Evans, I told them that I would brief the case and discuss it with my law partners, which I did. When they returned three weeks later, I told them that, in my opinion, the various categories under which some women were admitted to A&M, and others denied, was an illegal system of classification prohibited by the equal protection clause of the fourteenth amendment to the U.S. Constitution. How could you admit a woman because her father had a job at A&M, but not a woman whose father worked for the highway department and lived in Dallas? How could you defend the admission of a woman to a fully state-supported institution because she lived in Brazos County, where A&M was located, but not from any of the other 253 counties in Texas?

Our first decision was how to confront the issue. The obvious choices were to introduce a bill in the legislature or to seek a court judgment by filing a friendly lawsuit. Neither was desirable. Both would be sensational. They would attract media attention and inflame passions, both pro and con, and a lawsuit would be expensive. We decided to follow a third course—to seek an opinion from the state attorney general, which would generally be regarded as law unless overturned by a court decision or an act of the legislature. By contrast, an AG's opinion would be inexpensive, and probably very low profile. With the approval of the A&M board, I filed an application with Attorney General Waggoner Carr for an opinion about the legality of A&M's admission policy. Carr had succeeded Will Wilson, and I was on good terms with him. In fact, I had helped him raise money in his campaign for office.

After I made the request, several weeks passed without action until Rudder and I met with Carr in his office. Carr agreed to an unusual procedure to deal with our request for an opinion. Normally, in handling such requests, a committee of assistants to the attorney general was formed, and one member would agree to draft an opinion that would be reviewed by the whole committee. The A&M request would be handled differently. Without a public announcement, the opinion committee would conduct an informal hearing similar to a court hearing, with me and another lawyer presenting the viewpoints of the opposing factions of the A&M's board of directors. I would represent the five directors led by Sterling Evans, who believed the law required the full admission of women, which President Rudder also favored. I have always believed Rudder's presence, his broad base of respect, and his determination to force the issue influenced Waggoner Carr's decision to allow this unusual procedure.

On September 9, 1965, we gathered for the hearing before the attorney general's opinion committee. The only news-media person present was Sam Kinch of the *Fort Worth Star-Telegram,* and his account did not get much attention, which was what we wanted—little or no publicity. The opposing attorney, Dee Kelly, argued that A&M's board of directors was within its discretionary power to accept "certain women relatives of students, faculty members and employees." I argued that the admissions policy was discriminatory and emphasized that admitting women only in selected arbitrary classes violated the U.S. Constitution.

When Waggoner Carr issued his opinion a month later, he agreed with me that the exclusion of applicants for the sole reason that they were not wives or daughters of staff members or students, or widows or daughters of deceased staff members, was discriminatory and an unreasonable class distinction and, therefore, illegal. And the attorney general's ruling was the law until overturned by a court order or by the legislature. Thus, to comply with the law, Texas A&M would have to change. If the admissions policy was not changed, it was only a matter of time before a woman who had been denied admission sued A&M and cited the attorney general's opinion to support her contention. The opinion would be powerful persuasion for any judge or jury. The U.S. Civil Rights Act of 1964 was not a factor in my argument or in the attorney general's opinion.

Months went by before the A&M board could agree on the exact wording of an admissions policy that abided by the AG's opinion not to discriminate against women. Meanwhile, I got a lot of telephone calls and correspondence, nearly all disapproving, alleging that I had forced unwarranted change on a hallowed institution. At the time, I was president of the Texas Exes. One letter said I was a Longhorn ruining A&M and another that I was guilty of treason—against whom I was never sure. In my view, it was an honor and a privilege to represent institutions like the University of Texas and Texas A&M University, and criticism was just part of the job. I treated A&M with the same respect and effort that I gave the University of Texas. I did the best I could do, and I did not benefit financially.

Suppressing Aggie Joke Books

A few months after the adversarial hearing about the admission of women before the attorney general's opinion committee, A&M's board chairman, Sterling Evans, was in our firm's office visiting with Mr.

Clark and dropped by to talk with me about another issue. Mr. Evans was troubled by the notorious "Aggie Joke" books, which had begun appearing on newsstands statewide a couple of years before. They were inexpensive to produce, merely saddle-stitched or stapled in the spine rather than bound. The jokes were mostly adapted from ethnic slurs. Published anonymously, the books had become widely circulated.

Sterling Evans thought they were affecting A&M's image and discouraging students who might otherwise apply for admission. Most Aggies seemed to think that an overzealous UT fan bent on ridiculing A&M was behind them, and Evans wanted to stop them. However, he knew it would be almost impossible in a straightforward legal procedure because of First Amendment freedoms. I told him I would check around and let him know what I found. I had a simple idea. I just walked along Congress Avenue and looked on the shelves of newsstands and bookstores. I found a bookshop that had several of the books, and I asked the owner for the business address of the sources. There were two publishers: a man in Houston and a married couple in Dallas. The couple in Dallas had an office in a downtown high rise.

While in Dallas for a meeting, I went to their office and just walked in. I came face-to-face with the woman and explained—oops! I had come there by mistake, a wrong address. But I stayed long enough to look around and see that they were publishing the joke books, among other tasteless materials. Back in Austin, I went to see Waggoner Carr, still the attorney general. He was receptive to doing something, and decided to issue what is known as an "Attorney General's Letter," which is not a search warrant or restraining order, but a written statement of interest in an activity. Carr then sent an assistant to Dallas to call on the publisher. A similar thing was done with the publisher in Houston, and both stopped putting out the offensive books.

Of course, this did not stop the publication of Aggie joke books for all time, but it did for a while. A&M's Association of Former Students investigated and found that the man in Houston had attended the University of Houston and the husband in the Dallas couple had attended Texas Christian University. I was glad that neither of the culprits was a Longhorn or an Aggie.

With John Dabney Murchison, board chairman, Delhi International, Inc. 1977. The company was founded by his father, Clint Murchison Sr.

I got one of the first personalized license plates when the legislature authorized them in 1965. Charmaine was as pleased as I was.

The "jet set" in Arkansas for the 1965 game. We traveled in Clint Murchison Sr.'s DC-3, the "Flying Jennie."

With my friend UT head football coach Darrell Royal. Darrell was the first coach to invite me to attend team practices.

The dedication of the Lila B. Etter Alumni Center, April 1965. I was president of the alumni association at the time and had co-chaired the fundraising committee. This was an important occasion as indicated by the attendees, left to right: UT Austin president Norman Hackerman, Regents chairman Frank Erwin, Congressman Jake Pickle, unknown, Sterling Holloway, Jack Blanton, Jack Maguire, and me. Former governor Allan Shivers is at the podium and further to the right are UT System chancellor Harry Ransom and former Regents chairman W. W. "Bill" Heath.

The 1989 dedication of the expanded alumni center: As I cut the ribbon, Texas Exes president Mike Cook and executive director Roy Vaughn look on.

I received the Distinguished Alumnus Award from the UT Ex-Students Association in 1991.

With Coach Mack Brown at a practice session. He said, "Frank has been to more practices than I have." *University of Texas Athletic Department.*

Coach Mack Brown occasionally asked me to make a pep talk to the team after practice. Here we are inside the bubble. I always ended with "One, two, three, I love Texas." *University of Texas Athletic Department.*

The Rose Bowl, January 4, 2006, when UT won the 2005 national championship, beating USC 41–38. *Photo courtesy of Adam Blum.*

An interview from the sidelines at DKR–Texas Memorial Stadium. *University of Texas Athletic Department.*

Mack Brown admires the commemorative tile I dedicated at the alumni center to his 2009 team that played for the national championship, losing to Alabama 37–21 in the Rose Bowl. *University of Texas Athletic Department.*

Congratulating Charlie Strong when he was appointed UT's head football coach, January 6, 2014. *University of Texas Athletic Department.*

DKR–Texas Memorial Stadium, Veterans Day, 2008. *University of Texas Athletic Department.*

With Claiborne "Clay" Johnson, inaugural dean of UT Austin's Dell Medical School, 2014. *Photo courtesy of Adam Blum.*

With UT System Chancellor Bill McRaven on the day his appointment was announced, August 21, 2014. *Photo courtesy of Adam Blum.*

Speaking to UT ROTC cadets, 2006. *Photo by Marsha Miller, the University of Texas at Austin.*

Speaking at the Frank Denius Veterans Memorial Plaza on the UT Austin campus when I was awarded the Legion of Honor by the French government, May 25, 2012. *University of Texas Athletic Department.*

With my great friends and traveling companions to all UT football games, Valerie and Ted Koy. *Photo courtesy Valerie and Ted Koy.*

I was extremely flattered when Edith and Darrell Royal attended the Legion of Honor award ceremony, May 25, 2012. *University of Texas Athletic Department.*

Charmaine and I enjoyed traveling with Nancy and Kerry Merritt. Here we are in 2002 in Paris, where Kerry and I hired a driver to take us to battlefields of both world wars while our wives did what women like to do in Paris.

With my entire family in Normandy near Bayeux, 2001. Left to right: Frank McGill, Charmaine Denius, me, Beth Denius, Charmaine McGill, Gordon McGill, Parker McGill, Reagan Denius, and Woffie Denius.

Standing at the orientation table in the Normandy American cemetery in 2001. I am explaining the invasion to my three grandsons.

The monument to the Thirtieth Infantry Division atop Hill 314 near Mortain, France.

The Normandy American cemetery where 9,387 of our war dead are buried, from a trip in 2001.

Mortain, France. May 27, 2014, at the victory parade commemorating the seventieth anniversary of the battle for Hill 314.

The Frank Denius Fields at the University of Texas at Austin. *University of Texas Athletic Department.*

The Heep Foundation

After twenty-seven years with the Looney & Clark law firm, I left the firm in 1976 to set up my own office. I was increasingly involved with corporate boards of directors, both in governance and in management, leaving me with little time to fulfill the expectations of a senior partner in a dynamic and growing law firm. In addition to my duties as chairman of the Southern Union Gas Board of Directors, I was soon to become CEO of the corporation. My responsibilities with the Cain Foundation were also increasing, as Uncle Wofford's health declined. For these reasons, I set up my own office, with me as the only attorney. I did not intend to take new cases, but to devote myself to philanthropy and corporate activities, particularly to Southern Union Gas. Nonetheless, I had a few cases, most of which were referred to me by lawyers with whom I had formed strong relationships over the years. One was Mr. Raybourne Thompson, a senior partner in the firm of Vinson & Elkins in Houston, which, as I stated earlier, kept the Looney & Clark firm on retainer.

The case I want to relate illustrates two accomplishments that are important to me. The first is that I enabled a client to achieve her goals; the second, that I employed legal strategies that benefitted Texas A&M University as well as my client. The case involved the assets of Herman F. and Minnie Belle Heep. Raybourne Thompson represented the Heep family's business interests, which were principally oil, gas, and ranching, on behalf of his law firm. I had seen Mr. and Mrs. Heep on social occasions in Austin and was aware of their home and ranch in Hays County, a few miles south of Austin. I was also generally familiar with Heep oil and gas activities through contacts in the industry and casually from their managers, who had offices in the same building on the same floor as the Looney & Clark law firm.

When Raybourne Thompson called, he told me that he planned to retire and that Mrs. Heep was his client, Mr. Heep having died on February 10, 1960. Mrs. Heep had asked him to recommend an attorney for her in Austin, and he had recommended me. Raybourne and I had worked closely together in several lawsuits involving the Texas Railroad Commission. He told Mrs. Heep my background, including that I had been a senior partner with the Looney & Clark law firm, and she asked him to contact me for her.

Mrs. Heep came to see me the first time in late 1976. I told her I would be honored to represent her in any matter for which she might need legal advice. Initially, her concerns were about making gifts to several relatives. Then she asked me to do some tax work for her. Gradually, my assistance to Mrs. Heep dealt with personal as well as business matters. My ability to advise her compelled me to delve deeper into her family issues. She wanted to help a number of people who had worked for her for years, and she wanted to help certain members of her family, some with outright gifts and others with trusts. I made an exhaustive study of the assets that she owned personally and those still owned by the estate of her late husband, which were in trust, and of the oil and gas properties that were allegedly their community property. Only with this information could I advise her as to provisions she should include in her last will and testament to legally accomplish what she wanted for her family and other beneficiaries.

An important event in representing her occurred when she had a serious illness that required surgery. Although in a weakened condition, Mrs. Heep survived the surgery and resumed living in her ranch home south of Austin. Fortunately, she had a very clear mind, because we had major estate-planning issues to work through that required her participation. Given her weakened condition, I would go to her home about two o'clock in the afternoon two or three times a week and talk with her until about five o'clock. I usually took a secretary to help me prepare, or amend, the documents in the way that Mrs. Heep wanted them. We necessarily discussed in detail many personal things that she wanted to accomplish. Underlying our discussions was the lucky coincidence that Mrs. Heep and my wife, Charmaine, had gotten acquainted by going to the same beauty parlor for a number of years. Their rapport no doubt made Mrs. Heep feel comfortable discussing sensitive matters with me.

Our discussions confirmed that she wanted to include Texas A&M in her gift plans. Mr. Heep had served as a director on the A&M governing board from 1957 until his death three years later. During his lifetime they had made annual gifts to A&M—inter vivos types of gifts—that she wanted to continue, as well as providing for a substantial gift from her estate. I helped her with those and, when representatives of A&M came to visit her, I usually attended their meetings. When I had finally got Mrs. Heep's will and estate plan exactly as she wanted them, she came to my office and signed the documents in the proper manner, with witnesses in the presence of a notary public.

Practicing law is an ongoing exercise in surprises, and one was coming. Out of the blue in July 1984, soon after Mrs. Heep had signed her new will and estate plan, her stepdaughter and three step-grandchildren filed a suit contesting both Mrs. Heep's separate and her community property interest in the entire estate. The suit contended that her only property right was a life estate in the home and ranch in Hays County. (The ranch was actually two separate plots, amounting to about five thousand acres altogether, referred to here simply as "the ranch.") The stepdaughter was a child of Mr. Heep and a wife before he married my client, Mrs. Minnie Belle Heep, in 1933. Bear in mind that Mr. and Mrs. Heep were married twenty-seven years and she had not remarried since his death in 1960. Meanwhile, she had looked after the ranch, of which she was a part owner. She had an estate for life in the entire ranch, although Mr. Heep had acquired part of it before they married, which was now in his estate. Her life estate included the part of the ranch that was in her late husband's estate, as well as her separate portion of it, which had been acquired after their marriage and was, therefore, community property.

Mr. and Mrs. Heep's financial transactions were complicated by the fact that he used a bank in Tulsa, Oklahoma, for his oil and gas business, and the Capital National Bank in Austin for all other interests; in fact, he was a director of the latter bank at the time of his death, and I took his place on the board. Mr. Heep used the Tulsa bank for his petroleum business because Austin banks lacked in-depth knowledge about drilling, exploring, and producing oil and gas. His Tulsa bank had the expertise he needed and made the kind of loans that he required. This dual banking complicated the determination of what was Mr. and Mrs. Heep's separate and community property, which was the crux of the lawsuit.

The lawsuit against Mrs. Heep was filed by attorneys of the Fulbright & Jaworski law firm in Houston on behalf of the plaintiffs, who were represented in Austin by Mr. Roy Minton and his law firm. The suit was an effort to recover all of the income from oil and gas that Mrs. Heep had received from the date of Mr. Heep's death until the lawsuit was filed, which was a period from 1960 until 1984, and subsequent years. The fact that substantial oil and gas income was derived from Heep properties in Borden County, Texas, became a factor in settling the case. The plaintiffs also claimed that none of the approximately five thousand acres south of Austin known as the Heep Ranch was community property, but was all separate property of Mr. Heep's at the time of his death, and, as I stated earlier, that Mrs. Heep's only interest was a life estate. These were the principal issues in the lawsuit, which became progressively complicated and was obviously an extremely important matter for Mrs. Heep. As plans evolved to defend her, Mrs. Heep left most decisions to my discretion, and I kept her informed as the suit developed.

The lawsuit lasted from 1984 until 1991. While negotiations and proceedings were unfolding, I was serving as interim president of Southern Union Gas Company, which took up much of my time. To help me with the case, I engaged the Brown & Maroney law firm in Austin to help me and worked primarily with Mr. Jack Maroney and Mr. Will Barber. (Officially, their law firm was Brown, Maroney, Rose, Barber & Dye.) They were trial lawyers, which I was not, although in the first years of my career, Mr. Looney assigned me cases that gave me enough experience to become one, if I was so inclined. As the Heep case developed, it seemed to me that every fundamental law in Texas was involved. It was the most complex case I was ever involved in, and I drew heavily on what Edward Looney had taught me. He emphasized knowing not only the law, but your client—every possible thing, for two main reasons, one positive and the other negative. The positive was to be able to construct your arguments to optimize success in achieving the client's goals. The other was to avoid surprises in the courtroom, which, Mr. Looney said, were usually damaging to the client.

In a sensitive conversation, Mrs. Heep confided that she was afraid of her stepdaughter, although she had virtually raised her. The stepdaughter lived in San Antonio, occasionally visited the ranch, and sometimes dropped in to see Mrs. Heep unexpectedly. When Mrs. Heep knew she was coming, I would hire an off-duty peace officer to park his car nearby on the highway, hoping to intimidate the stepdaughter, if she contemplated anything rash. On occasion, I sat with the peace officer to familiarize myself with the scene.

In other discussions, Mrs. Heep confirmed her continuing interest in Texas A&M, and her desire to benefit A&M through her estate planning. She had discussed it with Mr. Heep before his death, so it was really their joint decision. As a part of the strategy to defend her position in the lawsuit and to clarify her gifts for Texas A&M, I conceived the idea that we should establish a nonprofit corporation called the "Herman F. Heep and Minnie Belle Heep Texas A&M Foundation." Mr. Maroney and Mr. Barber enthusiastically endorsed the idea, and their firm drew up the papers to create the foundation. With Mrs. Heep's concurrence, I proposed it to Texas A&M's general counsel, Mr. Jimmy Bond, who got it approved by the A&M board of regents, which appointed Mr. John Lawrence as their attorney of record for this new foundation. Mr. Lawrence was perfect, strictly looking after the interest of his client and not infringing on my responsibilities in preparing for trial. I got the foundation chartered under Texas law as a nonprofit support organization for Texas A&M University, and I obtained a parallel IRS designation of the foundation as a 501(c)3 nonprofit corporation in support of Texas A&M. This meant that the foundation's income and assets could go only to Texas A&M.

In this way I brought Texas A&M into the suit as a codefendant. Then I had Mrs. Heep transfer 10 percent of her ownership in the ranch to the new foundation, which gave A&M a vested interest in the outcome of the case. Texas A&M was now an active party defendant, a vital and necessary party, to the lawsuit.

Anticipating going to trial, I hoped Mrs. Heep's gift would make jurors more sympathetic to her, inclined to appreciate her as a generous and unselfish lady (which she was), rather than as a wealthy, self-centered widow, as our opposition would probably portray her. Related to A&M's participation in the suit, there was a Texas statute stipulating that when a private foundation or nonprofit corporation in Texas is involved in litigation, the attorney general is by law automatically a party representing the interest of the state. Jim Mattox was then Texas attorney general. A&M was the state agency with a material interest in the lawsuit and wanted their designated private attorney, Mr. Lawrence, to look after their interest; in effect, to assume the role of the attorney general in the suit. This required the attorney general's concurrence, which the A&M regents successfully obtained without any help from me. A&M's attorney was present at all proceedings and at the taking of all depositions.

Not long after Mrs. Heep conveyed the 10 percent interest in the ranch to the new foundation, an attorney for the Fulbright & Jaworski firm, which had filed the original lawsuit on behalf of the plaintiffs, called me to object to my bringing Texas A&M into the suit. I told the attorney that Mr. and Mrs. Heep had a long history of giving to A&M and that I had only formalized a major gift in Mrs. Heep's estate plan. I was glad to have fielded the lawyer's objection because it confirmed that our opponents were concerned about the strategy we were using to defend Mrs. Heep.

We, the attorneys for Mrs. Heep—Jack Maroney, Will Barber, and I—conferred often, surfacing and discussing every conceivable consideration that could affect the outcome of the forthcoming trial. One issue was the best way to present the necessary documentation—like the previous wills of both Mr. and Mrs. Heep, their tax returns from 1933 to 1960, his estate tax returns, and hers since his death—in front of a jury in a way that was understandable and memorable. I interviewed a Los Angeles company called Legal Presentations on how best to present evidence to a jury electronically. We tentatively agreed to have six television monitors in the courtroom: two monitors for the jury, one for the witness stand, one for the judge, one for the defense table, and one for the plaintiff's table. Everything would be electronically programmed on the monitors so that viewers could see side by side the documents and how the changes evolved over a period of time, both in the estate planning and taxes. The cost of the electronic presentation was estimated between $750 thousand and a million dollars. Another issue was finding a courtroom in Austin of sufficient size. It would have to be spacious as there were so many parties. Everyone had a lawyer, including each of Mrs. Heep's three step-granddaughters as well as their mother, the stepdaughter.

Another topic was the role of the Vinson & Elkins law firm, which as

I stated earlier, had handled Heep interests before Mrs. Heep engaged me to help her. We realized that during the time that Vinson & Elkins had represented the estates of both Mr. Heep and Mrs. Heep, the firm had represented competing legal entities, at least with the filing of the lawsuit. This was a significant mistake by the firm. Vinson & Elkins had represented Mr. Heep's estate and probate matters as well as the settlement of taxes, both estate taxes and income taxes, and done the same for Mrs. Heep after his death in 1960. As a result, Vinson & Elkins was a necessary party to her defense. And the only way that could be done was to join the Vinson & Elkins law firm as a party defendant in this big lawsuit.

Jack Maroney and I flew to Houston, met with Vinson & Elkins attorneys, explained the situation, gave them a copy of our pleadings, and told them it was necessary for their firm to come into the lawsuit as a party defendant. They recognized what they had done, and accepted it, although I am sure they would have preferred not to be a party to the lawsuit. Nonetheless, they became a major party to the lawsuit. If Vinson & Elkins had not participated, I could have been guilty of negligence in representing Mrs. Heep.

Leading up to the trial, many depositions were taken by both sides. I was determined to get the deposition of a certain accountant, whose testimony was important to Mrs. Heep's defense, because he knew that Mr. Heep had comingled monies from his oil and gas ventures with his personal accounts at Austin's Capital National Bank. The comingling included money he had borrowed from his Tulsa bank. This was an important issue because under Texas law, when separate property and community property monies are comingled, the entire amount becomes community property. I located the accountant and, assisted by Will Barber, took his deposition in an office of the Brown & Maroney firm, in the presence of a lawyer from Roy Minton's law firm, which almost assured that Roy would know about it. As a witness, the accountant confirmed that Mr. Heep had used money he had borrowed from the Tulsa bank to pay community obligations. I have always thought the accountant's deposition was a factor in Mr. Minton's decisions about the case, which, as you will see, ended on favorable terms for Mrs. Heep.

As the date for the trial drew closer, Mr. Minton requested that he take Mrs. Heep's deposition. Mrs. Heep, at her age, was not in the best of health but, after she and I discussed it, she agreed. I agreed on two conditions. The first was that her deposition would be in a hotel room adjacent to a room where she could rest during intermissions; and, second, that we would start at one o'clock in the afternoon and quit about five o'clock. Mr. Minton and his associates, representing the plaintiffs, conducted those depositions over a period of thirteen days of actual testimony before a court reporter and video cameras. Will Barber and I represented Mrs. Heep; Mr. Lawrence, the attorney for the Texas A&M Foundation, was also present. All of this was done before the actual settlement discussions occurred.

The depositions were quite a trying experience for Mrs. Heep. I regretted that she had to endure them, and I wished Mr. Minton had been more sensitive to her condition. I tried to provide her every convenience during rest periods throughout the thirteen-day ordeal. I dreaded it, but as I explained to her, her deposition was a necessary part of the process of defending herself in the lawsuit. She was straightforward and her sincerity was obvious, altogether a good witness, which was probably a factor in Mr. Minton's subsequent decision to seek arbitration (in legal terms, alternate dispute resolution) rather than go to trial. That's what he did: he asked for a court authorized arbitration proceeding under and pursuant to the Rules of Civil Procedure. His request was approved and we went into arbitration. The arbitrator was Judge Jim Meyers, a former state district judge in Travis County, who personally supervised the negotiations.

The negotiations began about 6:30 in the evening when all the attorneys and their clients met with Judge Meyers, at least twenty of us altogether. Only Mrs. Heep was absent, but she had authorized me to negotiate on her behalf. My group included Will Barber, Jack Maroney, Bill Pargaman (a young partner in their firm), John Lawrence, and me. After instructions from Judge Meyers, each group went to a separate room. Judge Meyers shuttled from one group to the other, urging and cajoling, carrying proposals back and forth, and recounting reactions to them, sometimes interjecting his ideas or a clarification. Only from Judge Myers could my team and I sense whether we were progressing toward a settlement.

160

It became apparent that the lawsuit would be settled with financial payments to the plaintiffs, and that there were three major revenue sources for the money: the insurance carriers for Vinson & Elkins, the Vinson & Elkins law firm, and from Mrs. Heep, subject to my concurrence on her behalf. I thought we had settled when the three aforementioned defendants agreed to pay $14 million to the plaintiffs, but the plaintiffs insisted on $15 million. The difference would have to come from Mrs. Heep, who was asked to contribute more than $1 million. Negotiating for her without calling her every few minutes, I offered $500,000 to be paid out of future revenue from oil and gas income from properties in Borden County. In other words, not a personal liability of Mrs. Heep for $500,000, but as a liability on future income from oil royalties and the sales of oil and gas from properties that Mr. Heep had left her. If such revenues did not materialize, then the plaintiffs would not be paid. But that was not enough for the other side. They insisted on another $500,000 that would bring the total cost to $15 million, and Judge Meyers leaned on me to come up with it.

After considerable discussion among my team of lawyers, I agreed to $1 million, all of which would be payable out of future oil and gas revenues from Borden County properties and not as a personal liability of Mrs. Heep. Thus, the final settlement rose to $15 million paid to the plaintiffs: $14 million by the Vinson & Elkins insurers and Vinson & Elkins itself, and $1 million from Mrs. Heep paid from future royalties income. For me, it was important that she had no personal liability. I never knew how the $14 million was divided between Vinson & Elkins and their insurance carriers.

It was midnight when Judge Meyers announced that a settlement had been agreed on and recommended that we meet the next day to sign the implementing documents. I discussed the situation with my group of lawyers—Mr. Maroney, Mr. Barber, Mr. Pargaman, and Mr. Lawrence—and decided that we should have a court reporter come right then to take under oath the agreement of the parties so there would be no dispute the next morning or at any subsequent date as to what the agreement was. Judge Meyers agreed and got a court reporter out of bed at 1:00 a.m., who came and took down the all parties' dictation in Judge Meyers's presence. All the proper legal proceedings were prefaced and each party agreed to the presentation of their participation in the settlement agreement. By the next day the court reporter had transcribed the settlement documents, which were duly signed by all parties. Judge Myers ruled that the Borden County property was never community property of Mr. and Mrs. Heep, but had been owned by the plaintiffs since Mr. Heep's death, although Mrs. Heep had paid taxes on the income, which amounted to more than $700,000. Keep in mind that these were taxes paid on revenue derived from property that the judge ruled she did not own.

The next day I went to see Mrs. Heep to describe in detail the settlement agreement. But before I went out to see her, I visited with her certified public accountants, the firm of Maxwell, Locke & Ritter. With Mr. Ritter and Mr. Locke, I discussed that since Mrs. Heep, in making the settlement out of future income, was agreeing that from 1960 until the date of the settlement she had paid an income tax personally on that money and now, because of the settlement, she would not be the owner of the oil and gas interest and not have that income due her personally, although she had taken the proper depletion allowances from her income taxes. I know this is difficult to explain, but basically I asked Tom Locke and Mark Ritter to help me with a claim of right to be filed with the IRS so that we would recapture the $700,000 income taxes paid by Mrs. Heep on revenue that was not hers. The IRS accepted the claim, which eventually benefitted Texas A&M in the amount of the money that was recaptured. Over the next several years we were able to recover more than $700,000 from the IRS, again all to the benefit of Texas A&M.

When Mrs. Heep passed away in 1993, all of the assets—other than gifts that she gave to her family—went to the Heep Endowment in the Texas A&M Foundation. Mr. Maroney, Mr. Barber, and Mr. Pargaman were of tremendous help in strategic planning and in the preparation for trial as well as in taking depositions. They are not only fine lawyers, but men of character with extraordinary personal qualities. They understood Mrs. Heep's position and were completely sympathetic to her.

Upon Mrs. Heep's death, her assets transferred to Texas A&M and were eventually sold for about $20 million. By 2014, the Heep Endowment in the Texas A&M Foundation was valued at almost $32 million and had paid out more than $13 million to Texas A&M University for a variety of programs of national significance. I cannot prove that the strategic move of bringing the Texas A&M Foundation and Texas A&M into the lawsuit determined the outcome, but it had a material impact on the settlement and accrued to the benefit of Texas A&M. In recognizing the gifts of Mr. and Mrs. Heep, the A&M regents named their renowned Soil and Crop Sciences and Entomology Center in College Station for Minnie Belle and Herman F. Heep. I attended the dedication ceremony. No one was more pleased than I was by the A&M governing board's expression of gratitude for Mr. and Mrs. Heep's generosity.

CHAPTER 16

'Til Gabriel Blows His Horn!
You Can't Have Texas Without the Exes

W hen I got back to the University of Texas in the fall of 1945, I had to complete the third year of a B.B.A. degree plan to be eligible for admission to the law school. Under this plan, when you graduated from law school, you were awarded both a business degree and a law degree. I completed law school in two and a half years, and graduated with both degrees in January 1949.

By then, my attachment and loyalty to the university had grown from mere affection to devotion, as liberally as I have been able to express it. Wanting to maintain contact with friends, and reciprocate in some measure for what my university had done for me, I joined the Ex-Students Association (henceforth Texas Exes or the association). I went to the office, then located in the Texas Union, and gave John McCurdy, the executive director, a check for twenty dollars. The annual dues were ten dollars a year and the additional ten dollars was for membership for my fiancée, Charmaine Hooper. Mr. McCurdy's office was only an assortment of desks inside the front door of the Texas Union, an inadequate setup even then. I could not have imagined that I would have an important role in eventually acquiring suitable space for the association. Neither did I appreciate that on that very day, I had volunteered for a lifetime to preserve, protect, promote, and proclaim the importance and greatness of the University of Texas.

In those days the big event of the year for the Texas Exes in Austin was a fish fry on Lake Austin in August before the football season began. Initially, I sold tickets to the fish fry. We'd invite an assistant football coach to attend and speak to us about the upcoming season. In 1956, we advertised our annual gathering as a countywide meeting on March 2, and we met on the campus in the Regents' Room of the Main Building (now the Lee Jamail Room). The speaker was Leroy Jeffers, a lawyer from Houston, with the law firm of Vinson & Elkins, who was chairman of the University of Texas Board of Regents. Only about ten people attended, and three of them were the staff members of the Texas Exes. Our fare was simple hors d'oeuvres and soft drinks.

In fall of 1956, the University of Texas had a terrible football season, winning one game and losing nine. By December the board of regents and President Logan Wilson had a nationwide search underway for a new head coach. They settled on Bobby Dodd, the famous Georgia Tech coach, and he agreed to accept the position, but stipulated that he had to notify his governing board before a public announcement was made. However, when the *Austin American-Statesman* broke the news that he was coming, Dodd was embarrassed and withdrew from consideration. The burden of making progress with the search then fell to former head coach and athletic director Dana X. Bible, an advisor to the board of regents. Between 1937 and 1946, Bible had brought the Longhorn football program to national prominence, unforgettably when a team photo was the front-page feature in *Life* magazine in 1941. He recommended Darrell Royal, then the thirty-two-year-old head coach at the University of Washington. The regents interviewed Coach Royal and announced on December 28 that he would become our head football coach. Darrell completely disarmed them, charming them with his down-home manner, folksy wisdom, and knowledge of the game. He also impressed them as a quick study, able to call each of them by name after meeting them for the first time. They did not know that he had prepared for the interview by researching the background of each regent. He wrote each of their names on a card and memorized it. Such preparation was typical of Darrell Royal.

I went to see Coach Royal in his office at Gregory Gym the next day, December 29, 1956. The local Texas Exes had promoted me from selling fish-fry tickets to planning our get-togethers. I introduced myself to Coach Royal and asked him to be the guest speaker for our March 2 meeting. He immediately accepted. Since he was from Oklahoma, I had to explain that March 2 was Texas Independence Day, the date in 1836 when Texas declared its separation from Mexico and became the Republic of Texas. Coach Royal and I hit it off and became instant friends. He spoke to us in the Crystal Ballroom of the Driskill Hotel in downtown Austin. A record number of more than 450 people attended. I introduced him, and later he said, "Frank, if you want to come to any of the practices, you'll be welcome." That had never happened before. I accepted his invitation and have been going to football practices ever since. In 1959, I asked Lyndon Johnson, then majority leader in the U.S. Senate, to be our March 2 speaker. My law firm was doing considerable business with him and his family. He was well received. Several hundred people attended, and the event was a huge success. In the span of three or four years, we had progressed from only ten attendants to hundreds of people attending the March 2 gathering.

By 1958, more space and a larger staff were imperative for the Texas Exes to serve the growing number of alumni, if only to handle their inquiries. The regents and the president of the Texas Exes, John Holmes of Houston, appointed a committee that included me to review possibilities for additional facilities on the campus. By then, after a decade of practicing law in the politics of the capital city, I was convinced that the university would always require strong leadership to protect and promote its interests, which would require a vigorous alumni association that was significant and meaningful. Consequently, the association needed a permanent and suitable home to carry out its functions.

When the committee convened in the Texas Union for our first meeting in early 1959, Jack Maguire had succeeded Mr. McCurdy as executive director. To help resolve the space problem, university president Logan Wilson offered temporary space in the basement of the Home Economics building (now Gearing Hall) and indicated that in the long term, we could occupy the former home of Major George Littlefield, the Victorian mansion at Twenty-fourth Street and Whitis, a campus landmark. The Littlefield Home was an excellent location. At the time, it was fully utilized by the university's three ROTC programs—army, air force, and navy. Large naval guns (nonoperational) painted the dark gray of warships were mounted on concrete pads in the yard around the outside of the building. In 1964, ROTC was scheduled to move to a new building on the north side of Gregory Gym. Our committee was favorably impressed with the Littlefield Home, and we hired an interior decorator to advise us about how it might be adapted as offices for the alumni association.

Since the Littlefield Home would not be available for five years and the association needed more space right away, the offices were moved from the Texas Union to the basement of Gearing Hall, as I stated above. Despite the limitations, we had more space for the expanding services and programs for members. We also had an agreement with the university for the association to manage alumni records. The staff now numbered twelve, and we had new-fangled office equipment like key-punch machines, card sorters, and collators. Assuming responsibility for the management of alumni records was an important breakthrough for the Texas Exes because it truly made us an operational partner with the university in the increasingly important function of fundraising and public relations. Furthermore, the university paid us for the service because the administration and the regents needed the information for quality assessment purposes. It was important to know who among more than two hundred thousand former students had actually graduated; in what fields they had taken their degrees; the progress of their careers; and how to contact them.

While the association was undergoing this transition, Governor Price Daniel appointed Thornton Hardie of El Paso to the board of regents (March 1957 to January 1963). I knew "Judge Hardie," as we lawyers called him as a matter of respect, because he and I served together on a corporate board of directors. Not long after he became the regents chairman in March of 1961, he asked me to meet with him during a forthcoming trip to Austin. In addition to the business he wanted to discuss, I wanted to talk with him about the challenges facing the Texas Exes. At the time, I had three capacities with the association: I was the representative from Austin to the executive council, an officer of the association, and a member of the committee to improve the space situation. Although we now had more space in the Home Economics basement, I heard the staff call it a "mole hole," which was conceivable because it was underground and hard to find. Some people worried that it might become the association's permanent home.

When Judge Hardie arrived in Austin, I picked him up at the airport and took him to the location of the current Alumni Center. It was a pretty shabby area. Trash and beer bottles left over from weekend parties along Waller Creek were removed on Monday mornings. When I said, "This is where we should build the Alumni Center," he replied, "Frank, you must have lost your mind." But as we walked around the area, he came to appreciate the location—along a stream that could be beautified and across San Jacinto Boulevard from Memorial Stadium. After initial misgivings, Thornton Hardie caught the vision and, at his invitation, I began discussions with the board of regents for the leasing of the ground space by the Ex-Students Association for the construction of the Alumni Center. In November 1961 the board agreed, and we signed a long-term ground lease agreement permitting the association to use the space that I had shown Judge Hardie earlier in the year.

We still had to raise money for the construction. John Holmes, Jack Maguire, and I started the fundraising program, chaired by Sterling Holloway. Holmes was still president of the association, and we flew around the state in his plane to meet with local alumni chapters. More than four thousand Texas Exes eventually contributed. When I became president of the association in the spring of 1964, my number one goal was to complete the project. When we had raised about twelve million dollars, we still needed about a million dollars to finish out the building and to furnish it. The board of regents came to our rescue. The board held in trust a fund set up by the family of a former student, Lila B. Etter. The purpose of the trust was broadly stated to benefit the university. The regents agreed to transfer funds from the trust to the association, and we named the building the Lila B. Etter Alumni Center. Construction began in 1964, and we dedicated the Alumni Center on April 3, 1965. Former governor Allan Shivers presided at the ceremony. It was a proud day for the association and for me. As president of the association, my role was to present the key to the building to the chairman of the board of regents. Presentation of the key symbolized the fact that since we had intentionally constructed the building on University of Texas land, the university actually owned the building and leased it to the Texas Exes.

Another hot issue that came up in 1964 was a proposal to demolish Memorial Stadium and build a new stadium nine miles north of the main campus on the university's 475-acre tract in northwest Austin that is now the J. J. Pickle Research Campus. Advocates for the move maintained that the university was out of space on the "Forty Acres," hemmed in between Guadalupe on the west, Red River on the east, Nineteenth Street (now Martin Luther King Jr. Blvd.) on the south, and Twenty-sixth Street (now Dean Keeton) on the north. These boundaries would change dramatically within a few years, especially with the expansion to the east. The advocates, many well placed, took the issue all the way to Governor John Connally, himself a Distinguished Alumnus of the association and graduate of the law school. To counter them, Jack Maguire, Coach Royal, and I embarked on a personal campaign to persuade the regents that Memorial Stadium should remain where it was. We invited each member of the board of regents individually to a private lunch in the new Alumni Center where we explained the history of the stadium and the importance of its location to students and alumni. Our reasons were nostalgic as well as tangible. Coach Royal was persuasive in his argument for keeping the stadium where it was. High on his list of concerns was the well-being of student athletes. The stadium was near Moore-Hill Hall, where most athletes lived; rehabilitation facilities for injured athletes were in the stadium; and the time that would be required for them to commute to the north Austin location was incalculable and would dramatically increase over time.

The regents decided in late 1965 that Memorial Stadium should remain where it was and, at the same time, approved its expansion with an upper deck on the west side and the renovation of classroom and offices within the stadium known as Belmont Hall. In 1963, Governor Connally had appointed Frank C. Erwin Jr. of Austin to the board of regents. Frank was a longtime friend of mine, and he emphatically favored the project. He would serve on the board until 1975 and was its chairman from 1966 to 1971. I was still president of the Texas Exes when the board of regents appointed engineering professor J. Neils Thompson and me to co-chair a committee to raise the funds for the stadium. Professor Thompson was chairman of the UT athletic council, the standing committee that governed intercollegiate athletics. Although Darrell

Royal was officially the director of athletics, Professor Thompson and the athletic council were responsible for making policy decisions that determined the future of the overall athletic program. He was an evangelist for the benefits to the university of intercollegiate athletics, and the perfect partner for me in fundraising.

We got a ruling from the Internal Revenue Service that all donations made to the university to expand and enhance the stadium would be tax deductible. To my knowledge, this was the first time that *all* contributions for the construction of athletic facilities were deductible from tax-liable income. We set about to raise the money; it was another labor of love for me. With some of the money we raised, we created the Two Hundred Horns Club on the ninth floor of the stadium's west side as a 501(c)3 tax-exempt nonprofit organization called the Longhorn Educational Foundation. I did the legal work to obtain the tax-exempt status for the foundation, which has been folded into the university Athletic Department and no longer exists as an entity. Under the umbrella of the foundation, we created the Centennial Club, which has been greatly expanded. Originally, it had two hundred members with private seating, food, and beverages available. From the beginning, we had more applications for membership than we could accommodate.

The financial health of the Texas Exes was closely related to intercollegiate athletics, which relied on the Exes to help market ticket sales. Many people joined the Ex-Students Association because of the priority accorded to members over nonmembers in purchasing football tickets. The order of priorities was printed on the ticket application distributed by the Athletic Department. First priority was for lettermen (men with outstanding records in athletics); second was the faculty; and, third in priority was members of Ex-Students Association. If you were a member, you'd check that square on the application, anticipating you'd be third priority in preference for the right to purchase tickets to games in Memorial Stadium. Memorial Stadium was not the size that it is today, however, and seating capacity was limited. Someone raised the issue of what "priority" actually meant, and I appointed a committee of the executive council to review the issue with the Athletic Department. The committee reported that the priority was real, but that it did not assure access to the better seats in the stadium. And we immediately had a decline of about four thousand members. That became our challenge—to rebuild the number of members of the Ex-Students Association. Jack Maguire and I spent a lot of time with the association's executive council discussing what we should do. We formed a membership committee and were able to regain the four thousand we had lost and increase the total membership to about sixteen thousand. I know those numbers do not seem large in comparison to later standards, but they were significant then, and the survival of the association was at stake.

The association also had the challenge of converting records from microfiche to a fully computerized system to maintain alumni records for the university. On the cutting edge of technology at the time, it was a new adventure in management that involved raising substantial sums of money to acquire computers, the staff learning new skills to use them, programming the computers to "talk" to the computers at the university, and sharing data with appropriate university personnel for immediate access to the records. After several meetings with the board of regents and the president of the university, the regents agreed to compensate the Texas Exes for the record keeping. The effort was a win-win situation for all parties.

Another important development in the history of the Ex-Students Association was the creation of the Distinguished Alumnus Awards that are granted annually to former students who have distinguished themselves professionally and by service to the University of Texas. The motivation to create the Distinguished Alumnus Awards was that the university was prohibited by law from granting honorary degrees, except with specific authorization by the Texas Legislature. Lacking the ability to award honorary degrees while wanting to recognize high achieving and prominent alumni, the idea of the Distinguished Alumnus Award began to be considered. The concept was put together at the Headliners Club in a meeting of several association officers, Jack Maguire, and myself in 1957. It was approved by the executive council, and in 1958 we made the first awards in a very upscale, black-tie event at the Crystal Ballroom of the Driskill Hotel before a sold-out crowd. The first recipients included Sam Rayburn, Speaker of the U.S. House of Representatives, and Walter Prescott Webb, a distinguished professor of history at the university. Until then, the university had awarded only one honorary doctorate, to Vice President John Nance Garner in 1935. Since the first DAAs were awarded in 1958, the association has awarded more than two hundred, while the university has awarded but three honorary doctorates, to President and Mrs. Johnson in 1964, and to President George H. W. Bush 1990. In 1991, I received a Distinguished Alumnus Award, which I regard as one of the most significant honors of my life.

One of the important customs of the Texas Exes is an annual gathering of former presidents for wide-ranging discussions about the well-being of the association, about the university, and about the relationship between the two. The Texas Exes and the university are independent, but interdependent to some extent, and certainly mutually beneficial. I have not missed a meeting of former presidents because the discussions concern serious issues for the present and the future. Generally, they focus on how the Texas Exes:

- Connect and engage supporters of the university with each other;
- Support students and encourage their achievement;
- Recognize alumni accomplishments;
- Remain strong financially; and,
- Make the association indispensable to the university.

In listening to other past presidents and reflecting on my own experiences, I have reached the overriding conviction that the association best serves the university apart from the university. To put it another way, the independence of the Texas Exes from the university is essential for it to serve the university in the best possible ways. Independence allows the association to be an advocate for the university when, as often happens, political influences prohibit or inhibit employees (the president and even the regents) from speaking out. This often occurs when the state legislature is enmeshed in the appropriations process, but there have been other significant episodes. One was the U.S. Supreme Court's 1996 decision in the Hopwood case, which prohibited university officials from using race as a consideration in admissions policies. At the time, many feared the limitation would lead to the "re-segregation of higher education." To avoid defeat in efforts to diversify the student body, the Texas Exes organized an outreach program for minority students and raised more than ten million dollars in scholarship funds to attract some of the state's top students. In 2003, the Supreme Court reversed its decision in the Hopwood case. In 2012, the Texas Exes helped establish the new medical school at UT Austin by working successfully to encourage Travis County voters to vote for the Central Health Proposition 1, which was not initially popular as it raised the ad valorem tax rate by five cents. I was actively involved in this initiative from the beginning, and I am proud of its success.

Only a few universities have independent alumni associations like ours, among them the University of North Carolina-Chapel Hill, the University of Michigan, and the University of Virginia. An independent association of volunteer alumni can do things for the university that the university cannot do for itself. Independence does not mean resistance to change or improvement, but it does mean we are fully vested in the University of Texas in many positive ways without being officially part of it. Remember the slogan, "You can't have Texas without the Exes," and, as I see it, the "Exes without Texas." Count me in "'Til Gabriel blows his horn."

CHAPTER 17

Integrating the Campus:
The Regents and Leon Jaworski

I N NOVEMBER 1961, the University of Texas System Board of Regents appointed Leon Jaworski of Houston and me as special defense counsel in a suit to force the university to admit three African American students to segregated dormitories. I want to be clear that the issue was not about admitting them to the university, but admitting them to a dormitory that was segregated. Jaworski, later to achieve lasting fame as the Watergate prosecutor, was then president of the Texas State Bar and the American College of Trial Lawyers. He was exactly twenty years older than me. He preferred to be called "Colonel," the rank he attained in the army while prosecuting war crimes in the United States during the war and in Germany immediately after the cessation of hostilities. When I say he prosecuted "war crimes in the United States," I mean bringing to justice fanatical Nazi prisoners of war in this country who brutalized and, in some instances, killed fellow German soldiers who cooperated with American authorities in charge of their POW camps. In 1961, Jaworski published a book, *After Fifteen Years,* recounting his experiences as a war crimes prosecutor that I recommend for its lessons about the corruption and evils of Nazism. In terms of professional standards and performance, Leon Jaworski was generally acknowledged as the pre-eminent trial lawyer of his generation, and I felt privileged to work with him.

My participation in this case was the first of many instances in which

I was privileged to assist the regents and the university with a challenging legal issue. Usually, the board of regents contracted with my law firm, which assigned me to the case. In the coming decades, I would help the regents acquire land, reconcile disputes, and negotiate contracts, as well as with litigation. Sometimes, I was asked to serve on a committee or to investigate a problem and report back, as with the Brackenridge Tract of land on the west side of Austin, which I will discuss later. In these cases I did not benefit financially for my services. If my law firm collected a fee for my services and allocated a portion of it to me, I reimbursed the university in like amount.

The case was styled *Leroy Sanders, et al. vs. Harry H. Ransom, et al.* Leroy Sanders was a student. Dr. Ransom was chancellor of the University of Texas System. The other defendants were the regents, UT Austin president Joe Smiley, the director of housing, and the managers of the residence halls. The plaintiffs had retained a local civil rights lawyer, Sam Houston Clinton, who asked the court to take jurisdiction under the authority of the Fourteenth Amendment to the U.S. Constitution and order the desegregation of all university dormitories. Clinton's petition maintained that the university's policies denied blacks "their rights, privileges, and immunities as secured by the constitution and the laws of the United States." Five years earlier in September 1956, the university had begun "admit[ting] qualified applicants on all levels without reference to race," but certain extracurricular activities and dormitories remained segregated. More than twenty-one thousand students were enrolled in the university. There was dormitory space for three thousand.

Before Jaworski and I could go to work on the case, a public controversy erupted when Will Wilson, the attorney general of Texas, objected to our appointment. Wilson argued that he should be the board of regents' lawyer because, by statute, the attorney general normally represents all state agencies, and the University of Texas is a state agency. He used strong language in his protests, denouncing several regents by name and telling newspapers our appointment was an encroachment upon his position and authority. Eventually, the issue was settled in favor of the board of regents, on the strength of a precedent from the late 1930s when previous regents had hired Dan Moody, a former governor of Texas, to represent them. Since the regents were apprehensive about the suit and its ongoing negotiations, they could have feared it might become a political football if Wilson was involved. He held a statewide elected office and had already announced that he intended to run for governor the next year, 1962—which he did, and lost. Obviously, he was more political than the regents wanted in a case that was already highly publicized. They wanted to resolve this matter as a legal process rather than as a political spectacle. In this, they were mindful that the university has many constituents—alumni, students, and faculty, the people of Texas, and the legislature —whose respect for the institution and how it conducts is business was important.

Some people interpreted the regents' decision to hire Jaworski and me as an effort to "maintain segregation at all costs." If so, no one told me. Neither Colonel Jaworski nor I were privy to what the regents said in closed meetings, and we definitely did not work on the case with an attitude of perpetuating segregation. Our client was the University of Texas System Board of Regents, which we represented in a professional way.

Since Jaworski was in Houston, I did most of the legwork in Austin—getting depositions and meeting with regents, plaintiffs, and the plaintiffs' attorney—while keeping Jaworski informed. In a fortunate coincidence, I knew the plaintiffs' attorney, Sam Houston Clinton, from having helped settle an estate in his family. He had run for office in Travis County when Austin was a close-knit community, and most lawyers were acquainted to some extent. I could talk with him in a personal way as well as in a legal way. In our conversations, it became clear that the black students wanted more than to desegregate the dorms. They also wanted to integrate the band, eating facilities, and all extracurricular activities. In effect, their real goal was the complete integration of the university in every aspect, socially as well as legally.

I conveyed the gist of my conversations with Mr. Clinton to Jaworski, and then to the chairman of the board of regents, initially Thornton Hardie of El Paso until Judge W. W. Heath succeeded him in December 1962, a year after the suit was filed. Judge Heath was my neighbor in Austin, so we were readily available to each other. Heath and Hardie would discuss my conversations with Mr. Clinton and then instruct me about how to proceed. Clinton did likewise with his clients, and there was a lot of back-and-forth between us. Part of the regents' quandary was deciding whether a particular action on their part would have an unintended consequence; would it enhance integration or segregation. This was the early 1960s, and we were attempting to solve a problem that involved conflicting attitudes about social relationships between blacks and whites that were more rigid and fixed than they were only a few years later.

Jurisdiction for the case was the federal court, and the judge for the Austin district at the time was Ben H. Rice Jr. He had served as the federal judge in Austin since before I was admitted to the bar in 1949. We had a number of pretrial hearings before Judge Rice in open court as well as in his chambers. The meetings in chambers usually included Colonel Jaworski, me, and the attorney for the plaintiffs. Judge Rice outlined his thoughts with respect to the trial process, the timing of the trial, and the pretrial discovery that we entered into. On some occasions, I met *ex parte* with Judge Rice in his chambers—in private with no others present. He advised me that the parties to the suit should not propose a motion to set the trial date without his prior approval. I can almost hear him saying, "I am relying on you to apprise the court of developments in this case." He did not want any surprises. He enforced a high level of decorum in his court, and I followed his instructions to the letter and showed him the utmost respect. When I entered his chambers, I always remained standing, even after he invited me to sit down.

Mr. Jaworski and I drafted an answer to the suit on behalf of the university; I went over it with Chairman Heath, who, in turn, reviewed it with the board. When the regents approved, we filed it in the court on behalf of the University of Texas. More discussions with Judge Rice followed. We did some pretrial discovery and took the depositions of the plaintiffs. Then came a surprising revelation that certain professors in the UT School of Law were assisting the plaintiffs with research and briefings. In an attempt to stop it, the board of regents issued a press release warning the law faculty that "any member . . . who directly or indirectly assists the Plaintiffs in this suit would be guilty of disloyalty to his employer and subject to dismissal or other disciplinary action." Page Keeton, dean of the law school, wrote to Regent Thornton Hardie that this was "an improper means of communicating a direction to a partic-ular faculty regarding proper conduct on their part." When the regents announced new rules under which the administration could fire a tenured professor, Professor Gus Hodges, a highly respected senior member of the law school faculty, informed the board that such attempted intimidation could result in the resignation of the entire faculty. These incidents may have influenced regents' attitudes and, therefore, the final settlement, but they did not distract Jaworski and me in our efforts to find a solution to which all parties could agree. We paid no attention to news media accounts.

While much of this case was handled in chamber meetings with Judge Rice, in pretrial hearings, and other meetings, Jaworski and I met with Bill Heath—and occasionally with the entire board—to outline possible defenses and the implications of various settlements for the university. We discussed the nationwide status of integration or desegregation. We thoroughly briefed the regents on those issues. Then they deliberated in private without Jaworski or me. After those closed-door meetings, Chairman Heath usually asked me to meet with him, and he would tell me what the board was willing to do to resolve the litigation. I was more available to him than Colonel Jaworski in Houston. My credibility with the plaintiffs' attorney was important. He and his clients had to trust me in order for negotiations to proceed and, ultimately, to succeed. The same was true of my relationship with Heath and affected how forthcoming he would be with me. Whenever I met with Clinton, I conveyed the regents' position, which he reported to his clients. That's how our discussions were carried out, all the while anticipating that eventually we would go to trial, but hoping that we would not.

Eventually, Chairman Heath gave me an outline of the board's position that paralleled Jaworski's and my thinking. He authorized me, after discussions with Jaworski, to tell Mr. Clinton that, if his clients would dismiss the lawsuit, the board of regents would completely integrate the University of Texas on an agreed timetable and accomplish his clients' objectives. I did as he asked, and when I heard from Mr. Clinton the next time, he had conferred with his clients, who had agreed to dismiss their suit against the university without prejudice. The board of regents then went about implementing the agreement. The practical meaning of dismissal without prejudice was that the plaintiffs could have reinstigated their suit if the university did not fulfill its commitment. The plaintiffs did not lose or waive their rights or privileges when they dropped their suit in May 1964.

Soon after, we entered the mutually agreed time period during which the University of Texas was progressively desegregated in all aspects. We knew that not every problem had been solved or anticipated. Years of adaptation and cultural change within the university lay ahead, but our litigation had established the legal and policy basis for integration to proceed. In November 1963, two years after the suit was filed, the regents unanimously ordered desegregation of all student activities with the exception of women's dorms, still pending in federal court from the original law suit. Until the plaintiffs dropped their suit the following May, the court had jurisdiction over the dormitories, originally the central concern of the suit. When the Civil Rights Act of 1964 was enacted in July of that year—a law that generally prohibited discrimination against minorities and women in schools, workplaces, and public accommodations—the University of Texas was already in compliance.

I have often been asked what were my true feelings about the facts of the case. Was I privately on the side of the plaintiffs while representing the defendants? I can say that in my law practice I never tried to impose my personal thoughts on a case in litigation unless asked by my client. And that's what I did in this case. My objective was to represent the University of Texas Board of Regents in the best manner, legally and otherwise, that I could. I believe Colonel Jaworski's attitude was similar to mine.

CHAPTER 18

Brackenridge Tract, Campus Expansion, and Frank Erwin

O NE OF THE MOST CONTROVERSIAL and valuable real estate hold-
ings of the University of Texas is the so-called Brackenridge
Tract, approximately 345 acres of land along the east side of the
Colorado River in Austin about three miles west of the campus proper.
Originally 503 acres, the land takes its name from its donor, George W.
Brackenridge (1832–1920), who gave the unimproved raw land to the
university in 1910 and 1911 and made the University of Texas Board of
Regents its stewards. Then accessible only by wagon or horseback, the
expansion of metropolitan Austin and the explosive population growth
of Central Texas has since made the Brackenridge Tract an island of
mostly open green space in the heart of an intense urban area that is
expanding both outward to suburbs and up with downtown high-rise
office and apartment buildings. As Austin grows, the increasing monetary value of the Brackenridge Tract is incalculable.

About three-fourths of the tract is ideal for open space or parkland,
which is the impassioned goal of neighborhood groups and environ-
mentalists, with whom members of the Austin City Council tend to
agree. One the other side, there are real estate developers and investors
who see the Brackenridge Tract as a virtual gold mine that they want
to exploit.

However, the Brackenridge Tract belongs to the University of Texas
at Austin, which requires an ever-increasing stream of revenue to be an

institution "of the first-class," as charged in the state constitution, and to further its aspirations for world-class status, as it is recognized in many global rankings. In my association with the university I have learned that excellence is a moving target that constantly rises. That's because institutional excellence is always about competing with peer institutions that have similar aspirations to scale the ladder of worldwide recognition and appreciation. As I have often said, I want the University of Texas to be the best in the world in whatever it undertakes. For this, an endless flow of money is required. I believe the board of regents is ethically and legally bound to use the Brackenridge Tract for academic purposes or to generate revenues that support the educational mission of the university, as Mr. Brackenridge clearly intended. I am a citizen of Austin, and my home is near the Brackenridge Tract, but I do not think the University of Texas is obligated to provide recreational green space for me and my fellow citizens. Some 141 acres of the tract are now used as a golf course by a contract with the City of Austin that will expire in 2019. To my stated conviction, I want to add that I believe the Brackenridge Tract can be developed for multiple uses and generate substantial revenue for the university, but I do not have a plan to accomplish it.

Before going further into my story, I should tell you why I became involved with Brackenridge Tract issues and controversies. The ultimate reason is that George Brackenridge was a shrewd philanthropist as well as generous with the University of Texas. When he gave the land to the University of Texas, he placed a clause in the deed that the tract would revert to Jackson County, Texas, for the benefit of its free public schools if the University of Texas did not use it for the purposes stated in his gift deed. I believe he knew exactly what he was doing. He had definite ideas about the use of his gifts and had excellent legal assistance in writing those ideas into the deeds. For example, he gave the City of San Antonio the park that bears his name, with the contingency that if certain stipulations were not abided by, the title would pass to the State of Texas for the benefit of the University of Texas.

In the early 1960s, the regents planned to build student housing on a portion of the Brackenridge Tract. They wanted to finance the project by selling revenue bonds backed by the tract itself. That's when they discovered the significance of Mr. Brackenridge's reversion clause. It "clouded" their deed and the bonds could not be sold. At that point, January 1963, the regents engaged my law firm to clarify the title, and the case was assigned to me. Thus, I became the board's special counsel to validate the bond issue and to clear other contingencies to obtain fee simple title (absolute ownership) to the Brackenridge property for the University of Texas Board of Regents.

I filed a suit in the 126th District Court of Travis County on behalf of the University of Texas to validate the revenue bonds that the university wanted to issue. In April 1964, the court approved the relief sought by the regents, who then issued $1,800,000 in revenue bonds to construct two hundred units of married-student housing. Nevertheless, the university still needed to remove the "cloud" from its title to the Brackenridge Tract so it could use the property for the ongoing development of the university. Judge W. W. Heath, the board of regents chairman, asked me to review the issue and brief the regents on how to eliminate the contingent remainder for Jackson County that Colonel Brackenridge had placed on the title. I prepared the documents and presented them to Judge Heath and the board of regents. We then began negotiating with Jackson County's Commissioner's Court, whose main negotiator was the county judge. The point man for the University of Texas was W. H. Bauer, a regent with strong connections to Jackson County. I assisted Mr. Bauer. The negotiations resulted in the university paying Jackson County fifty thousand dollars to relinquish the county's interest in the property and transfer it to the university. While this was obviously a good deal for the university, I think it was fair for Jackson County, because I cannot envision a board of regents violating the covenant with Colonel Brackenridge to use the property forever for the benefit of the University of Texas. So the chances of Jackson County ever receiving title to that property were unlikely. From my perspective, fifty thousand dollars out of the blue to Jackson County was a good deal for them.

These developments involved negotiations and court hearings over several years. In late 1966, the Jackson County Commissioners formally conveyed their interest in the Brackenridge Tract to the board of regents. In October 1967, the District Court in Travis County declared that the board held fee simple interest in the tract.

While I was working as special counsel to the board of regents on problems related to the Brackenridge Tract, Governor Connally appointed Frank C. Erwin Jr. to the board in March 1963. He immediately took a strong interest in the Brackenridge Tract and was instrumental in the enactment of a series of bills that clarified and formalized the authority of the University of Texas Board of Regents over the Brackenridge Tract.

Almost forty years after I served as special counsel to the board of regents to clarify the university's title to the Brackenridge Tract, the board brought me into the issue again. James Huffines, the regents chairman in 2006, appointed me to a ten-member task force chaired by my friend Larry Temple to recommend "the best and most prudent ways to utilize [the Brackenridge Tract] to the maximum benefit of the University of Texas at Austin." First among the task force's findings and recommendations was that the board of regents has a "legal and ethical obligation" to carry out Colonel Brackenridge's mandate "to use the tract for the benefit of the educational mission of the university." That has been my judgment since I first studied the Brackenridge Tract in 1963. Because the land has become extraordinarily valuable, it will continue to be controversial, certainly as we approach the year 2019 when the City of Austin's contract to operate a golf course on the grounds will expire.

Frank Erwin

Since Frank Erwin was one of the most influential of my contemporary advocates for the university, I want to say more about him. In his confirmation hearing before a committee of the state senate, he expressed my philosophy exactly when he said his goal for the university was "to be the best in classroom, in laboratories, on the football field, everywhere." If Frank Erwin was anything, he was an advocate! He argued for and defended any project or organization that interested him, none more so than the University of Texas. At times he tried to be diplomatic, but it did not come naturally to him. Frank had brains, and he respected brains. No one could push him around. A Phi Beta Kappa graduate, he understood that a true, comprehensive university included the arts and humanities, libraries, museums, and prized collections, as well as vocationally oriented professional schools—and he tried to make them all better. As an undergraduate he was an outspoken supporter of President Homer Rainey when the regents wanted to fire him, which they finally did in 1944. After Frank went off to the navy in 1942, he wrote an impassioned letter to *The Daily Texan* urging students to "Keep up the fight for Rainey and the University," saying when he and others "return[ed] after the war, they would continue the fight for freedom." His closing line was "Give 'em Hell!!!" Which was exactly the opposite of his attitude toward students, deans, and presidents who disagreed with him a quarter-century later. Remember that he fired Arts and Sciences dean John Silber; and that while Frank was highly active as chairman of the board of regents, the distinguished Norman Hackerman resigned as president of the university to accept the same position at Rice University; and the esteemed Harry Ransom retired as chancellor of the UT System.

Erwin and I had been friends almost from the get-go when we got out of law school. I fully supported him when he organized the Longhorn Club, over the objections of Dana X. Bible, then UT director of intercollegiate athletics. We had offices in the same building and had a personal relationship as well as a legal one. I once represented him in an amusing incident involving Kappa Sigma, his UT social fraternity. The fraternity was one of his passions. The Kappa Sig House was located on West Nineteenth Street (now Martin Luther King Jr. Boulevard) facing straight up University Boulevard toward the UT Tower. To cordon off a construction project on an adjoining lot, the contractor built a fence between his building site and the Kappa Sig property. When Frank looked over the scene, he concluded the fence encroached on fraternity property, and he kicked it down. He actually kicked it down on the ground. Then he called me because he anticipated a complaint, perhaps a hearing, about what he had done. He was in the right, and nothing came of the incident, except that the contractor rebuilt the fence so that it did not encroach on Kappa Sig property. Like Admiral Farragut, Frank's attitude was, "Damn the torpedoes. Full steam ahead!"

While Frank Erwin and I agreed on many issues, I disagreed with his idea to have numerous universities of Texas across the state, when the University of Texas System was expanding under his leadership in the late 1960s and early 1970s. I favored a UT System, but with one, and only one, institution called the University of Texas, the one in Austin. I argued with Frank about retaining the name of the University of Texas without adding "at Austin." But Frank felt that developing the UT System with institutions belonging to the system in the various geographic areas of the state would be in the best interest of higher education and for the University of Texas System. He believed the collective influence of the several institutions would be helpful both in developing a state-wide system and in lobbying the legislature and other state agencies. My attitude has not changed, but time moves on, and I relate now to UT Austin, which has a special cachet. Yet I am proud that my diploma is inscribed with "The University of Texas."

Although Frank was opinionated, in my judgment he always had the best interests of the university at heart. At the same time, he was often intolerant of those who disagreed with him, whether faculty, students, administrators, or other board members. He cared more about what got done rather than how it was done. Frank "grew" during his twelve years on the board of regents (1963–1975), the last six as chairman. In the long term, his influence greatly enhanced the university and one only needs to review the historical development of the campus to see that we were lucky to have him.

Campus Expansion: East and South

I was still special counsel to the board of regents when Frank Erwin succeeded Bill Heath as chairman in 1966. He and I were in agreement that the "Forty Acres" required more ground space, and that one area to get it was east of Red River Street (now Robert Dedman Drive), which was then the eastern boundary of the campus. I want to emphasize that university property on the east side ended with the football stadium and that the university was entering a period of tremendous growth. As student enrollment increased from about thirty thousand to fifty thousand, more classrooms and laboratories were needed. Planning was underway for the Bass Performing Arts Center and the Bates

Recital Hall. Those two additions alone would require the entire area known for generations as Clark Field, where the New York Yankees had once played the Longhorns, and famous for its limestone cliff and goat path in left center field, where the carillon now stands. Gregory Gym was inadequate for intercollegiate basketball. Winning national championships in football in 1963 and 1969 heightened the enthusiasm of UT sports fans, a clear signal that the athletic facilities should be expanded. Frank Erwin and I were of like minds about prospects for growth and the elbow room that the university would require in the future.

We were not thinking about limited or gradual addition of campus facilities, but about very large enrollment growth with the arrival of the baby boomers and especially the dramatic impact of Lyndon Johnson's presidency on the university campus. Erwin was a political confidant of LBJ, and I had represented Johnson business interests for many years. Both of us visited the White House from time to time, and we were privy to discussions about the likelihood of the Johnson presidential library and museum being built on the campus. At the same time, President (later system chancellor) Harry Ransom and professors like Bill Livingston and Emmitt Redford were intent on expanding the government department's bureau of public affairs into a full-blown school to honor President Johnson's legacy, which is exactly what happened.

Therefore, at the direction of the board of regents, I began investigating piece by piece all property within these boundaries for acquisition by the university: Red River Street on the west (now Robert Dedman Drive), Nineteenth Street (now Martin Luther King Boulevard) on the south, Interstate 35 on the east, and Twenty-Sixth Street (now Dean Keeton Street) on the north. Within this area, there were many private homes, several fraternity and sorority houses, numerous boarding houses, duplexes, and rent houses. Longstanding and strong supporters of the university owned some of the property, among them John B. Holmes, a Distinguished Alumnus in 1965, who had built exceptional student housing units there. Another was the home of the distinguished university naturalist and writer, Roy Bedichek, at 801 East Twenty-Third Street, which is now part of the parking lot for the LBJ Library. Negotiating sales prices was often a sticky proposition, like with the lady who agreed to sell if we assured her that the magnificent live oaks that stood around her home would be preserved, which they were, and can now be seen to the west of the Joe C. Thompson Conference Center. In planning this entire development, we were mindful of Mrs. Lyndon Johnson's intense interest in preserving trees. When the ground was leveled in the area around the LBJ School, we saved trees by leaving them either on high mounds or in pits with walls around them to hold back the soil.

For decisions about these individual properties, I conferred with Frank Erwin, and he supported my recommendations to the board of regents. In a number of cases, I recommended more money than the appraised value or the acceptance of an unusual condition in order to obtain clear title to a property. We did not exercise the university's constitutional right to condemn property, although I was authorized to do so, and the threat of it brought some reluctant owners to the negotiating table. In this way, the entire area between Robert Dedman Drive and Interstate 35 became part of the campus, making space for the Thompson Conference Center, the LBJ Library, the Mike A. Myers Track and Soccer Stadium, and Sid Richardson Hall, which houses the LBJ School of Public Affairs, the Dolph Briscoe Center for American History, and the Teresa Lozano Long Institute of Latin American Studies—and, I am proud to say, the practice fields that were subsequently named for me.

Later I negotiated the purchase of land east of Interstate 35 that became Disch-Falk Field. Still later I represented the regents in dealings with the City of Austin to acquire the acreage south of MLK Boulevard and north of Fifteenth Street between Red River and Trinity, except for the area around two buildings that the university already owned—Arno Nowotny and John Hargis Halls. The city had purchased the land from private owners for redevelopment through the federally funded Urban Renewal program. The city could have retained the Urban Renewal acreage, and the five-member Austin City Council was split two-to-two with one undecided member about keeping it or deeding it to the university. The undecided member was Mr. Ben White, with whom I had gotten well acquainted through his friendship with former mayor Tom Miller, who had passed on a few years earlier. Meanwhile, I had helped Mr. White in his election campaigns, and eventually he voted to convey the land to the university, which became the basic footprint for the UT Austin Dell Medical School. This acquisition also made room for the

School of Nursing, the Collections Deposit Library, the Trinity Parking Garage, and the land where now stands the Frank C. Erwin Special Events Center and the Denton Cooley Practice Facility. In these ways, I participated in acquiring property that made possible the development of the campus as it came to be.

CHAPTER 19

Longhorn Football and the Game of Life

My passion for Texas Longhorn football is in my blood and beyond my control. It burns in me like an inherited trait. I cannot do anything about it and would not if I could. It is part of my life, and I love it!

I recognize that not everyone is as enthusiastic about athletics, especially football, as I am. Actually, I think you can argue for intercollegiate athletics both factually and emotionally. An obvious fact is that no other function allows the alumni, students, and other constituents to relate to the university in such large numbers. In practice, athletics are useful for teaching the importance of preparing, competing, overcoming obstacles, and putting forth your best effort until the final whistle blows. You have probably noticed that people who are successful in competitive sports are often successful in competitive occupations, like law or business.

In many ways, football is a metaphor for life. "Life is a contact sport," I like to say. That may be an exaggerated figure of speech, but in both life and football you get knocked down, and if you don't get up, you lose. If you quit, you will be beaten every time because there are always players on the opposing team who want to win, and they will whip you if you let them. To carry the comparison further, in my life there have been more "thirds and long," than "seconds and one." Football fans know that "third and long" is a predicament while "second down and one yard" to go for a first down is a good situation to be in.

Football is more important to people in Texas than in most other states because of the competitive heritage of the state. Texas came into being by fighting for its independence as a nation and winning against the odds. The "can do" competitive spirit of Texans is rooted in our history.

During the war, when I dreamed about coming home and returning to the university, I thought a lot about Longhorn football, but the hope that inspired me was the possibility of earning my degree, completing law school, passing the bar exam, and working as a lawyer. Academics was then, and remains, my primary interest in the university. In fact, if all of the numerous gifts I have directed to institutions in the University of Texas System and to Texas A&M were totaled, the tally would show that far more money has gone to academic, medical, and research activities than to athletic programs. I take great pride in the endowments I have helped create. Having thus clarified that my commitment to academic endeavors surmounts athletics, I want to elaborate on a few of the rewarding intersections of my life with Longhorn football.

In the fall of 1945, I got out of the army a few weeks before the OU game, played then as now on the second Saturday in October in Dallas during the state fair. Since I didn't have a ticket, I listened to the game on the radio. Games would not be televised for another decade. My favorite sportscaster before the war, Kern Tips, was still doing the games on the radio for the Humble Oil and Refining Company. His vivid and original descriptions challenged listeners to create a mental image of what had actually happened on the field. If a ball was fumbled in the handoff between a quarterback and a running back, he might say it was a "malfunction at the junction," and you'd have to imagine what that looked like. His unpredictable, colorful narration kept you engaged with the game, compelling you to hang on his words for more. If a quarterback was dropped for a loss, he'd say, "He had to peel it and eat it that time." While you were trying to figure that one out, he might say a receiver who caught a low-thrown ball "was pickin' 'em off the daisies." With me listening on the radio, we won the 1945 OU game, 12 to 7, and I have been to every OU game since then! And this is 2015. The first home game after

I got back to the university was against Rice on October 27, and we lost 7 to 6, our only loss of the season. Since then, I have missed only one game in Memorial Stadium, against Missouri on October 18, 2008, when I went to Dallas to receive an award from the Congressional Medal of Honor Society.

My return to the university coincided with the Bobby Layne era in Longhorn football and baseball. In the annals of competitive athletics, Layne deserves to be remembered for two reasons. The obvious thing was his athletic ability, which was demonstrated by the records he established. More importantly for me, however, he personified the American spirit at the end of the war. The war shaped my values in ways that enabled me to identify with many of his most admirable qualities. He combined physical ability with charismatic leadership and competitiveness in every game situation. To be around him was to sense that he was bold, confident, capable, intensely competitive, and dominant. Truly a winner, he was therefore indispensable for his teammates.

Layne became an athletic legend shortly after he enrolled in the university at the age of seventeen in the spring of 1944. He played baseball that spring and, as a freshman in the fall, he quarterbacked the Longhorns to within one point of the Southwest Conference championship. During his sophomore season he spent eight months in the United States Merchant Marine and played in only four games, one of which was a 12 to 7 victory over SMU for the SWC title. The next year, 1945, I went to all UT games, including the Cotton Bowl on January 1, 1946, where the Longhorns beat Missouri 40 to 27. In that game, Layne completed eleven of twelve passes for two touchdowns and scored four times himself. He was an All-SWC selection all four years at the university and an All-American after his senior year. Layne also excelled as a baseball player. In four seasons he compiled a record of thirty-nine wins and seven losses as a pitcher, including twenty-eight consecutive wins in SWC play. In 1946, he threw two no-hitters and struck out eighty-four batters, a conference record that stood for thirty years. His admirers would say, "Bobby Layne never lost a game. Time just ran out on him."

Charmaine and I married in Athens, Texas, on Saturday, November 19, 1949, on the weekend after the TCU game and five days before the Texas A&M game on Thanksgiving Day. She and I went to both games.

Texas lost the TCU game 14 to 13, but won the A&M game in College Station, 42 to 14. Charmaine liked football and supported my indulgence as though we had made a prenuptial agreement that she would. You may recall that I saw her for the first time at a football game. She knew that, when she got me, she also got football. She enjoyed the social whirl that went with Longhorn football, and there was a lot of it.

In the early years of our marriage, I was a busy young lawyer, anxious to please my clients and the senior partners of our firm, Everett Looney and Edward Clark. At home, she and I were creating the ambience and comforts we wanted in our apartment at 2511 Enfield Road, furnished initially with surplus tables and chairs from the Kappa Alpha house and a few other pieces that Charmaine and my mother selected. Although Longhorn football was in the picture and I went to the games, our family was the most important "game" in town, particularly after our son Frank Wofford Denius, called "Woffie," was born August 19, 1952. When "Little Charmaine" was born on April 9, 1956, Charmaine and I thought we had the perfect family. And we did.

Darrell Royal

The won-lost record for Longhorn football hit rock bottom in 1956, when the Horns won one game and lost nine, the worst record in team history. The lone victory was over Tulane in New Orleans by the unimpressive score of 7 to 6. Earlier I told the story about the UT regents appointing Darrell Royal head coach on December 28, 1956, and that I went to see him the next day in his Gregory Gym office. Coach Royal and I hit it off immediately, and we became close friends. He was the first Longhorn coach with whom I had a close relationship. Not only were he and I friends, but our families became good friends, all of us— Edith Royal, Charmaine, and the children. Darrell and I liked to play chess, and Sunday evenings worked for both our schedules. We'd have supper in one of our homes and then play chess, just the two of us. Darrell invited me to attend team practices, and, before long, he invited me to be on the field during games, standing behind the Longhorn bench. I traveled with the team. He attached no conditions to these unprecedented invitations, but I promised him that I would never repeat what

I heard him or any assistant coaches say and that I would never discuss offense and defense strategies with him, except in chess.

Darrell was a hands-on head coach in ways that are probably not possible for his modern-day counterparts. That was because his playing years occurred before free substitution was permitted and special teams were developed. Consequently, he had played most positions on both the offense and the defense. He had quarterbacked, punted, kicked extra points, held the ball for extra points, and played defensive back and linebacker. When he prepared his assistants and key players for their next game, he told them in detail what he wanted them to do, describing his game strategy and how the other team would probably react to it. On the practice field, when he was showing a ball-handler proper movement or explaining a certain blocking technique, you might hear him say, "This play can win the game for us," and sometimes it did. He was a thinking man's coach. He exemplified the fact that good coaches have a demanding job of being a parent, teacher, pastor, psychologist, and taskmaster, all at the same time.

As Darrell Royal integrated me into the Texas football family, he put me in contact with players and their parents on a personal level. If his players had issues with law enforcement in Austin, I was often their pro bono advisor. Several times Darrell asked me to investigate rumors that one or more players had been involved in a fight or had disturbed others, perhaps with loud music or public profanity, as some young men are wont to do. Since I knew the Austin police chief and a number of APD officers, my inquiries were discreet as well as unofficial. About halfway through the 1963 national championship season, Darrell heard that one of his players named "Ernie," whose last name was uncertain, had created a fracas at the Villa Capri Motel, now the location of the Frank Denius Fields. He was concerned that "Ernie" might be his star fullback, Ernie Koy Jr., and asked me to find out. To his relief, I determined that the Ernie involved in the fracas was not fullback Ernie, but another student who was friends with several players.

Until agents began representing players aspiring to play professional football, I negotiated contracts for them with NFL executives. Two contracts that I negotiated were especially interesting. In 1967, I helped a

Longhorn lineman, tackle Diron Talbert, reach a contractual agreement with the Los Angeles Rams. (The team later moved to St. Louis.) Diron told me he wanted a Buick Riviera as a signing bonus. Diron stood six feet five inches and weighed about 275 pounds, very large for the time. I said, "Diron, you cannot get into a Riviera. You need a Lincoln Continental." He agreed and the Rams gave him a new Lincoln Continental. Shortly before Diron was to leave for the Rams' preseason training camp, I got a call from George Allen, the Rams' famous head coach. He said, "Frank, are we still friends?" When I said we were, he said, "Well, I need a favor. Ask Diron not to drive his new Lincoln Continental to camp. If he drives that car out here, I will have to buy forty-four of them." In other words, every player on the team would demand one. Diron went along with Coach Allen's request.

The beneficiary of another memorable contract negotiation was Bill Bradley of Palestine, Texas. Bill entered UT in 1965 and became the starting quarterback the next year. A versatile athlete, his running and passing skills gained him selection as a high school All-American. He was a talented infielder and could have had a professional career playing baseball, but chose to attend college, a decision in which Darrell Royal was instrumental. In football, Bill could punt, kick extra points, kick off, return punts, and throw passes or kick with either hand or foot. His left-footed punts were difficult for opponents to catch because the spin on the football was the reverse of the spin from a right-footed man, which the vast majority of punters were. Also, punt receivers had difficulty judging where the ball would come to ground because it curved in the opposite direction from those off a punter's right foot. This versatility earned Bradley the nickname "Super Bill." In 1968, when Texas introduced the wishbone formation on offense, Coach Royal made James Street the quarterback, and Bradley moved to defensive back, while continuing to punt, kick extra points, and return punts. As a defensive back he set the Texas and Southwest Conference record for the most interceptions in a game when he picked off Texas A&M four times in the last game of the season. His final game as a Longhorn was the 36 to 13 win over Tennessee in the Cotton Bowl. He was drafted by the Philadelphia Eagles as a defensive back, and I negotiated his contract, inserting an add-on clause to his base salary for any game chores he performed other than as a defensive back. So, if he kicked, passed, or punted, extra money was added to his base salary. When the Eagles capitalized on his versatility, his salary rose enough that after three years, he was one of the highest paid defensive backs in the NFL. Super Bill was selected for the All-Pro team, and got "bonuses" for playing any position for the Eagles other than defensive back. Words are inadequate for me to express the satisfaction I got from doing such favors for student athletes.

My special pride in Duke Carlisle's career as a Texas Longhorn begins with the fact that he was also from Athens, and our families were longtime friends. In our hometown, he was given the noble-sounding nickname "Duke" to distinguish him from his father and grandfather, who were also named Emmett. In 1961, Duke's sophomore year, he saw playing time as a third-string quarterback and defensive back. In 1963, he started every game at quarterback and led the team to the national championship with an 11-0 record. On Sunday evenings Charmaine and I were delighted that he often came to our home for hamburgers. Then he'd take Little Charmaine and Woffie to a movie, which, incidentally, would be a violation of the NCAA's current rules.

The Flying Jennie

When Darrell Royal coached his first Texas game, it was against the University of Georgia in Atlanta on September 21, 1957, and I took fifteen friends to the game. It happened this way. I was already going to some out-of-town games, when Clint Murchison Sr., my client and family friend, offered an incentive that made going to them an airborne party with friends. Uncle Clint had a twin-engine Douglas transport plane, a DC-3, called the "Flying Jennie" that was outfitted to carry sixteen passengers in comfort. Clint told me to use it when he wasn't, which was most of the time because his menagerie of airplanes included later models. His pilot and copilot came with the plane. At the front of the passengers' cabin, the "Flying Jennie" had a bar and a seating area with a divan. At the back, there was a restroom and card tables. Our first trip was to Atlanta for the Georgia game, which Texas won 26 to 7. The 1957 Longhorns compiled a 6-4-1 record, and played Ole Miss in the Sugar Bowl on New Year's Day 1958. I think we went to all of them.

Since I did not drink, I was usually the bartender on the "Flying Jennie." Otherwise, my friends mixed their own, which was better for them because I did not know the difference between liquors and mixes. My ignorance about booze and cocktails had memorable consequences. On a trip to New Orleans in 1958 to play Tulane, Ed Clark asked me to mix him a scotch and water, but I inadvertently mixed scotch and vodka. He was so busy talking that he drank it without noticing the difference—until later, of course. Since I liked to attend the team's pre-game warm-ups, which began several hours before the game, we went straight from the airport to the Sugar Bowl, where we were admitted on the strength of Darrell vouching for us. It was an exciting game, which Texas won 21 to 20. According to my companions, I got pretty rambunctious, prompting Wally Scott to say, "From now on, we're gonna draw black and white beans to decide who has to sit by Frank." For a similar reason, Darrell pulled me aside during halftime in Fayetteville in 1965, and said, "Frank, one of the officials says you are too demonstrative and are a distraction from the game. You need to be more conservative, or we may draw a penalty." I restrained myself, calmed down, stayed away from the sidelines—and we lost, 27 to 24 when Arkansas scored a touchdown with ninety seconds left on the clock. Go figure!

Grateful as my friends and I were for the "Flying Jennie," a younger generation would be surprised at our tolerance of flight conditions in an airplane designed in the early 1930s. The DC-3 was a "tail-dragger." It had a tail wheel, not a nose wheel. This meant that when it was on the ground, the fuselage slanted up putting the nose about fifteen feet in the air and the tail almost on the ground, making it awkward to enter and walk through. It cruised at barely 200 mph, as compared to today's 500 mph. The cabin was not pressurized, and, therefore, not air-conditioned. We bounced along in the turbulence of 8,000 to 10,000 feet rather than at 35,000 feet above most of it. An apt nickname for the DC-3 was "gooney-bird." When we took our "gooney-bird" to the West Coast for Cal-Berkeley games, the flight time was about ten hours, allowing for headwinds and two stops. Once there, we dined handsomely in San Francisco, where the incense of John Burns's favorite Indian restaurant almost suffocated us. Going to the Miami game, our pilot did not fly over the Gulf of Mexico, but stayed over land, making the trip almost as long as to San Francisco. When the big, lumbering DC-3 carried us to

UCLA and USC games, we stayed overnight in Las Vegas, compliments of a friend of Charles E. Green, editor of the *American-Statesman*. On a trip back to Austin from Lubbock, an engine caught fire and we made a forced landing in Sweetwater. Fortunately, a qualified radial engine mechanic was available, and we were soon on our way. After Clint Murchison died in 1969, his son John Dabney Murchison continued loaning me the plane, but the engine trouble foretold the end of our days in the air. By 1974, replacement parts for the DC-3 were difficult to find, and our fun came to an end, but not before we had crisscrossed the country from Massachusetts to Washington state, Florida to California, loyally following the orange and white. Among others who traveled on the "Flying Jennie" were Harry Whittington, Noble Doss, Walter Bremond III, Bob Present, Jerry Bell, Clyde Copus, Morgan Nesbitt, Joe Greenhill, Jim Langston, John Coates, W. W. Heath, Duke Carlisle, Horace Crommer, Grogan Lord, and Tom Miller Jr. The "Flying Jennie" was so much fun that I only regretted that I could not take more friends to more games.

One of the great moments in my history with Longhorn football occurred in December 1963 when I was present in New York City for the award of the MacArthur Bowl to the University of Texas for winning the national championship, our first national championship. The trophy is presented annually by the National Football Foundation and College Hall of Fame to the outstanding team of the season, one of the most coveted awards in college football. On the invitation of Coach Royal, I was a guest at the banquet. Darrell asked me to travel with David McWilliams, one the team's tri-captains, who was making his first trip to the Big Apple. Darrell wanted to be sure that this young man from Cleburne, Texas, actually got there to receive the prized bowl. David and I flew up on Braniff Airways, landed at LaGuardia, and took a cab to the fabled Waldorf Astoria Hotel, where the banquet was held.

Wales Madden, perhaps the youngest UT regent ever appointed and a truly distinguished alumnus, and McWilliams accepted the trophy on behalf of the university. Wales and his wife, Abbie Cowden, were dear friends of mine for years. General Douglas MacArthur personally presented for the last time the bowl named after him. The occasion was sad, emotional, and historic. After a long, extraordinary, and vigorous life of serving our country, the five-star general was obviously frail and in poor health. He died in April 1964.

I was also privileged to be there in December 1969 at Darrell Royal's request when the MacArthur Bowl was presented to the university for winning the national championship in the famous "Big Shootout" with the University of Arkansas. This, too, was a sad occasion. Darrell was already in New York for press conferences when he learned that Freddie Steinmark, the team's gifted defensive back and punt return specialist, then at the M. D. Anderson Hospital and Tumor Institute in Houston, had been diagnosed with a bone sarcoma and would have his left leg amputated. Darrell called and asked me to represent him, so I flew to New York as he flew to Houston to be with Freddie and his family. I got there in time for the banquet, where team tri-captains, James Street, Ted Koy, and Glen Halsell accepted the trophy. After the banquet in New York, I accompanied the team captains to Washington for a White House reception, where President Nixon proclaimed the Longhorns national champions. I sat next to Gerald Ford, then the Republican minority leader in the House of Representatives and destined to become president in August 1974, when Nixon resigned. Mr. Ford, who had played center on the University of Michigan team from 1932 to 1934, told me, "You're lucky to be here. If my team had not beaten Ohio State, Texas would not be the national champions." I could only agree. Michigan's 24-12 victory was a big upset. Ohio State had gone into the game ranked number one in the nation and was shooting for its second consecutive national title.

Given my close association with Darrell Royal, I have a few observations about him, some of which are well known and others that may not be. I will begin by telling you that he knew the importance of his players' academic success and hired the first "brain coach" for football players at any major university in the country. A conservative play-caller, his preference for running and punting rather than passing was popularized by his saying, "Three things can happen to you when you throw the football, and two of them are bad." His remarkable ability to foresee how a high school player would probably develop during his college years gave direction to his recruiting efforts. He developed special teams to a greater extent than any previous Longhorn coach and made his colorful language a useful teaching tool because it was so memorable. For example, he told a defensive special team, "Punt returns will kill you before a minnow can swim a dipper." If he talked about competing and winning, he'd say. "Horseshoes is the only game in which you get points for getting close." He realized he was primarily a teacher, but at the same time a counseling psychologist for his players—and how he spoke to them on the sidelines was an important part of counseling. What he said was usually heard only by the player he was talking to. He was keenly aware of game situations and willing to act on his hunches. His decision to replace Bill Bradley at quarterback with James Street was intuitive and led to a national championship because both men found the niche where they could make the greatest contribution to the team. James Street told the story about Darrell's instructions just before the Arkansas game in 1969, the famous "Shoot-Out" that we won 15 to 14. "Remember," Royal told Street, "when we score the first time, go for two points." James could not believe it. "At that point in the season," Street remembered, "we were running through everyone. Why go for two? How did Coach know to do that?" Intuition is the best answer. It was the only time that Darrell attempted a two-point conversion during the entire season. Darrell's decision to insert the ailing Freddie Steinmark for the last play of the same game was inspired. He wanted Freddie on the field not only for his skill as a defensive back, but for his spirit and his impact on other players who admired him. At the time, Freddie's pain was thought to be only a deep bruise.

I was not surprised when Darrell retired at the end of the 1976 season. The won-loss record (four wins, four losses, and one tie) was a factor, but he was weary and utterly disgusted with the cheating in two aspects of the game. One was the corruption in recruiting players, essentially "buying" them by providing them and their families with unlawful gifts—cars, money for their families, and jobs without duties—which he refused to do. The other issue was the sophisticated and organized spying on Longhorn practices by friends of Oklahoma coach Barry Switzer, which Switzer later admitted was true, but disclaimed responsibility. Many of Darrell's assertions about recruiting violations were confirmed by subsequent investigations. He told me that he took a "box of statements signed by people who had firsthand knowledge of recruiting violations" to the NCAA, and the NCAA refused to act on them. Disgusted, his response was, "Well, gentlemen, we will beat them fair-and-square." Deep down, the unsavory recruiting practices gnawed on him so much that he could no longer tolerate it. It was no coincidence that Frank Broyles, Darrell's close friend, rival, and counterpart at the University of Arkansas, chose to retire in the same year. When Switzer succeeded Tom Landry as head coach of the Dallas Cowboys, an insightful sportswriter aptly described him as "the unLandry." Tom Landry was an extraordinary gentleman and a Distinguished Alumnus of UT Austin.

Another consideration at the time was friction between Darrell and two powerful political figures: Frank Erwin and Allan Shivers, former governor and the current regents chairman. Entering the 1976 season, Texas had lost five straight games to Oklahoma. Erwin was incensed and insisted that Darrell do whatever was required in recruiting to beat Oklahoma. That meant buying players, and Darrell refused. Instead he put maximum effort into winning the 1976 OU game, only to have it end in a 6 to 6 tie. He was bitterly disappointed, and Erwin was infuriated. Contributing to Darrell's disgust, in the summer of 1976, Shivers attempted to mediate the animosity between Royal and Switzer by arranging a meeting between the two in Dallas. With the assistance of friends in Oklahoma, Shivers set up the meeting without telling Royal. When informed, Darrell refused to participate, saying he would see Switzer in the Cotton Bowl the second Saturday in October, and only then. Switzer pushed the envelope on every rule and guideline of ethical conduct. Shivers was not accustomed to rejection. And he was not pleased that Darrell counted among his friends country-western singers Willie Nelson and Larry Gatlin. So Erwin and Shivers were on his back, criticizing him. This was long before statues were erected to Willie and he became one of the many faces of Texas. Darrell had an affinity for guitar-playing songwriters and singers who changed country music in the 1970s and 1980s. He admired their ability to say a lot in a single line, as he did. He was loyal to his friends. He understood ordinary folk and their music and empathized with them. To understand Darrell Royal, never forget that he had been disparaged as an "Okie" when his family had migrated to California from the Oklahoma Dust Bowl during the Great Depression. He identified with people who were looked down on as lesser than, not as good as, and not as important as others. That's one reason why he and Earl Campbell's mother got along so well.

Darrell's mainstay assistant, Mike Campbell, did not want him to retire in 1976. He kept saying, "Coach, we are going to have a great team next year." He was thinking primarily about the defensive unit. But Darrell had had enough and was succeeded by Fred Akers, who had a spectacular season in 1977, winning every game of the regular season, only to lose to Notre Dame in the Cotton Bowl, which knocked the Longhorns out of another national championship. I had known Fred since Darrell hired him as an assistant in 1966. On the day he and Diane arrived in Austin, Darrell and Edith hosted them for dinner with Charmaine and me. In the Akers head-coaching era, I continued to be very familiar with team developments as he invited me to attend practices. Akers' ten-year record 86–31–2, is third best in UT's history. He did well against Oklahoma, winning five, losing four, and tying one game.

David McWilliams succeeded Fred Akers in 1987 and remained through the 1991 season. I was well acquainted with David from his playing days under Coach Royal from 1961 to 1963, when the team compiled a record of 30–2–1, won the national championship that I described earlier, and three Southwest Conference championships. He, too, made me welcome to attend practices, and I was close to the team. David is a great person, and I had high hopes for his tenure as head coach. Looking back on his tenure, I wish that he had been more demanding of his assistant coaches. He may have been too loyal to them. That said, my high esteem and respect for David is undiminished.

John Mackovic succeeded David McWilliams at the beginning of the 1992 season and lasted through 1997. I was never close to Coach Mackovic, although he continued Darrell's custom of inviting me to practices, and I went. Mackovic was a sophisticated person, known for his appreciation of fine wines and vintage automobiles, and there is nothing wrong with either. He had an excellent understanding of the game and was a brilliant offensive strategist, which may explain ESPN's hiring him as an analyst. In coaching seventy-one Longhorn games, he won forty-one, lost twenty-eight, and tied two. With no initiative on my part, I became an unofficial messenger to him for the UT Austin administration as his disappointing 1997 season unraveled to a record of four wins and seven losses. The season opened well enough with a 48 to 14 victory over Rutgers in Austin. The fourth game was the high point, beating Oklahoma by a score of 27 to 24. However, for the wrong reason, the second game was one of the most memorable in Longhorn history. Unranked UCLA came to Austin and did everything except grill BEVO steaks, winning 66 to 3. It was the worst loss ever at home for Longhorn football. Californians celebrated their victory by calling it "Rout 66" after the famous road that ran from Chicago across the continent, ending at the Pacific Ocean in Santa Monica near the UCLA campus. Despite this, orange-blooded fans might remember that under Coach Mackovic, the Longhorns won the last Southwest Conference championship in 1995 and the first Big 12 championship in 1996.

By chance, a few days later I had an appointment with UT interim president, Peter Flawn, whom I had known for years from serving with him on the Capital National Bank board of directors. I wanted to talk with Peter about the university's admissions policy for entering freshmen. Before I sat down, he began the conversation with, "What do you think about Coach Mackovic?" He added, "I don't think his players will play for him." I declined to discuss the coach and team situation because I had come prepared to suggest the possibility of capitalizing on the ethnic and racial diversity of the 254 counties of Texas in the university's admissions policy as a way to achieve diversity on the campus.

Three weeks later Oklahoma State whooped us 42 to 16 in Stillwater. As prospects for the season declined, an emissary from the administration (whom I prefer not to name) asked me to talk with Coach Mackovic about the situation. I agreed and made an appointment to see him. Feeling like an ambassador without portfolio, I began the conversation by saying, "In practicing law, I never ask a question in court that I do not already know the answer to. But I am breaking my rule today and want to ask you, 'Why don't you hire the best defensive coordinator in the country to come here and help you.'" He replied, "We already have the best defensive coordinator in the country." Thus rebuffed, I asked, "How about hiring the best high school coach you can find to help with recruiting?" Mackovic replied, "We do not have a vacancy on the staff." His final season ended with a 27 to 16 loss at the hands of Texas A&M.

Longhorn fans were treated to a memorable and humiliating scene as the waning seconds of the game ticked off the clock at Kyle Field. Aggie fans on the second deck in the west stands unfurled a huge banner with this message: "Aggies for Mackovic. Four more years! Keep John." But it was not to be. Three days later, November 29, 1997, President Flawn fired Coach Mackovic.

Whatever may be said about John Mackovic's career, which included being head coach of an NFL team—the Kansas City Chiefs—he did not recruit well in Texas. It was a conspicuous deficiency that should be remembered in the selection of head football coaches and their assistants. He did not understand the importance of high school coaches, of befriending them, accommodating them, and relating to them in a way that made them feel good about their graduates choosing the University of Texas. I have a unique perspective on this issue, because from 1961 to 2012, I was the attorney for the Texas High School Coaches Association, founded in 1930 to enhance the professionalism of coaches and their schools. The association's motto is to "help coaches help kids." I have known many high school coaches, and I understand the conditions of their employment, and the pressures and temptations under which they work. Woe be to the Longhorn coach who does not cultivate friendly and professional relationships with high school coaches.

Mack Brown

Mack Brown and I hit it off from the get-go and remained close. I saw him for the first time at a news conference on December 4, 1997, when athletic director DeLoss Dodd introduced him as our new coach. I did not have a chance to talk to him, but when I got back to my office I had a message that he had called. At his invitation, I went to see him the next day. I sensed immediately that he appreciated history and believed in the importance of tradition. He had already reached out to Darrell Royal, whom he had idolized as a high school player. He would build a relationship with Darrell that was important to both men. Mack got sage advice from Darrell about coaching in Texas and getting along with UT football stakeholders. When Brown took the Texas job, Royal told Brown he had to repair a fractured support base, develop new ties with Texas high school coaches, and shrug off criticism. "One other thing," Mack said Darrell told him. "You've got to win all the damn games."

While he was building bridges to Darrell and me, Brown also built relationships with lettermen and high school coaches. He identified with the coaches and recognized their importance to his goals. He genuinely admired them, and he treated them with the utmost respect. He had grown up close to his grandfather, a legendary high school football coach in Tennessee, who had inculcated him with a love for the game and an appreciation of high school coaches. His father had also coached high school football in Tennessee.

Mack reintegrated both Darrell and me into the Longhorn football program. In a real sense, Darrell and I were history and embodied tradition, which Mack linked to winning and education. We were welcome at the practices, and he named me honorary coach. I sometimes traveled with the team. Over his sixteen years, he asked me to speak to the team many times, memorably before several OU games, and the team gave me game balls. Players hugged me. At the first practice after 9/11, Mack and I stood with the entire team around us, and I led the kids in singing "God Bless America." When the last note was sung, they called out together, "I love Texas." And tears flowed. In every game since 9/11, the team has run onto the field carrying the American flag. Mack made several trips to Iraq to visit troops in the field. On occasion, he wanted me to tell the team about my war experiences. Once I told him, in front of the entire team, "Coach, if you had seen me running across Omaha Beach, you would have offered me a scholarship." He told people that I had made more practices than he had.

After each practice session, Mack would gather the team around him and talk about important issues other than football, topics like schoolwork, class attendance, and good citizenship. Then he might ask a visitor to speak. When he asked me, he'd say, "Mr. Denius, get in there and break 'em down." He nicknamed his special teams the "Frank Denius Special Operations." Mack was an authentic person. His conduct, character, and personality were on view as he invited "outsiders" to practices. These included parents of players, UT Austin presidents, former players, war veterans, high school coaches, and Eddie Joseph, executive director of the high school coaches association. President Bill Powers and his wife, Kim, traveled with the team. Mack promoted burnt orange and white in unprecedented ways. To get an idea of what I mean, just compare photographs of spectators in the stadium before Mack Brown came and a couple of years after he arrived, and you will see that in the later years the bleachers are filled with burnt orange shirts and blouses, many emblazoned with "Come Early, Stay Late, Be Loud, Hook 'Em Horns." I saw them all over Texas as never before. As Mack believed in winning, he also believed in having fun. His players loved him, and he loved them. His 158–48 record over sixteen seasons, with ten or more victories in nine seasons, reflects their mutual respect.

College football changed a lot in the twenty-two years between the end of Darrell Royal's and the beginning of Mack Brown's coaching careers at Texas. In that interval, 1976 to 1998, the NCAA modified several rules that promoted the offense and produced bigger numbers on the scoreboard. Spectators preferred explosive, high scoring games over the "three yards and a cloud of dust," as the saying goes. A major change relaxed the rules that limited how offensive linemen could use their hands against the defensive linemen. I have studied this change because I have a strong interest in the defensive game—the strategies, the techniques, the preparation, all of it. In the Royal era, 1957–1976, the rules required an offensive lineman to keep his hands within the defender's body frame; an offensive lineman could not grab the defensive lineman in front of him. I can remember hearing Darrell emphasize this rule in practice sessions; otherwise, the offensive lineman would draw penalties. Relaxing the rule enabled the offensive linemen to better protect the quarterback, which, in turn, enabled the quarterback to engineer more touchdowns. In Mack Brown's era, 1998–2013, the relaxed rules allowed an offensive lineman to touch, to hold, even to reach around the man in front of him—to keep the defender from getting to the quarterback. That's why uniforms fit tighter and are slicker now than they used to be.

The desire to protect the quarterback and stimulate scoring also led to tightening the rule on how late the defenders could tackle the quarterback. Nowadays, if a defensive player hits the quarterback after he has thrown the ball, the defense will be penalized unless, of course, the officials fail to see the infraction. With such assurance, the modern quarterback can focus more on his receivers downfield, who have benefited from another rule change that restricts defensive backs from blatantly interfering with them after they have advanced more than five yards beyond the line of scrimmage. This change has put a premium on speedy downfield receivers who can get behind the defensive backs. In another rule change that also favors the offense, a defensive back will draw a penalty if the downfield judge thinks he has gone for the receiver rather than for the ball coming toward both the receiver and the defender. These rule changes have produced new techniques in blocking, the rise of the spread formation, and brought about changes in the kinds of players needed for some positions, like three hundred-pound offensive linemen, who need not be agile, but to take only take a step or two to the right or left, then grab, hold, and push the opposing linemen trying to come through. I have already mentioned the opportunities that these changes created for speedy downfield receivers to play, all of which has led to high scoring, explosive games.

Ethics and Ideals

As the University of Texas has matured and grown in international prestige, standards of performance have risen. The standards express the ever-emerging institutional culture, which the wise coach will study and adapt to his or her method of operation. The performance level is high for coaches at UT Austin, both in competing on the playing field and in conduct off the field. The potential for a coach's influence is profound. Male or female, a coach often embodies character traits that players will emulate, especially players who do not have a comparable person at home. Although I am thinking about all coaches, the head football coach has the highest profile and is subject to the closest scrutiny. Given the external demands on a head coach, she or he must insist on similar behavior by assistants, because they also make decisions that reflect on the athletic program and the university.

Intercollegiate athletics operate on the margin of the university, far from the core academic areas where the fundamental institutional values are formed. Extra effort may be required for a coach, particularly a newly arrived coach, to gain a sense of ethical expectations on the Forty Acres, and to recognize the boundaries of acceptable conduct, personal and professional. Coaches are confronted by ethical decisions about adhering to rules, and about their relations with players, faculty, and donors, who are sometimes overly eager to support their program. A special dilemma is whether to tolerate and exploit a talented but immature youngster on the playing field, or to discipline him or her, hoping to help the player along the path of long-term growth and development as a worthy citizen. These decisions are not clear cut, but that's the way it is with many ethical choices. In ethical decision-making, the institutional culture is a factor, and the University of Texas is no ordinary institution. We always want to be number one in the field of ethics as well as competitive on the playing field.

For a long time I have thought every new student and employee should have a short course on the exceptionalism of the University of Texas. By emphasizing exceptionalism, I imply that superficial or perfunctory adherence to rules and principles is not sufficient. Our university must be, and usually is, in the forefront of institutions that are admired for setting standards and making the proper decision, even when the institution may appear to suffer or be disadvantaged in the short term.

My short course on the exceptionalism of the University of Texas begins in the old Regents Room in the Main Building 212, now the Lee Jamail Academic Room. The Main Building is large, complicated, and contains numerous symbols that represent the history of the university, of the state of Texas, and of Western Civilization. In its high silhouette against the sky, the building is a cultural icon of the university and an emblem of higher education in the state. Symbols and inscriptions around the Main Building are clues to inform us—its champions and advocates—about how it came to be, and the values on which it was founded.

The Lee Jamail Room extends majestically upward through two stories, inspiring awe and admiration. When I was legal counsel to the regents, we usually met there, and I have attended numerous gatherings of university commissions in the same location. On occasion, I have sat quietly in the august ambience of the room. Aside from its elegance, the room is memorable for the gilded inscriptions on the ceiling that express the ideals and hopes of the university's founders and leaders in its formative years. I have been inspired by their pronouncements about knowledge and education. Harry Yandell Benedict, president of the university from 1927 until he died in office in 1937, stated a truism to be kept in mind by those in authority in their every deed: "Public confidence is the only real endowment of a state university." A. W. Terrell, a regent in the early twentieth century, combined faith, teaching, and patriotism in saying, "Those who serve best both God and country are those who wisely instruct youth." O. H. Cooper (1852–1932) considered the university "the noblest concrete embodiment of the best spirit of Texas." Probably the most frequently cited inscription is Mirabeau B. Lamar's insight that "Cultivated mind is the guardian genius of democracy," which is printed on official documents and diplomas, and appears on the university seal in its Latin rendering: *Disciplina Praesidium Civitatis*. These words from the state constitution challenge us to be the best—"The Legislature shall establish, organize, and provide for the maintenance, support, and direction of a University of the first class."

This challenge, embedded in the fundamental law of Texas, defies complacency and defines a never-ending quest for excellence. It reminds me that the university is not a corporation, not the NFL, the NBA, or IBM, whose bottom line is financial, but an educational institution whose success is ultimately measured in the achievements of its graduates long after they have left the campus. This is true, even if they make football their vocation, as Tom Landry did. Although Landry was an All-Southwest Conference fullback and defensive back at the University of Texas in the 1940s and played professionally for the New York Giants, he is most remembered as the very proper gentleman and head coach of the Dallas Cowboys from 1960 to 1988. Even so, he was quick to acknowledge that the personal discipline instilled in him as a student-athlete on the Forty Acres transformed his life and was the foundation of his career. For his conduct, integrity, and achievements in both his playing years and his subsequent career, Landry can be considered a model for Longhorn football players.

The exterior of the Main Building informs us that the university's mission embraces the arts and humanities as well as science and technology. On the east and west walls you see the names of great thinkers who explained and framed the classics of Western Civilization for our society and the names of the earliest universities in Europe and the United States, along with the University of Mexico, the oldest university in North America. These designations tell us that the University of Texas is not a special-purpose institution, but has been from its inception a comprehensive university of highest aspiration in the truest meaning of the word. If these connections seem remote and abstract, you can come to earth nearby by looking under the eaves of Garrison Hall, where there are more than thirty symbols to remind us of the university's roots in the unpretentious soil of Texas. The symbols are cattle brands made famous in an epochal period of our history about the time of the university's founding in 1883 by ranchers like Charles Goodnight, Sam Maverick, José Antonio Navarro, and George Littlefield—cattleman and banker— whose monetary gifts funded much of the construction costs for the Main Building and Tower.

In the long history of the university, not everything has been done as we, with perfect hindsight, may wish it had been done. The university is no more perfect than its countless constituents, each with high expectations. Since their expectations usually differ, they are impossible to meet. Always, some of us will be disappointed with incidents or trends that please others. None of us can have our way all the time, but that is not a reason for any of us to diminish our support of our university. Think of it this way: we are the crew of the same ship, working together, striving to move forward. Faced with headwinds and heavy seas, we may tack left or right, but we stay the course, steering toward the same goal, which is quality in all endeavors. The university is always a work in progress.

CHAPTER 20

The Greatest Legacy

THE RICHEST INHERITANCE OF MY LIFE has been the family legacy of giving with no expectation of return. I may have been born with the inclination, but I definitely acquired the habit from my uncle, Wofford Cain, and he got it from his uncle, Reagan Wofford, the brother of my Grandmother Cain. Reagan Wofford (1870–1923) planted the seed of family generosity, nurtured it, and became the role model for Wofford Cain in both philanthropy and business. Although Reagan Wofford died two years before I was born, he deserves acknowledgment because his extraordinary influence on the family continues to this day, most significantly in the Cain Foundation, which Wofford Cain created in 1952.

For similar reasons, Reagan's two sisters—my Grandmother Cain and Aunt Sha—deserve mention for their influence. They were ethical, pursued the educational opportunities available to them, and, with the retrospection of decades, I can say they were truly wise. They shaped those of us lucky enough to be around them, especially me and my first cousin, Jimmy Cain, son of my mother's brother, John. You may remember from an early section of this book that Aunt Sha recommended that both Jimmy and I go to Schreiner Institute, a military boarding school and junior college in Kerrville, Texas. I went there at the age of thirteen. She paid my tuition and bought my uniforms. My experience at Schreiner Institute was immeasurably important. It was the beginning of six years of military training before going to war, which probably saved my life together with the lives of comrades who were with me. I am certain that the discipline instilled in me has been a factor in all of my pursuits.

To the extent that our family has achieved material wealth, Reagan Wofford started it; he was the progenitor. When his father, Bushrod William John (B. W. J.) Wofford, was killed in a farming accident in 1891, Reagan left Southwestern University shortly before graduation and returned to Athens to take over his father's mercantile store and farms. Reagan became a genuine entrepreneur with investments in banking, ranching, farming, and oil and gas. He moved to Dallas, where he was prominent in business and banking circles. Never married, he died suddenly in 1923 at the age of fifty-one while serving barbecue to friends at his estate north of Dallas. The estate is now the site of the Presbyterian Hospital of Dallas. A eulogist referred to Reagan Wofford's "vast wealth" and the "large sums of money" he had spent "to assist individuals and enterprises," concluding "we have lost a greater friend than is generally recognized." His final will and testament designated the husbands of his two sisters—my grandfather Smith Cain and my uncle Chick Coleman—as the co-independent executors of his estate. It was an indication of his devotion and trust in his family.

Reagan Wofford and his sister Sally encouraged their nephew Wofford Cain to go to college. He graduated from Texas A&M with a degree in civil engineering in 1913. To help pay his expenses, Reagan gave Wofford a job in a cotton compress plant in Italy, Texas. He was Wofford's hero and role model in business and citizenship. Reagan believed that a good businessman should give back to society, to the church, and to family. He inculcated Wofford Cain with two fundamental values—generosity and the importance of education—and Wofford did the same for me.

This background information explains much about the creation of the Wofford and Effie Cain Foundation in 1952, and the accumulation of the wealth that has made it significant. Wofford Cain had a long record of personal philanthropy before he created the foundation. He had funded a chapel for the First Methodist Church in Athens in honor of his father and had numerous students on scholarship at Texas A&M. He would often say, "The greatest gift you can give anyone is an education." Even today, almost forty years after his passing, the Texas A&M website carries this quotation from him: "A&M afforded me the opportunities I have had in my life. I have tried to help A&M, in turn, to help others." Those last three words, "to help others," sum up Uncle Wofford's attitude toward people and society. He wanted the best for young people and believed financial grants in the form of scholarships were the best vehicle to unleash their potential. "Educate and encourage others to give" was virtually his motto.

Financial assistance for students has continued as a major interest of the foundation. Uncle Wofford created the foundation on the assumption that it was the best assurance that his wealth would continue to benefit people after his death. It was his gift to the family and through them, to untold numbers of other beneficiaries. He made his family responsible for its stewardship. In recent years we have kept membership on the board of directors to my son, daughter, John Cain of Athens, and me. Our decisions are guided by the knowledge that we are guardians of the legacy of Reagan Wofford and Wofford Cain. Our responsibility for the foundation has fostered important conversations among us about our beliefs and the kinds of activities we should support with foundation monies.

I was not a founder, but at Uncle Wofford's request I reviewed the proposed bylaws and articles of incorporation for the foundation, which was chartered in Texas as a nonprofit corporation 501(c)3 private foundation in 1952. In the same year, we obtained a letter from the IRS approving it as a 501(c)3 private foundation, subject to federal codes. Uncle Wofford made me a director of the foundation from the beginning, and, since then, the foundation has been the principal recipient of my monetary donations. It is the main medium through which my philanthropy has been expressed. As a consequence, my personal philanthropy cannot be separated from the Cain Foundation's.

In the first few years, the directors met in Uncle Wofford's office in Dallas at least annually in compliance with the law. He was chairman of the board; Effie Cain and I were members; and the fourth member was his friend, John Kilgore. We did not make many grants. Uncle Wofford called me occasionally to discuss grants he was considering.

The foundation's very first grant was to the Scottish Rite Children's Hospital in Dallas. It was not large, but it was significant. The hospital's chief fundraiser was Mr. John Kettle. Twenty-five years earlier, in 1929, Mr. Kettle was the executive vice president of the First National Bank who recommended to bank president Nathan Adams that they should cover the $100,000 "hot check" Wofford Cain and Clint Murchison had written to the City of Albuquerque in their successful bid to get the gas contract that led to the creation of the Southern Union Gas Company. The grant to the Scottish Rite Children's Hospital began a pattern that has characterized many Cain Foundation gifts ever since—there is usually a story behind the gift, a personal connection of some kind to a friend or to a family member.

Uncle Wofford died in 1977, and the foundation was the main beneficiary of his separate property in his estate, which was valued at about forty-eight million dollars. After the IRS approved the distribution of the assets in 1982, the foundation was capable of functioning as a freestanding entity. The principal assets from his estate were stock in Southern Union Gas, other stocks and bonds, and land, including some in downtown Dallas, which the foundation still owns. Uncle Wofford had oil and gas properties from which royalties still accrue to the foundation. Aunt Effie succeeded her husband as foundation CEO and, as her health failed, I succeeded her, and we moved the offices to Austin. When Aunt Effie died in 1999, about sixteen million dollars of her estate came to the foundation. They had no children, but she had other heirs.

Between the mid-1980s and 2014, the Cain Foundation gave away about $120 million and yet had assets of $130 million. In broad terms, about 38 percent of the money went for scientific and medical purposes, 36 percent for education, 11 percent for human needs and services, and 6 percent each to religious and cultural institutions. In my years as a director and CEO of the foundation, I have learned that giving away money intelligently is not easy. It is a challenging task that involves study, analysis, and reflection.

The city of Athens, Texas, has been a major beneficiary of the Cain Foundation. It was Wofford Cain's hometown. He grew up in Athens. His character was forged there, heavily influenced by family and friends. The same is true of me. Both of us were fortunate to grow up in this easygoing and modest East Texas town with so many friendly and authentic people. Appropriately, the foundation made its first major gift, some $6.5 million, to establish the Cain Center, a civic and recreational facility in Athens. I proposed it to Aunt Effie in 1982, when she was still actively participating in the foundation's business decisions. She readily agreed. The Cain Center is situated in a grove of oaks on the outskirts of the city, surrounded by the eighty-five-acre Cain Park. Eventually, the foundation committed about eight million dollars to the project.

Other Cain Foundation gifts benefitting Athens have gone to the Trinity Valley Community College and to the East Texas Arboretum, where we have contributed to two major enhancements. In 2001, we moved the 1850s cabin home of our forebearer, Bushrod Wofford, about twenty miles and restored it on the grounds of the arboretum. Called the Wofford House Museum, it is a reminder of early pioneer days, complete with period furnishings. The Wofford House Museum has a seasonal garden and is frequently the scene of reunions, weddings, and receptions.

Recognizing and bringing to public attention the men and women who have served in our country's armed forces is a major interest of mine and of the Cain Foundation. Thus, the foundation made another gift to the East Texas Arboretum by funding the construction of the Henderson County Veterans Memorial and Plaza, which I proposed and designed. Dedicated on Veterans Day in 2013, the memorial honors military veterans from Henderson County who have fought in any of America's wars, beginning with the Civil War, including those who fought for the Confederacy. Individual names of more than nine thousand veterans are chiseled in polished steel-gray marble panels embedded in the memorial's two red brick walls arrayed in a half-circle around an open plaza, with generous space allowed for additional names. Standing between the walls is a tall column crowned with the bronze sculpture of a large bald eagle with outspread wings as though soaring above the plaza. Two shorter flagpoles stand in front of the column, each with a smaller but exact replica of the eagle on the column. The eagles were sculpted by Paul Tadlock, of New Braunfels, Texas. Mr. Tadlock took the eagle statuary to the scene and directed the installation of each, assisted by Bob McDonald, the project superintendent. Mr. McDonald, an Athens native and dedicated civic worker, oversaw construction of the memorial. He was my perfect partner for the project. In a massive undertaking, volunteers in Athens compiled the veterans' names.

In nature as well as in these sculptures, the bald eagle represents freedom, strength, and grandeur. That's why it was selected as our national emblem and appears on the Great Seal of the United States, on our coins, and on other official seals. And that's why I like it. I wrote the inscription for a plaque at the base of the eagle's column: "In glory and with eternal gratitude to all veterans whose legacy is our freedom." It is my earnest hope that the Henderson County Veterans Memorial will forever remind our fellow citizens and visitors from afar of the debt they owe to military veterans who have served to protect and preserve freedom for all of us. Speaking of visitors from afar, the Cain Foundation has also contributed to monuments erected in Europe on battlefields where Americans fought during World War II. Several such monuments can be seen along the route of my Thirtieth Infantry Division across France, Belgium, and Holland. They are funded through the federal agency responsible for them, the American Battle Monuments Commission.

Until recently, it was accurate to say that the University of Texas Southwestern Medical Center at Dallas had received more money from the Cain Foundation than any other beneficiary. Uncle Wofford and Aunt Effie lived in Dallas and made numerous gifts to UT Southwestern before the foundation was fully funded. When they became ill late in their lives, they were treated at UT Southwestern. Since they had helped Southwestern, it was only natural that we should continue their legacy. I personally initiated the foundation's first gifts to Southwestern by proposing them to then-president Dr. Kern Wildenthal. The result has been the Cain Foundation funding of cutting-edge research and clinical care in fields ranging from dementia to arthritis, cancer, diagnostic imaging, mobility, hearing and vision loss, urology, and angiogenesis—the physiological process through which new blood vessels form from preexisting vessels. Our gift to create the Cain/Denius Comprehensive Center in Mobility Research funds clinical research in areas such as multiple sclerosis, spinal cord injury, and stroke. The multiple sclerosis program provides comprehensive, interdisciplinary health care for patients and families with MS. In addition, the research has focused on mechanisms that cause the disease. The spinal-cord-injury program's primary purpose is to develop ways to promote nerve repair. The laboratory includes innovative programs involving repetitive training on treadmills to strengthen and retrain damaged neurons, and research on regeneration of injured cells. UT Southwestern's stroke center, one of the most prominent in the nation, includes comprehensive treatment and research programs. By 2014, the Cain Foundation had given more than nineteen million dollars to the UT Southwestern Medical Center at Dallas.

Perhaps the foundation's most conspicuous gift to Southwestern is the Cain Conference Center for meetings and seminars on the top floor of the Seay Biomedical Building on the North Campus. The location is singularly appropriate in that Wofford and Effie Cain were close friends of Sarah and Charles Seay, the Dallas philanthropists for whom the Seay Biomedical Building is named. Acting in concert, the two couples gave generously to Dallas civic groups and schools, to the Park City YMCA, as well as to the Southwestern Medical Center. Other medical institutions that have benefitted from Cain Foundation benevolence are the UT MD Anderson Cancer Center in Houston, the Baylor College of Medicine in Houston, and the UT Health Center in Tyler. In each instance, the gift memorializes a friend or relative who benefitted from services rendered by the receiving institution.

For my entire adult life, I have been an activist in helping the University of Texas at Austin pursue its objectives. Active as I have been, it is significant that the Cain Foundation's first gift to UT Austin, made in 1986 to the College of Liberal Arts, was the initiative by my aunt, Effie Cain, to honor her friend, Virginia Linthicum, the second wife of Clint Murchison Sr. Our family's history of involvement with the university connection is strong and multigenerational. My wife, Charmaine, attended the university. Before the Cain Foundation was activated, she and I contributed directly to various UT endeavors, notably to the Texas Exes Outstanding Award for K–12 teachers. Our son and daughter as well as their spouses graduated from the university. My interest and commitment to the University of Texas is not to any one part, but to all of it. That's been a major commitment for my entire adult life.

The Cain Foundation's numerous gifts to the university have varied widely in the amounts, but always for carefully considered purposes.

The Denius-Sams Gaming Academy in UT Austin's Moody College of Communication offers unique professional development opportunities for students who know how to make games and want to acquire skills to devise, produce, or direct a game—and much more. Created on the initiative of my son, Wofford Denius, it is unique among academic game-development programs in the level of financial support for students. The foundation has supported a variety of programs and projects in the Harry Ransom Humanities Research Center, notably the acquisition and exhibit of the David Douglas Duncan Photography Collection. In 2014, the foundation helped fund the Ransom Center's World War I exhibit, which received favorable reviews in this country and in Europe. For our family, the Charmaine H. Denius Seminar Room is a special venue in the Ransom Center. The foundation also contributed to the Thomas M. Hatfield Seminar Room in the Dolph Briscoe Center for American History.

In the early 1990s, a promising series of undergraduate courses concerned with World War II came to my attention. Called the Normandy Scholar Program, faculty from several departments of the university organized the courses in the UT College of Liberal Arts, after then governor Bill Clements suggested to UT president Bill Cunningham that the university should have a program for students to concentrate on the war, particularly the battle of Normandy. Governor Clements had served in the war and was encouraged in his initiative by Anthony Stout, head of the Battle of Normandy Foundation, chartered in Washington, D.C., which held out the promise of continuing financial support for the program. Cunningham gave development of the project to Bill Livingston, his senior vice president and my longtime friend, who told me about it. I was immediately interested. Like me, Bill had been an artilleryman in the European theater and had fought across France and Belgium and into Germany until he was wounded by an enemy mine that exploded under his foot.

Bill Livingston, with his extraordinary background as a gifted teacher and talented administrator, was the ideal advocate and organizer for the Normandy Scholar Program, both on the campus and in France. He recruited faculty from history, literature, journalism, and European civilization for a multidisciplinary approach that would afford students an overview of the historical, cultural, and intellectual influences leading to the war as well as its strategic and operational history. Continuing legacies of the war were also considered. In cooperation with leading citizens of Caen, the university town and governmental center of Lower Normandy, the Livingston group prepared a logistical plan that enabled students to begin their studies on the campus in Austin and complete them "over there" in close association with French people, some of whom who had lived under the German occupation. This was important to me because I have felt a close affinity for the French people since my first visit to their country in 1944, involuntary though it was. Their gratitude for the United States is genuine, and I feel keenly about the bonds between our two countries. Among the university faculty who got the program going under Bill Livington's leadership were professors Bob Divine, Roger Louis, Jean-Pierre Cauvin, Francoise De Backer, Lance Bertelson, Don Graham, Tom Hatfield, and Martin Blumenson, a visiting scholar and noted biographer of General George S. Patton.

From its beginning in 1990, student testimonials indicated the program was a huge success. Many students said it was a life-transforming experience. When the Battle of Normandy Foundation unexpectedly collapsed, the Cain Foundation made a commitment to create an endowment that would subsidize the program perpetually. How pleased I was when the University of Texas Board of Regents attached my name to the program, designating it as the Frank Denius Normandy Scholar Program, and Randy Diehl, the dean of Liberal Arts, put my name on the program's seminar room. Since its beginning, the itinerary of the scholars has expanded to include northwest and central Europe, starting out in London and ending in Poland, while retaining a focus on Normandy. I meet with the students each spring before they leave for Europe and when they return. They come back speaking with a voice and with a look in the eye that indicates they have had, as they are inclined to say, an "awesome experience." Many have told me that the program has made an enduring change in their lives, and that they now think more about freedom and the importance of defending freedom. I do not have the words to fully express the satisfaction I get from listening to these students. Their reactions to the program remind me of the changes that came over me when I came home from the war. Ironically, I was then twenty years old, about the same age as today's Normandy scholars are when they complete their studies in Europe and return home. I always tell them to make giving back to the university part of their life plan. There is an unhealthy misconception that UT Austin is a very wealthy university when, it fact, it is increasingly dependent on donations.

Another area in which I have been able to give back to the university is athletics. The spacious area on the UT Austin campus known as the Frank Denius Fields resulted, oddly enough, from a lawsuit settled by the university in May 1993 concerning Title IX of the Civil Rights Act of 1964. When the act was amended in 1972, the following provision was added: "No person in the United States shall, on the basis of sex, be excluded from participation in, be denied the benefits of, or be subjected to discrimination under any education program or activity receiving federal financial assistance." This language in Title IX required all universities receiving federal funds to offer equal opportunities for women and men in all programs, athletic as well as academic. Eventually, a suit was brought against UT Austin challenging whether it had met its obligations under the law. In settling the suit, the university agreed to add three women's sports: soccer, softball, and rowing. However, we did not have adequate facilities for them. At the time, there was no Mike Myers Stadium for soccer and track or the Red and Charline McCombs Field for softball. Furthermore, the football team did not have satisfactory, conveniently located facilities, and actually practiced in two places: Memorial Stadium for an artificial surface and the intramural field for grass. The intramural field was several miles north of the campus. In order to practice on a natural surface, the entire team had to be bused to the intramural field, which was not only inconvenient, but consumed time that could be better spent practicing or studying. And once the team got to the intramural field, there were no lockers or dressing rooms or rehab facilities. Obviously, the football program needed additional and enhanced athletic facilities in a more central location near Memorial Stadium. I was interested in helping resolve these problems.

In a nationwide context, in the early 1990s college athletics were in a state of flux, and conference realignments were part of it. In 1991, Arkansas left the Southwest Conference in favor of the SEC, and other SWC institutions were rumored to be leaving. At the same time, there were discussions about forming the Big 12, which was announced in February 1994. With visionary leadership, our athletic director, DeLoss Dodds, saw these changes not as a crisis, but as an opportunity "to change our lives" and create athletic facilities second to none. DeLoss got me together with Mack Rankin and Corby Robinson on Tom Hicks's jet to visit the University of Tennessee and the University of Georgia to see their new facilities, everything—suites, locker rooms, upper decks, trophy rooms, skyboxes, and playing fields. We were positively impressed and encouraged DeLoss to develop a proposal that would result in outstanding facilities for our university. The UT athletic council agreed and made similar recommendations that were endorsed by the administration, which the board of regents approved. One of the recommendations was to build practice fields for the football team on the current location between Red River Street and Interstate 35. The Cain Foundation then chipped in to help the university build the practice facility, and subsequently the regents named it for me. It was a great honor for my family and me. Maybe the regents heard about Mack Brown's quip that I mentioned earlier, "Frank has been to more practices than I have."

UT Austin's football stadium has been expanded several times since its original opening in 1924. It has been dedicated and rededicated three times to our war dead: in 1924, upon completion of the original stadium; in 1948, in honor of the men and women who died during World War II; and in 1977, in memory of all veterans in all wars fought by the United States. A major expansion and modernization began in 1996 when the stadium was officially named for Coach Royal, making it the Darrell K Royal-Texas Memorial Stadium. I was invited to participate in planning the renovation and expansion, a privilege that included being chairman of the Stadium Veterans Committee, composed of alumni who have served in the armed services, and charged with planning dedications to veterans, particularly those in the stadium on the game day closest to Veterans Day, November 11.

From the beginning of the DKR-Texas Memorial Stadium expansion and renovation, the Veterans Committee wanted the university to memorialize veterans more conspicuously than in the past. We wanted the new memorial to be readily visible to students and visitors to the campus. By contrast, although the 1924 memorial was impressive, it was inside the stadium at the top of the north end-zone seats, where few people ever saw it. I was particularly interested in a statue. I wanted the new memorial to include a life-sized representation of an American soldier in the combat gear of a World War I doughboy, holding a replica of a Springfield rifle with a fixed bayonet. Such a statue would continue the heritage established with the original dedication of the stadium to the dead of World War I, and would recognize that America's participation in that war signified our arrival as a power to be reckoned with on the world scene. After an unsuccessful search for a doughboy statue, perhaps from a deactivated army post, the Cain Foundation funded a bronze statue exactly as I wanted it, sculpted by Paul Tadlock, who had made the eagles for the veterans memorial in Athens. On Veterans Day 2009, UT Athletics dedicated the Frank Denius Veterans Memorial Plaza at the northwest corner of the stadium grounds with the doughboy statue in the center mounted on a block of red Texas granite. The huge plaque with the names of 5,246 Texans who died in World War I, dedicated in 1924, was moved from inside the stadium and is mounted on the wall behind the statue. In front of the statue there are flowerbeds in the design of the famous Longhorn icon. A plaque beneath the statue has the same inscription as the Athens memorial: "In glory and with eternal gratitude to all veterans whose legacy is our freedom." I was extremely proud to have the plaza named for me. The location is perfect. It is a constant reminder of the old adage that "eternal vigilance is the price of liberty." My expression for the same idea is, "Every generation must pay a price for our freedoms." In 2012, when the French consul came from Houston to award me the Legion of Honor (Chevalier distinction) for my participation in the liberation of France in 1944, I selected the plaza for the ceremony. People tell me the plaza is a favorite place for campus visitors and group and bridal photographs.

In the same way that the Cain Foundation and I want to memorialize veterans, we also want to help those who suffer from injuries that have occurred since the "War on Terror" began after the attacks on the United States on September 11, 2001. As a conduit and agent for this effort we have partnered with a national nonprofit, nonpartisan organization known as Building Homes for Heroes. This group constructs or modifies homes and gives them to disabled veterans and their families, for whom the struggles of everyday activities is an ordeal, often requiring several people to help the wounded veteran. The Cain Foundation's entire board of directors has attended dedications of these mortgage-free homes and seen the difference they make in the lives of women and men who have sacrificed so much for all of us. Philanthropy, too, makes a better country for all of us.

I have wanted UT Austin to have a medical school since 1957, when Austin mayor Tom Miller appointed me to a committee to investigate the possibility. Since then, I have believed the university had to have a medical school to truly achieve tier-one status. To realize this dream, I had to wait until 2012, when Travis County voters approved a tax rate increase for Central Health, the countywide hospital district, and committed thirty-five million dollars each year to support the medical school. Soon afterward, the Michael and Susan Dell Foundation pledged fifty million dollars to establish the school, which was then appropriately designated the Dell Medical School by the board of regents. The regents also committed $334 million for construction. In 2011, I asked the medical school's organizing committee for a menu of their needs that the Cain Foundation might fund. We chose to create an endowment of one million dollars to help the related teaching facility, Seton Hospital, establish residencies for medical students. Later, and more significantly, the foundation gave ten million dollars to create the Frank and Charmaine Denius Distinguished Dean's Chair in Medical Leadership. The foundation's board of directors, and I, wanted the medical school dean to have the necessary financial resources to build and maintain a preeminent institution. I understand that the endowment is the highest amount ever committed for a chair at the university. Philanthropy is increasingly important to the University of Texas.

Earlier I wrote that the Cain Foundation was my Uncle Wofford's gift to the family and through them, to untold numbers of other beneficiaries. Wofford Cain knew the satisfaction that a giver obtains from helping others, and he made it possible for us, his successors, to have similar experiences. By making philanthropists of us all, he compounded his gift by virtually forcing us to contemplate our purpose in being, a reflective process that has enhanced almost every aspect of our lives. My philanthropy, like all philanthropy, is an expression of personal values, enabling me to say that the three great loves of my life have been my family, my country, and the University of Texas. I do not know Winston Churchill's record in philanthropy, but I agree with a comment attributed to him that "We make a living by what we get, we make a life by what we give."

In another parallel to Reagan Wofford and Wofford Cain, I have continued our family's traditional relationship with the Presbyterian Church, whose learned pastors have helped me a lot. Over the years they planted the idea in me that everyone should expect challenges and hardships, and, as a corollary, that how we deal with them makes all the difference. All of us have crises, large and small, sometimes real and other times imagined. That is certainly true of me, although compared to most people, I have had it pretty easy. I have seen many people who were hungry and without shelter, but I have never been one of them. How grateful I am to have been born into a kind and generous and prosperous family, had a loving wife and children, devoted friends, and a most interesting career. Yet not a day passes that I do not face uncertainties or have worries, usually subtle forms of suffering or pain, perhaps associated with my concern about the well-being of someone I know, or of myself. "I hope my eye examination is okay." "I hope my secretary's test goes well today; she was upset over the last one." People lose their jobs. They suffer losses on the stock market or in the courtroom. Marriages fail. Loved ones die and we grieve. Even small anxieties build up—"If this traffic does not get moving . . .." What I am trying to say is that life is difficult, in spite of its rewards and satisfactions. If you doubt that, just think of the number of people you know who see a counselor for their problems, physical as well as psychic, and often for both.

I believe there is a purpose in our hardships, because they demand persistence and determination to overcome them. Adversity and difficulty often draw out qualities in a person that otherwise might never be realized and incorporated into a useful life. My favorite biblical passage tells us that hardship compels endurance, which produces character, and character begets hope, and hope does not disappoint us. Quite the opposite, in fact, hope sustains us. These verses remind us about the positive consequences of overcoming difficulty. This basic belief has guided me through my entire adult life. I earnestly hope my descendants will carry on with the values and spirit of Reagan Wofford and Wofford Cain, as I have tried to do.

"... we rejoice in our sufferings, knowing that suffering produces endurance, and endurance produces character, and character produces hope, and hope does not put us to shame, because God's love has been poured into our hearts through the Holy Spirit who has been given to us."

ROMANS 5: 3–5

Acknowledgments

FOR MY ENTIRE LIFE I have been encouraged and sustained by my steadfast and loving family. In acknowledging what they have done for me, I should begin with my maternal grandparents, Mattie Wofford Cain and her husband, Smith Cain, and their children: Uncle Wofford, Uncle John, and my mother, Frances Carrie Denius. They were the foundation of my life. In adulthood, they were succeeded by my wife, Charmaine H. Denius (1929–2014) and our family: our son, F. Wofford Denius and his wife, Beth Broz Denius; our daughter, Charmaine Denius McGill and her husband, Gordon; and our grandsons Parker McGill, Franklin Wofford McGill (1988–2009), and Reagan Denius.

I have been blessed with extraordinary friends and colleagues who have inspired and helped for my entire life. I cannot possibly name all of them all, but I want to name a few as well as apologize to those not cited here, some of whom are named in the narrative, in the index, and in the list of donors to the publication of this book. Growing up in Athens, Texas, my teachers endeared themselves to me, especially Jennie Boone, Ada Mae Norwood, and Coach Walker. Similarly, I became attached to my schoolmates in Athens from the first grade in 1931 through the fifth grade in 1937; and to those at Highland Park Junior High in Dallas in 1937–1938. Athens townsmen who influenced me included Winfield Stirman, Fred Stone, W. W. Spencer, Dick Derden, county judge Country "Turkey" Spencer, sheriff Jeff Sweetin, district judge Jack Holland, my lifelong friend Dr. Robert W. "Bob" Strain, and our family doctor, R. E. Henderson. Then as now, Dallas was the principal metropolitan area for East Texas, and special friends there were the family of Toodie Lee Wynne Sr. and Gus Bowen.

I owe much to the faculty and my fellow cadets at the Schreiner Institute in Kerrville, Texas, and the Citadel, the Military College of South Carolina, where I studied and drilled from 1938 to 1943. At Schreiner, I remember especially dean of students Major Martin, Professor Lynn McGraw, Professor of Military Science Captain W. O. Green, Coach Heinie Weir, and my buddies Jimmy Barton, Harry Carter, Tommy Melms, Billy Sunday, Dan Krausse, Alexander Waugh, Richard "Dick" Jones, and Dan W. Wagner.

When I returned from the war and entered the University of Texas in 1945, I began forming friendships that were important for the rest of my life, among them: Wales Madden, Hubert W. Green, Marty Bigger, Bill Thacker, Bob Ed Steele, Dan Wagner, fraternity brothers in Kappa Alpha, and many men associated with UT athletics, notably football lettermen, coaches, and athletic directors. In a similar way, I made countless friends through the UT Ex-Students Association from the moment I became a member in 1949. I never miss a meeting of former presidents of the Texas Exes.

In the law firm where I practiced from 1949 to 1975, Everett Looney was my mentor in the profession and Edward Clark in politics. Through them I came under the good and benevolent influence of Austin Mayor Tom Miller, the finest public servant I have ever know. Mayor Miller taught me how to be a good citizen, how to bring people together, and to project a vision for the future that people want to support. Other civic leaders in Austin that I admired and were important to me include James P. Nash, W. W. Bremond Sr., Raymond Todd, Ed Wise Sr., Mayor Roy Butler, Howard T. Cox, Mrs. Minnie Belle Heep, Theo Davis, Jack Maroney, William Pargaman, Will Barber, Pat Carlisle, Mayor Lester Palmer, Louis Shanks, John Burns, Ben White, and Jay Brown. The fact that Joyce L. Reynolds was my personal secretary from 1957 to 2004 signifies our congeniality and mutual confidence.

I learned much from fellow executives and directors of corporate boards, particularly D. F. "Doc" Neuhaus, John T. MacGuire, and

Jimmy Sewell, president of Delhi Oil and its spinoffs. In later years, Eric Hirschmann. We were companions in deliberations leading to important decisions that were not always easy. Those boards include the Delhi Oil Corporation, Southern Union Company, Delhi Taylor Oil Corporation, Delhi Australian Oil Company, Aztec Oil Corporation, Texas Capital Corporation, Telecom Corporation, Southern Union Production Company, Supron Energy Corporation, Capital National Bank in Austin, Texas Commerce Bank, Chemical Bank, Chase Bank, and JPMorgan Chase.

Since the 1960s I have been associated with the UT Austin Development Board and wish to express my appreciation to fellow members and staff. During the same period, I have known most of University of Texas System Regents and I want to thank them for their service, especially four chairmen: Thornton Hardie, W. W. Heath, Frank C. Erwin Jr., and James R. Huffines. I am grateful to Dr. Kern Wildenthal, former president of the UT Health Science Center in Dallas for showing me and the Cain Foundation how we could help the medical complex make emerging medical research and development accessible to more people.

I never had more fun than in the late 1950s and 1960s when Clint Murchison Sr., allowed me to use his airplane, a DC-3 nicknamed the "Flying Jennie," to take at least fifteen friends to out-of-town UT football games. My traveling companions varied but usually included Harry Whittington, Walter Bremond III, Alden Smith, Noble Doss, Woody Woodward, Warren Woodward, Jerry Bell, Morgan Nesbitt, Robert P. Present, Clyde Copus, Joe Greenhill, Edward Clark, John Coates, Jim Langton, W. W. Heath, Wally Scott, Duke Carlisle, John Burns, Charles Green, Dr. Horace Crommer, Grogan Lord, and Tom Miller Jr.

Lastly, I wish to express my gratitude to the pastors who have served the First Presbyterian Church in Athens and the Westminster Presbyterian Church in Austin. Their messages have consistently reminded me of the values inculcated by my family and shown by their examples the significant of servant leadership.

We all have our difficult moments, and I have always been comforted by their presence.

—Frank Denius

Note on Sources

THIS NARRATIVE OF FRANK DENIUS'S LIFE depended heavily on my interviews with him. Although Mr. Denius has a remarkable memory, I did not rely entirely on his recollection of any significant event, if I could find a written account that was created by another eyewitness shortly after the event occurred. When I discovered a discrepancy between his memory and such an account, I told him, and in every instance, he readily agreed to change the manuscript to reflect the written record. To be clear, if his recollection differed from the recollections of other witnesses who left no written record that I found, Mr. Denius's account was printed in this book. Throughout, I challenged him to substantiate his assertions.

Readers with special interest in World War II may want to know how I reconstructed Mr. Denius's experiences from D-Day to VE- Day. The storyline was based on the daily diary of his 230th Field Artillery Battalion, an official army record, and supplemented by an impressive publication also titled *On the Way*, an anecdotal chronology of particulars of his battalion's advance across Northern France, across Holland, into Belgium and finally to the Elbe River in the heart of Germany. *On the Way* was prepared by the battalion staff shortly after the German surrender in May 1945 and probably edited by Frank's immediate superior, Lt. John Jacobs, a journalism graduate of the University of Missouri, whom Frank admired and stayed in contact with after the war.

In addition to Mr. Denius's account of the ordeal at Hill 314 in Normandy in early August 1944 I drew on papers written by two company commanders who were there and after the war wrote scholarly papers describing their experiences while attending the advanced officer's course at the army's Infantry School at Fort Benning, Georgia. Because Mr. Denius was in close proximity to Lt. Ralph A. Kerley, Kerley's unpublished paper was particularly useful: "Operations of the 2nd Battalion, 120th Infantry, 30th Infantry Division at Mortain, France, 6–12 August 1944." In addition to Cpl. Frank Denius, there was a second artillery forward observer on Hill 314: Lt. Robert Weiss, who wrote a well-researched book about it under the title of *Fire Mission! The Siege at Mortain, Normandy, August 1944* (Shippensburg, Pa.: Burd Sheet Press, 2nd edition, 2002). A parallel story to the account in this book is an article by Kevin Hymel, "Strong Stand Atop Mortain," which appeared in the July 2012 issue of the *World War II Magazine*. With permission of Mr. Hymel and his publisher, his essay was integrated with mine. For the battle statistics, I used the U.S. Army's *Battle Casualties and Non-Battle Deaths in World War II. Final Report, 1 December 1941–31 December 1946*.

Perhaps the most widely read account of LBJ becoming Kennedy's vice presidential candidate was written by Robert A. Caro in *The Years of Lyndon Johnson: The Passage of Power*, vol. IV (New York: Knopf, 2012), 54–143. However, Caro did not interview Mr. Denius. Therefore, Mr. Denius's recollection is the version in this book, and it differs from Caro's account. Relatedly, Neal Spelce significantly clarified controversial issues about the operation of KTBC-TV Channel 7 in the late 1950s and early 1960s, then owned by the Johnson family and the only commercial network station in Austin until 1965.

The chapter on Mr. Denius's role as special counsel (with Leon Jaworski) to the UT System in the early 1960s lawsuit that resulted in removing the last policy obstacles to complete racial integration of the UT Austin campus benefitted from Dwonna Goldstone's *Integrating the 40 Acres: The Fifty-Year Struggle for Racial Equality at the University of Texas* (Athens, Ga., The University of Georgia, 2006), and various newspaper articles. Much of the historical context for and some of the detail of Mr. Denius's pro bono legal assistance to Texas A&M University was based on material in my biography of A&M's illustrious president, Earl

Rudder, *Rudder: From Leader to Legend* (College Station, Texas A&M Press, 2011).

In addition, Mr. Denius's recollections have been supplemented with information from the archives of the University of Texas and the National Archives. Since the Briscoe Center for American History is the repository for UT Austin, many historical records were virtually at my fingertips.

—Thomas M. Hatfield

List of Donors

T HE BRISCOE CENTER FOR AMERICAN HISTORY and The University of Texas Press gratefully acknowledge the support of many individuals in the preparation and publication of this book. Without their crucial material support, this account of the life of Frank Wofford Denius would not have been possible.

Linda and Thomas Barrow
Jack Blanton
Brorby Crozier & Dobie P.C.
Emily and Emmett Carlisle
Elaine and Don Carlton
Margaret and James Coleman
Mike Cotten
Sylvie and Gary Crum
Richard Dwelle
Syd and Guy Fisher
Priscilla and Peter Flawn
Amanda Beck Foster and Morris Foster
Lynn and Bill Fowler
Franklin Templeton Institutional
Dorothy Goddard

Claire and Steve Grant
R. Steven Hicks
Cinda and Thomas Hicks
Michelle and Brandon Holcomb
Patty Anne and James Huffines
Inman Foundation
John W. Jacobs Jr.
Pete Lammons
Betty Lord
Betty and John MacGuire
McCombs Family Foundation
Mike A. Myers Foundation
Nancy and Kerry Merritt
Jill and James Metzger
Mary Jo and Tom Miller
W. A. Moncrief

B. M. Rankin
Seton
Smith Asset Management Group,
   L.P.
Mary Couri Spence and Roy
   Spence
Judy and Charles Tate
The Coneway Family Foundation

The Utley Group, Inc.
TIW Corporation
Judy Trabulsi
Margaret and Dewitt Waltmon
Waukesha-Pearce Industries,
   Inc.
Marnie and Kern Wildenthal
Judith and Mark Yudof

Index

Denius refers to Franklin W. Denius